AF540843

Trends and Structural Behaviour of Indian Exports

TRENDS AND STRUCTURAL BEHAVIOUR OF INDIAN EXPORTS

P. R. JOSHI

1997
Discovery Publishing House
NEW DELHI - 110002 (India)

First Published - 1997

ISBN 81-7141-373-0

Published by :

Discovery Publishing House
4831/24, Ansari Road, Darya Ganj,
New Delhi - 110 002 (INDIA)
Phone : 327 9245
Fax. : 91-11-3253475

Laser Typeset by :

Debug Computer Services
Delhi.

Printed at

Tarun Offset Printers, Maujpur,
Delhi-53, Phone : 2260794

TO MY PARENTS

Contents

Acknowledgements

An accomplishment of any research work is not only an out-come of exclusive efforts of an individual alone, but of also the co-operation offered by many people in their various academic pursuits. In view of the same, I take this opportunity to acknowledge their co-operation extended to me in completion of the present study, on "Trends and Structural Behaviour of Indian Exports".

I express my deep sense of gratitude to Professor M.M Dadi, Head, Department of Economics, Faculty of Arts, M.S. University of Baroda, under whose guidance the present empirical study has been initiated and accomplished. However, I must confess that inspite of his busy schedule, he gladly spared his precious time at each and every stage of the present work and provided an invaluable guidance. Indeed, I owe a great deal to him for his unending and vigilant guidance to me.

I am equally, grateful to Professor V.N. Kothari, Professor of Economics, Department of Economics, Faculty of Arts, M.S. University of Baroda, for his invaluable suggestions and critical comments offered, so as to improvise the present study as regards, the relevant theoretical and empirical issues.

My thanks are also due to my colleagues, Professor N.M. Pandya, Professor of Economics and Dr. (Miss) B.S. Kantawala, Reader in Economics, for the discussion with whom, I have been benefitted a great deal.

I am also, thankful to Professor D.S. Pathak, Professor of Business Economics, Faculty of Commerce, M.S. University of Baroda, for his invaluable suggestions and comments with reference to an improvisation of the methodology of the present work. However, the responsibility of any error or omissions is of mine only.

I am also grateful to the staff members of Smt. Hansa Mehta Library (University Library), M.S. University of Baroda for providing me all types of library facilities.

I am also obliged to Indian Institute of Management Library, Ahmedabad, and Shri Bhaikaka Library, Sardar Patel University, Vallabh Vidyanagar, for lending me books and journals on inter-library loan scheme during the process of my work.

I am thankful to Shri Vinod K. Padaria, Word Processor Operator - cum - Technical Assistant, Shri B.C. Patel, Statistical Assistant and Shri V.M. Bhatt, Research Investigator, Department of Economics, Faculty of Arts, M.S. University of Baroda, for their statistical assistance most efficiently rendered to me, without whose help this work could not have been completed in time.

I express my deep sense of gratitutde to Shri Jashmin Zaveri for carrying out an extremely strenuous task of typing of this work to the best of his ability.

I am also thankful to my brother, Dr. D.R. Joshi, Teaching Assistant, Department of Applied Physics, Faculty of Technology and Engineering, M.S. University of Baroda for his unending help and encouragement extended to me at each and every stage of my work.

Finally, I would like to express my deep feelings of gratitude to my parents, Shri R.S. Joshi and Smt. J.R. Joshi and my wife, Smt. Daxa P. Joshi, who have all along been an unending source of inspiration, encouragement and enthusiasm. Indeed, I cannot adequately express in words that I owe to all of them.

P. R. JOSHI

1

Introduction

Importance of the Present Study

For a developing economy in general and Indian economy in particular, the foreign trade plays a very significant role in the process of economic development by providing external market outlets to domestically produced goods and required foreign exchange for development purpose of a country through exports and external resources for promoting developmental efforts through imports. The significance of the foreign trade as a transmittor of economic growth has been recognised in so much so that in the historical countext, it has been pointed out that international trade has substantially contributed to the economic development of the then developing countries.[1] Diametrically opposed to this view, it is argued that foreign trade has actually favoured the advanced countries of the world at the expense of underdeveloped countries and thus accentuated international inequality.[2] An another view adopts a neutral position and offers some special observations on the dynamic character of trade as a transmittor of economic growth.[3]

India being a developing economy, foreign trade occupies a place of strategic importance in the context of economic development along with other domestic economic factors with an inception of 'Economic Planning' in India. Subsequently after Independence, the Government of India resorted to various remarkable changes in its foreign trade policy, like export promotion scheme, bilateral trade and payment agreements and preferential import controls and import substitution in order to facilitate the developmental efforts and also to circumvent certain bottlenecks in the availability of productive resources.

It would be quite an admissible fact of experience that the

structure and composition of foreign trade of a country would certainly exhibit some spectacular changes over a period time in response to changes in the domestic economic policy and foreign trade policy. Therefore, there seems to be a clear prima facie case to examine the various aspects of India's export trade as detailed subsequently over a period of time particularly after the year 1965, which displayed major changes in our economic policy.

Objectives of the Present Study

In contrast to the studies mentioned above, the distinguishing character of our present study can be discerned from the objectives mentioned below :

[A] Price and Quantity Trends in Indian Exports

For each country, the recorded aggregates of exports are in terms of exports at current prices. If these aggregates are used over period of time , they indicate only the composite effects of changes in the volume of exports and prices. However, one of the significant problems that is frequently encountred in connection with the behaviour of commodity exports over time is to decompose the combined influence of two factors namely, price and quantity changes on the value of exports that is to ascertain how much of changes in the value of exports is accounted for by varying prices and similarly, how much of changes in the value arises because of changes in the volume of exports. This decomposition of changes in the value of exports due to price and quantity changes will enable us to examine in detail the relative importance of the two factors mentioned above and also to guess about the nature of demand for and supply of exports. This type of the analysis will be more relevant in formulating policy decisions regarding foreign trade policy of a country.

As regards exports aggregates of a country, it is a fact of reality that it comprises of a hetrogeneous groups of commodities for which there is no specific quantity measure common to all. But it is only through the construction of index numbers that it is possible to get a meaningful measure of changes in volume and prices of exports.

So far as the price and quantity indices are concerned, the Central Statistical Organization, Government of India has published price and quantity indices for different commodity groups and for different years. But these indices suffer from severe limitations. Firstly, these indices are available only for 29 groups of commodity exports with different base years for the year 1950-51 to 1976-77. Secondly for certain years, these indices are available at financial years and for other years they are available at calender years. These limitations make it - extremely difficult to compare their indicies for different years of the same commodity group.

Hence, the purpose of this study is to examine variations and trends in the price and quantity indices. This study attempts to construct price index number according to Paasche formula and quantum index numbers according to Laspeyres formula. Inspite of the fact that this study has adopted the same formula in the construction of price and quantum indices as is used by the Central Statistical Organization, Government of India, it has improved the methodology with regard to the number of commodities covered in the construction of index number and also with regard to the adjustment for the incomplete coverage of different commodities of exports.

With the above improvement in the construction of index number over the methodology adopted by the Central Statistical Organisation, this study has constructed the price index number and quantity index number for four major commodity groups of exports, i.e. consumer goods, intermediate goods for producing consumer goods, intermediate goods for producing capital goods and capital goods by aggregating value figures of 170 commodity groups of exports (i.e. all the commodities which are classified at 3 digit level of the RITC 1965 group) at current prices and at constant prices of 1970-71 as against 29 different commodity groups provided by the Central Statistical Organization, for the years 1965-66 to 1981-82.

[B] Agricultural Product : Some Issues

Another aspect of exports that needs to be examined is to analyses the trend in relative prices of agricultural products and manufactured products and also their relations with domestic prices. The importance of this study of this aspect lies in the fact that there has been widespread conviction that compared to prices of manufactured products, prices of agricultural products inexorably decline. As Singer argued "it is a matter of historical fact that ever since the seventies, the trend of prices has been heavily against sellers of food and raw materials and in favour of the sellers of manufactured articles"[4]. The analysis of the trend in relative prices of agricultural goods and manufactured products encompasses the following issues.

(i) Have the relative prices of exports of agricultural products and manufactured products changed over time ?

(ii) What are their trends ? What have been the relative positions of different prices over time ?

(iii) What has been the relation of prices of exports of agricultural products and manufactured products with domestic prices ?

[C] Structure and Composition of Indian Exports

As regards, the various important groups of commodities of exports we expect a change in their structure and composition in an event of divergence in relative price of different commodities. In connection with this, the following issues are examined.

(i) Whether the structure of exports has narrowed down or widened over a period of time ?

(ii) What has been the relative rates of growth of these groups ?

(iii) What has been the nature of change in the commodity composition of exports ?

(iv) What has been the degree of instability of commodity exports over time ?

[D] Structure of Exports : Micro and Macro Levels

In order to examine these issues, our analysis of structure of exports runs in terms of current prices and constant prices at macro (aggregated) and micro (disaggregated) levels.

In the macro analysis, the salient factures of exports and changes therein are examined in terms of the following :

(i) Share of export in NNP.

(ii) Share of exports in World exports.

(iii) Growth rates of exports : In order to estimate the growth rates of exports of different commodity groups, we have fitted a semi-logarithmic function to the exports of major commodity groups and also to the principal commodities of exports at constant prices for the years 1965-66 to 1981-82. Algebraically, it may be written as $Y = ae^{bt}$ Where, 'b' denotes the growth coefficient.

(iv) Instability index for exports of different commodites. After having analysed and reviewed the various methods for estimating instability index, this study has adopted the method as given by J.D. Coppock.[5] Known as Coppock's Log-Variance Method. This method of calculating instability index can be written as

$$V \log = \frac{1}{N-1} S[\log X_{t+1} - \log X_t - \frac{1}{N-1} S(\log X_{t+1} - \log X_t)]^2$$

Where N and X are there number of years and value of exports respectively and subscripts indicate the date.

Apart from the macro behaviour of trade activity, structural changes in exports are examined at micro level. The micro level analysis of structure of trade refers to commodity composition of exports. With reference to structural changes in the commodity composition of India's exports, this study has examined the following issues :

(i) What is the degree of concentration in the commodity composition of exports ? Has there been any changes in the degree of concentration over time ?

In order to calculate the commodity concentration index, we have used the formula as given by Michaely Micael[6] which is useful in analysing as to what extent the economic fortune of a country depends on one or few commodities is defined as $C = \sqrt{\Sigma(xi/xi)^2}. 100$. Where Xi referes to exports of ith item in India and X refers to total exports in India in some specified year this index is calculated at current prices as well as at constant prices at three digit level of RITC commodity groups of exports for the years 1965-66 to 1981-82.

(ii)[a] Is there any shift in the share of different commodities in total exports of a country over time ?

We have examined this issue with reference to India's major commodity groups of exports and principal exports at current prices and at constant prices.

(ii)[b] It is commonly argued that the economic development of an economy generally affects the pattern of exports of a country. In order to ascertain whether there is or not a relationship betweer the shares of different groups of commodity exports to total exports and the level of economic development of a country, we have fitted a beveriate regression model of the form Y = a + bx. Where, y and x refer to the percentage share of commodity exports to total exports and per capita income respectively to the time series date at current prices and at constant prices for the years 1965-66 to 1981-82.

[E] Direction of Exports

In response to changes in the foreign trade policy of a country, the direction of its export trade also undergoes a change. Therefore, to analyse the nature of changes in the direction of exports, this study has examined the direction of India's exports over time.

In view of the changes in the direction of exports, it is indispensable to examine the structural changes in world exports. Hence, this study examines the structural changes in the world exports by different groups of countries in terms of the following :

(a) Percentage share in world exports
(b) Growith rates of exports
(c) Instability of exports
(d) Percentage share of exports in national income.

[F] Trends in India's Foreign Trade

Since, foreign trade occupies a place of stratagic importance in the economic development of a developing country. India being under consideration, we intend to examine and analyse the trends in India's foreign trade during the period of 1966-67 to 1988-89 with reference to the issues furnished below :

(i) What has been the average percentage rate of growth of imports and exports per annum over time ?
(ii) What has been the trend behaviour of percentage share of exports in total world exports and gross national product ?
(iii) What has been the trend behaviour of percentage share of trade deficit in the gross national product ?

[G] Structural Behaviour of Indian Exports during the period of (i) 1970-71 to 1986-87 and (ii) 1965-66 to 1981-82 at Current Prices:

(i) As far as the structural behaviour of Indian exports during the period of 1971-71 to 1986-87, we intend to examine and analyse the structural behaviour of Indian exports by various commodity groups [i.e. Agricultural and Allied Products, Ores and Minerals, (excluding Coal), and others] in terms of their percentage share in total exports over period under consideration. This will enable us to know the change in the relative importance of each commodity group of exports in relation to total exports.

(ii) As regard, the structural behaviour of Indian commodity exports during 1965-66 to 1981-82, we intend to examine the following aspects :

[a] Traditional exports and non-traditional exports

[b] Primary exports and manufactured exports

[c] Traditional manufactured exports and non-traditional manufactured exports

[d] Indian commodity exports according to market environment, viz. monopolistic, oligopolistic, competitive and others.

[e] The direction of Indian exports according its regional destination.

[f] The Indian exports according to SITC commodity groups. With references to above, the following issues are intended to be examined :

(i) What has been the trend behaviour of percentage shares of each commodity groups of exports in total exports ?

(ii) What has been the average percentage rates of growth of exports per annum ?

(iii) What has been the nature of commodity composition of Indian exports over time according to market environment and SITC commodity groups of exports ?

(iv) Whether has there been a diversification or concentration of Indian exports ?

(v) What has been the nature of stability of Indian exports overtime ?

(vi) Whether has there been any relation between commodity groups of exports and economic development of India ?

Sources of Data

The statistics regarding the foreign trade of India are available in two series. The first series is published by the Directorate General of Commercial Intelligence and Statistics, Calcutta, regarding the foreign trade as registered by the custom authorities at Indian Seaports, airports and at land customs stations. The other series published by the Reserve Bank of India is based on the date collected from the information furnished to the Reserve Bank of India by the administration of exchange control. The foreign trade statistics as published by the Directorate General of Commercial Intelligence and Statistics in Monthly Statistics of Foreign Trade of India relate to the physical movement of goods in to and out of the custom territory of India, regardless of when payment is made or received.

Whereas the exchange control data record the value of current transactions when payment is made or received. Thus, stocks bought and accumulated by foreign buyers in India and Indian overeas would get reflected in to exchange control data but not in custom data. As regards, exports, the statistics published by the first series relate to exports and re-exports valued at f.o.b./f.o.r. from all the seaports, airports, and land customs stations of the country are based on declarations made by exporters as subsequently checked by customs officials. Further, exports and re-exports figures are credited to the country of final destination. However, it is significant to note that the statistics given in this publication differ from exchange control data compiled by the Reserve Bank of India owing to differences in timing, coverage and valuation of recording.

The present study uses the data given in the 'Monthly Statistics of Foreign Trade of India', Vol. I. Exports and Re-exports published by the Directorate General of Commercial Intelligence and statistics as detail quantitative break-down is available therein.

Moreover, this study also uses the data published in the following official publication :

(i) *'Economic Survey'*, Ministry of Finance, Government of India, New Delhi.

(ii) *'National Account Statistics'*, Ministry of Planning, Government of India, New Delhi.

(iii) *'Basic Statistics Relating to the Indian Economy'*, New Delhi.

(iv) *'International Financial Statistics'*, International Monetary Fund, Geneva.

Plan of the Study

Chapter 2 presents a brief survey of research work on India's exports trade.

Chapter 3 is designed to estimation of price and quantity indices of Indian exports.

Chapter 4 examines price and quantity trends in Indian exports by various commodity groups over time.

Chapter 5 is designed to examine and analyses the structural behaviour of Indian export at macro (i.e. aggregated) and micro (i.e. disaggregated) levels in money terms and in real terms.

Chapter 6 presents an overall view about trends in India's foreign trade in general and examines various aspects of India's commodity exports in particular with reference to its structural behaviour over time.

Chapter 7 presents main findings and conclusions of the study.

References

1. Robertson. D.H. "The Future of International Trade" in *Readings in the Theory of International Trade*. American Economic Association. Balackistone Co.. (1949).

– Haberler. G. *International Trade and Development*. Cairo. National Bank of Egypt. (1956).

– Cairncross. A.K. *Contributions of Trade to Development. An Essay in Factors in Economic Development*. George Allen & Unwin. London. (1966).

2. Singer. H.W. "The Distribution of gains between Investing and Borrowing Countries". *American Economic Review. Papers and Proceedings*. (May. 1950).

Myrdal. G. *Development and Underdevelopment*. Cairo. National Bank of Egypt. (1956).

– Prebisch. R. "Economic Development of Latin America". *Bulletin for Latin America*. (February. 1962).

3. Hicks, J.R. "Development and Trade" *Essays in World Economics*. Oxford. Clarendon Press. (1959)

– Nurkse, R. "Trade Theory and Development Policy" *Economic Development for Latin America*. H.S. Ellis Editor. New York. St. Matin's Press (1969).

4. Singer. H.W. *op.cit.* pp. 473-485.

5. J.D. Coppock. *International Economic Instability - the Experience after World War-II*. Mc Graw-Hill Book Co. Inc., (1962). Chapter-2, pp. 23-26.

6. Michaely Michael. "Concentration of Exports and Imports. an International Comparision". *The Economic Journal*. (December. 1958) pp. 722-736.

2

India's Export Trade : A Brief Survey

Introduction

In view of the problems of economic development of developing countries in general and India in particular, there has been growing amount of interest among academic community over a span of last two decades and a half to probe in to an analysis of various aspects of India's export trade.

Gupte's[1] work throws light on the problem of foreign exchange constraint of Indian economic growth, the role of exports in India's economic development and the nature of export performance of India viewed from short run and the long run.

With reference to the problem of foreign exchange constraint on Indian economic growth being suggestive of the fact that the three methods of relieving foreign exchange constraint viz. cushioning method, conserving method and augmenting method which have been practised so far in India are problematic in nature in terms of its consequences of India's economic development. Therefore, the only way to relieve the problem of foreign exchange constraint is to accelerate the export earnings, which is conducive to self sustained economic growth.

Further, it is pointed out that though Indian exports suffered from fluctuations, there is no evidence of its adverse effects on India's economic development. On the contrary, they had positive impact on India's economic development. They have played the role of quasi-capital goods sector through enabling India to import much needed developmental goods.

As regards the export performance of India, the study being

indicative of export pessimism revealed that the growth of Indian exports have been very sluggish during the period of first two plans on account of gross neglect of export promotion measures. During 1951-58 India's exports grew at an annual average rate of 0.028% ranked India 33rd among the 40 developing countries. Further, during the period of 1960-68, while the world exports grew at an annual average rate of 7.9% and the exports of the developed and developing countries grew at an annual average rate of 8.5% and 4.7% respectively Indian export growth rate has been 2.2% ranking India 43rd among 53 developing countries. This state of poor export performance in India was due to neglect of export promotion measures coupled with deficiency of demand and supply and domestic inflationary pressures in the economy brought down the competitive strength of Indian exports and growing competition in the world market.

Moreover, devaluation of Indian Rupee could improve India's trade balance during the period of 1966-67 to 1970-71 to the extent of 90.5% in terms of U.S. dollars and 66% in terms of Indian rupee. But this improvement in trade balance was largely due to decreases in imports rather than increases in exports. This state of unhealthy growth of Indian exports was due to fact that the devaluation of rupee failed to bring down the prices of Indian exports to a competitive level.

J.A. Rosario[2] examined the structure of India's export trade during the period of 1951-52 to 1965-66. As per his findings, the world trade during this period recorded a consistently high and relatively stable rate of growth. Whereas India's share in the world trade declined from 1.54% to 0.95%. Thus, India's share in the world trade suffered a severe set back. Further, India's exports reflected no consistent and upward trend, they moved up in spurts during 1959-60, 1962-63 and 1964-65. During the period of upswing a limited number of primary products made a distingushing contribution to export trade. Against these, the rate of industrial growth and commodity pattern of industrial output did not alter the structure of India's exports.

As regards, the salient features of the structure of India's export trade, this study revealed that the exports of primary products registered a remarkable rate of increase in comparision to manufactured goods. The increased earnings on account of increase in exports of primary products contributed a little in the beginning but added substantially latter on.

Further, the exports of manufactured goods increased at a much lower rate, than that of primary products. The manufactured goods exports continued to be dominated by textile materials. India participated in those commodities in which world trade experienced a lowest rate of growth. Further, there has been change in the pattern of jute and textile exports which reflected a fall in the exports of sacking, rise in the exports of carpet baking and speciality goods. The commodities like rayon, synthetic fabrics, woollen goods and ready made textile products were added. While the commodities like metals - iron and steel and crude products did make a noticeable contribution. Whereas engineering and chemical goods as a group failed to make a significant impact on the structure of Indian exports in spite of large subsidies offered by the Government of India.

In terms of concluding remarks, the study revealed that the export trade in primary product group, there has been more diversification which helped in stabilizing export receipts to a higher degree than at the beginning of the period. Further, the traditional products and new added primary products have been the major expansionary force in our export trade during this period.

Deepak Nayyar[3] in his study brought out the ficticious optimism that prevailed among the advocates of export-led growth as a strategy for development by examining the export performance of India during the period of 1970-71 to 1974-75 with due recognition of the implications of recent developments in terms of recent booms in prices of primary products, the sharp increase in prices of crude oil and a marked acceleration in the rate of inflation in India as these developments have an important bearings on India's export performance. In view of these recent developments, the claims made by the advocates of export-led growth have little substance. Further, India's export performance has been examined in terms of overall export trends, changes in commodity composition and market distribution of exports and also principal export goods industries. Moreover, the study analysed the factors underlying the growth in export earnings and also examined the impact of oil crisis, commodities boom and the rapid inflation on the export sector.

The findings of this study are suggestive of the fact that the remarkable expansion in the rupee value of Indian exports since 1970 is rather deceptive on account of global inflation and the steady depreciation in the exchange value. Hence, the growth of exports in real terms was considerably less. Moreover, the export expansion on account of new trade with Bangladesh and the commodities boom cannot be considered as the basis of export growth. In the wider context, the export growth looks even less impressive because the oil crisis and the sharp increases in the prices of India's major imports led to a marked deterioration in the terms of trade and a dramatic reduction in purchasing power of exports. As a matter of fact, India's ability to mobilise the external resources needed to finance development through export earnings declined significantly after 1973. As such, India's exports remain very much a problem of production. Therefore, it would be unrealistic to expect exports to grow at faster rate than real national income.

S.J. Patel[4] having examined the long-term trends in Indian exports for the period of 1928 to 1956 in terms of volume, composition and direction, projected a gloomy picture of the prospects of increasing traditional exports in future. The state of gloomy picture on export front as pointed out by him is attributable to the falling world demand for India's traditional exports as the main factor accountable for the relative stagnation of Indian exports, indicating the fact that the export promotion measures adopted by the Government are ineffective.

Whereas Benjamin Cohen[5] in his article commented on S.J. Patel's analysis of Indian exports. He argued that the stagnation of Indian exports has been due to the higher domestic production cost and rising domestic demand leading to a higher relative price of Indian exports in the world markets that to the falling world demand for India's traditional exports. Further, he pointed out that it is the reduced competitive strength of India's exports primarily due to price factor which has led to the falling share of Indian traditional export items in the world market. Moreover, the Government of India's export policy according to Cohen, reflected a conflict with domestic economic policies which contributed to the relative ineffectiveness of the measures adopted for promotion of exports. This state of affairs on export front calls for the formulation of an integrated strategy for export promotion in consonance with the doctrine of comparative advantage to be followed by the Government, if the objective of export promotion is to be effectively accomplished in future.

As regards, the competitiveness of exports, Samuel Paul and V.L. Mote[6] pointed out that the competitiveness of exports depends on non-price factors (such as, quality and service) and price factors. But it is the latter which is significantly a dominant factor in determing the competitiveness of exports. They presented a theoritical model for analyzing export competitiveness at micro level in terms of the factors which explain the net domestic-price/export-price differential. They carried out their empirical analysis of competitiveness of selected export products using Indian data and arrived at a tentative conclusion that in the short run, the pressure of domestic demand is a significant factor which limit the competitiveness of Indian exports.

Charan Wadhva[7] in his paper provides an analysis of the changing pattern of India's export performance during the period of 1951 to 1974 and examines the export performance with special reference to the contribution made by government policies towards promotion of exports.

Further, in view of the emerging opportunities for the new-non-traditional export products and project exports in the world market, the study emphasizes the need for formulating and implementing a new long-term strategy for India's exports, contigent upon an integrated planning at national level and export unit level with due recognition of linkages between export sector and the domestic economy. Moreover, it is also suggested that, since the present policy of export incentives does not provide greater incentives to industries with higher net foreign exchange earnings and vice-versa, the structure of export incentives is required to be modified by selecting the items in accordance with the criterion of "net" foreign exchange earnings.

Vijay Kelker and O.P. Sharma[8] examined India's export performance for the period of 1961 to 1974 in terms of macro-economic framework, pattern of growth of India's exports, identification of the determinants of the supply of exportables and the pattern of direction of India's export trade.

With reference to an analysis of India's export performance in terms of macro-economic framework, the study is indicative of the precipitous decline in share of India's exports in the total world exports i.e. the share of India's export in world exports which remained greater than 1% upto 1965, thereafter it remained less than 1%. Over a period of time it declined from 1.2% in 1961 to 0.50% in 1974. This decline in share as this study emphasizes has to be explained in terms of demand and supply factors. On the demand side, there has been decline in demand for India's exports of traditional products. Even among to underdeveloped countries India's export performance was not proportionate in volume and value terms due to a sharp rise in the unit value of exports of the underdeveloped countries in 1973 on account of the price hike of petroleum products which benefitted only the oil producing countries.

On the supply side, decline in India's share in world exports can be accounted for by reduction in the growth of supply of exportables and or reduction in India's export price competitiveness. At an aggregative level, India's supply capacity can be reflected by the ratio of exports to NNP. Given the foreign demand conditions, this ratio gets affected by domestic demand pressure on account of increase in population, increase in per capita income etc., and the level of domestic production. The domestic demand pressure has negative whereas the level of domestic production has positive impact on this ratio. India's export ability has not increased because of the exogeneous factors like drought during 1965-66 to 1966-67 and recession in 1969-70 to 1970-71 which depressed this ratio. Thereafter, this ratio reflected a rising trend implying thereby increasing ability of the country to generate exportable surplus. But this tendency has been counteracted by rapid growth in domestic demand for exportables leading to increase in domestic consumption resulted in to diversion of exportables to domestic market and reduction in exportable surplus. This is reflected by relative disparity in growth of domestic prices and export prices indicative of relative profitability of the two markets to the sellers. The inflationary tendencies in the country increased the profitability of selling in the home market vis-a-vis world market indicated the reduced competitiveness of India's exports in the world market.

As regards, the pattern of growth of India's exports, the study revealed that the share of three principal items viz. tea, jute manufactures and cotton textiles declined in India's total exports, whereas the share of cashew, tobacco, coffee, iron ore, leather goods and oilcakes increased. Further, the share of new manufactured items iron and steel increased but declined in 1974-75. Machinery and transport equipment group registered an increase. The share of sugar export in total exports increased during 1971-72 to 1974-75. Along with, other items, readymade garments, handlooms and other products showed an increase in their shares.

Among non-manufactures, marine products appeared to be fast expanding export earners. Fish and fish preparations continued to increase in its share upto 1971-72 but declined in 1974-75 due to supply constraints. Chemical, rubber and rubber products have much potential for export growth.

On the supply side of exports, domestic consumption, production and export price competitiveness are the three strong determinents of supply of exports. For tea, jute hessian, jute sacking, raw cotton and coffee, there was a reduction in export/production ratio, whereas this ratio fluctuated very sharply for sugar and cotton yarn.

Further, there was a negative trend in export/output ratio for tea, spices, raw cotton, coal and coke, except tobacco, coffee, jute manufactures and yarn, no items showed positive trend.

Increase in domestic consumption was an another constraint on supply of exports. Increase in population in India led to increase in production intake and thus reduced exportable surplus. In connection with this, consumption elasticities were higher for footwear, coffee, rubber tyres and tubes, bicycles, electric fans, iron ore, cotton yarn and finished steel. Thus in many cases, production as well as consumption operated as effective constraints on the supply of exportables.

India's capacity to export was weakened by increase in domestic demand. The profitability of exporting was relatively reduced by rising prices of exportables in the domestic market. Except tea, domestic price level severly affected the unit export price of coffee, cotton piecegoods, cotton yarn and jute manufacturers, whereas in case of some important exports goods viz. tea and cotton fabrics, raw sugar, raw cotton, coffee, pepper and tobacco, India faced a stiff competition in the world market.

None the less, the another important aspect of India's export performance was analysed in terms of change in the direction of exports. As regards, the direction of India's export trade there was a rapid growth in its exports to the socialist countries. Their share in India's total exports increased from 7.5 % in 1960-61 to 20.62% in 1974-75. Among the Socialist countries, the share of USSR in India's exports increased from 4.4% in 1960-61 to 12.60% in 1974-75. Thus the USSR emerged as the biggest importer of India's export goods.

Whereas the share of exports to U.K., India's most important trading partner in the fifties declined consistently from 26.13% in 1960-61 to 18.17% in 1965-66 and to 9.9% in 1974-75. the U.S.A.'s share on India's total exports increased from 15.52% in 1960-61 to 18.35% in 1965, but declined steeply to 11.35% in 1974-75. Japan emerged as a dynamic market for India's exports, its share increased from 5.35% in

1960-61 to 15.28% in 1973-74 but declined to 8.93% in 1974-75. In terms of directionwise exports, oil producing countries like Iran, Iraq, Saudi Arabia, Dubai and Kuwait emerged as an important export market for India. Whereas in terms of regionwise exports, Asia, Oceania and within this ESCAP accounted for largest share of India's exports, followed by ECM, the East European Bloc, North America and Africa.

References

1. Gupte, D.B. 'Exports in a Developing Economy : A Case Study of India' (unpublished) Ph.D. Thesis, Baroda, The M.S. University of Baroda (1973), Chapter VI, pp. 225-267.
2. Rosario, J.A. : "The Structure of India's Export Trade", *Foreign Trade Review*, Vol. III, No. 1 (April-June, 1968) pp. 66-84.
3. Nayyar Deepak : "India's Export Performance in the 1970s", *Economic & Political Weekly*, (May 15, 1976), pp. 731-743.
4. Patel, S.J. : "Export Prospects and Economic Growth : India", *The Economic Journal*, Vol., LXIX, (September, 1959), pp. 490-506.
5. Cohen, B. : "The stagnation of Indian Exports, 1951-1961", *Quarterly Journal of Economics*, Vol. 78 (November, 1964) pp. 604-620.

   "A Comment on S.J. Patel's Analysis of Indian Exports", *Indian Economic Journal*, (September, 1963).

   The Stagnation of Indian Exports, (unpublished), Ph.D. Thesis, Harward University, (June, 1963).
6. Samuel Paul and V.L. Mote : "Competitiveness of Exports : A Micro-Level Approach", *The Economic Journal*, Vol. 80, (December, 1970), pp. 895-909.
7. Wadhwa Charan : "India's Export Performance and Policy : 1951-74 and Planning for the Future up to 1981", *Some Problems of India's Economic Policy*, Tata McGraw-Hill Publishing Co. Ltd., New Delhi, (2nd Edition, Fourth Reprint, 1984), pp. 620-653.
8. Kelker Vijay L. and Sharma O.P. : "Trends and Determinants of India's Export Performance : 1961-1974", *Foreign Trade Review*, Vol. XI, No. 3, (October-December, 1976), pp. 283-311.

3

Price and Quantity Indices

Introduction

In spite of the fact that the Pre-Devaluation period reflected a relative stagnation in the value of India's exports, the Post-Devaluation period displayed the symptoms of increase in the value of exports. However, this increase in the value of exports over a period of time is attributable to the combined effects of changes in the volume of exports and of prices. In connection with this, one of the essential problems that is frequently encountred is to seggregate the composite effects of these two factors to determine how much of change in value is accounted for by varying prices and how much of change in the value arises because of changes in the volume of exports.

Further, the export aggregates of a country comprise of heterogeneous groups of commodities for which there is no specific quantity measure common to all. It is through the construction of index numbers that it is possible to get any measure of changes in volume and prices of exports.

In order to seggregate the composite effects of price and quantity changes on the value of exports, the present study is designed to construct price and volume indices for major commodity groups of exports* viz, consumer goods, intermediate goods for producing consumer goods, intermediate goods for producing capital goods and capital goods on the basis of commodities classified at three digit level of the Revised Indian Trade classification (RITC), 1965 group.†

---

* For scheme of Classification see, *Appendix Table - V-4*

† For RITC 1965 groups, see, *Appendix Table IV-3*

Moreover, it is also intended to undertake an analysis of the trend in the relative prices of exports of agricultural and manufactured products.

Index Numbers : Need for Construction

The need for the construction of index numbers finds its justification in the fact that price and quantum indicies for different commodity groups and for different years which are published by the Central Statistical Organization, Government of India suffers from two important limitations. Firstly, these indicies are available for 29 groups of commodity exports with different base year for the years 1950-51 to 1976-77. Secondly, for certain years, these indicies are available for financial years, whereas for others in calender years. These limitations make it difficult to compare these indicies for different years of the same commodity group. For the years, 1959 to 1973, price and quantum indicies are available at 1958 price level (i.e. calender year). However, these indicies are available for the years 1969-70 to 1979-80 at 1968-69 price level (i.e. Financial years) and from 1980-81 onwards at 1978-79 price level.

In view of the revision of Indian Trade classification, the base year for the construction of price and quantum indicies of different commodity groups of exports has been changed by the Department of Commercial Intelligence and Statistics from 1952-53 to 1958, and again to 1968-69 and thereafter to 1978-79.

In order to make the price index and quantum index comparable during the period of 1965-66 to 1981-82, the present study has attempted to construct these indicies at the 1970-71 price level for the major commodity groups of exports on the basis of the three digit level of RITC 1965 group i.e. 170 commodities as against 29 commodity groups provided by the Central Statistical Organization.

During the period under consideration i.e. 1965-66 to 1981-82, the Indian Trade classification has been changed twice, one in April 1965 known as the Revised Indian Trade Classification, Revision - 1 and another in April 1977 known as the Revised Indian Trade Classification, Revision-2. However, in the present study, we have used the RITC 1965 as the basis of commodity classification and accordingly the items classified in RITC, Revision-2 have been regrouped as far as possible in accordance with the RITC 1965, Revision-1 in order to establish correspondence between the two classifications.

Coverage of Commodities

As far as the coverage of items for computing index numbers is concerned, the present study marks an improvement over the indicies provided by the Government of India.

It becomes evident from Table 3.1 that the number of items included in the construction of index numbers in the present study is greater than the number of items included by the Government of India. It is pertinent to mention that the Government of India has not maintained consistency in the construction of price and volume indicies for different sections of the RITC group i.e. in some cases, the Government of India has considered the commodities at three digit level or four digit level or seven digit level. For sections 0, 1, 3, and 4 of the RITC group index numbers are constructed by the Government of Indian by considering the number of commodities at the three digit level of the RITC 1965 group, whereas for section 5 index numbers are constructed using the number of commodities at the four digit level of RITC 1965 group.

But for section seven, the index numbers are constructed by considering the number of commodities at the 7 digit level of RITC 1965 group. However, the present study has considered the number of commodities at the 4 digit level of the RITC 1965 group in order to construct the index numbers for the major commodity groups of exports on the basis of 3 digit level RITC 1965 group. As regards Section 7 it is impossible to consider the number of commodities at the 4 digit level of commodity group. There, for Section 7 it is considered here at 7 digit level of different commodity group having an identical quantity measure within a group of 4 digit level.

TABLE 3.1
Coverage of Items Included for Computing Index Number of Exports

Section	Exports	
	No. of Items[1] included	No. of Items in the Present Study
[1]	[2]	[3]
0. Food and Live Animals	61	72
1. Beverages & Tobacco	7	8

(Contd.)

Table 3.1 (Contd.)

[1]	[2]	[3]
2. Crude Materials inedible [except fuels]	91	75
3. Mineral fuels, lubricants and relevant materials	3	11
4. Animal and Vegetable oils and fats	5	11
5. Chemicals	34	61
6. Manufactured goods classified chiefly by materials	168	201
7. Machinery and Transport Equipment	93	106
8. Miscellaneous manufactured Articles	25	71
9. Commodities and transactions not classified according to kind	2	-
All Sections	789	616

Source 1 : Directorate General of Commercial Intelligence and Statistics, Calcutta, Govt. of India. *A Guide to Current Official Statistics of Trade, Shipping and Customs and Exercise Revenue of India,* p-46, Third Edition, 1978.

Construction of Index Numbers : Methodology

In order to compare exports in the current period with that revalued at 1970-71 prices the unit price index for exports is constructed according to Paasche's formula. Expressed in symbols, the formula can be written as follows :

$$P = \frac{\Sigma\, Pn\, Qn}{\Sigma\, Po\, Qn} \cdot 100$$

Where Po and Pn denote the price of an article in the base year and in the current years respectively and Qn denotes the quantity in the current year.

Thus the Paasche's formula for calculating the unit price index is nothing but the ratio of exports at current prices to exports at constant prices multiplied by 100. In this study, an attempt is made to estimate exports at the 1970-71 price level for the years 1965-66 to 1981-82. It is possible to estimate export at constant prices, if the quantity date of different commodities and the price per unit are available.

Adjustment for the incomplete coverage

As far as the estimation of exports at constant prices is concerned, it is associated with the following two important limitations :

(1) It is impossible to obtain quantity data for almost all commodities entering in to trade.

(2) In cases of some commodities which were exported during the years (i.e. 1965-66 to 1981-82) other than the base year, it is not possible to get unit price for the commodities in question.

With reference to the above limitations, the important question that arises as to what adjustment if any should be made in the final index to allow for incomplete coverage in commodity detail. The common practice that is prevalent among different countries is to make such an adjustment by assuming that price changes for the items not covered are the same as those for items which are directly included in the computation. Some of these countries make the adjustment only in the total index for exports i.e. price changes in all items not covered are assumed to be the same as the price changes shown by the aggregate of all items covered by the computation. Finland and Ireland are two countries adopting this method.[1] Other countries, adopt the same method, but apply to each major commodity class separately, there the assumption is that price changes in items not covered within each separate class are the same as price changes shown by the items included in the calculation for the class. The adjustment is exactly identical to the one as shown above, but since it is made for each class, the adjustment is different for one class than it is for another and the overall index is obtained by aggregating separately adjusted class index numbers. This method is followed by the United States, United Kingdom, Canada, Netherlands and Sweden amongst others.[2]

In case of India, according to Department of Commercial Intelligence and Statistics,[3] adjustments are based on the assumption that price changes in the items not covered in a section are similar to those shown by the items included in the calculation of index numbers for that section i.e. $P_i = P'_i$.

Where Pi is the unit price index for a given section in respect of the included items and P'_i is same for ith section (inclusive of all items).

The unit price index (P_i) for the included items in a section is given by the formula :

$$P_i = \frac{\Sigma \text{ Pn Qn}}{\Sigma \text{ Po Qn}} \quad \text{------} \; (1)$$

The index for the section inclusive of all items will be given by

$$P'_i = \frac{\Sigma' Pn\, Qn}{\Sigma' Po\, Qn} \text{ ------ } (2)$$

In the equation (2) the aggregate Σ' PnQn is known but the aggregate Σ' PoQn is unknown and it cannot be computed directly. Therefore, it is assumed that price changes for not covered items and for all the items are the same. Algebriacally, this can be shown as follows :

$$P_i = P'_i$$

$$\therefore \quad \frac{\Sigma' Pn\, Qn}{\Sigma' Po\, Qn} = \frac{\Sigma Pn\, Qn}{\Sigma Po\, Qn}$$

$$\frac{\Sigma' Po\, Qn}{\Sigma' Pn\, Qn} = \frac{\Sigma Po\, Qn}{\Sigma Pn\, Qn}$$

$$\Sigma' Po\, Qn = \frac{\Sigma Po\, Qn}{\Sigma Pn\, Qn} \cdot \Sigma\ Pn\, Qn$$

$$= \frac{\Sigma' Pn\, Qn}{\Sigma Pn\, Qn / \Sigma Po\, Qn}$$

= *Total Values of all other items in the section*
unadjusted index for the section

The above value of Σ ' PoQn is substituted in the equation (2) in order to obtain the adjusted index number P'_i.

As far as a section of RITC group is concerned, it includes a large number of commodities at four digit level reflecting large variations in the price changes among the four digit level of commodities of the RITC group. If the quentity data are not available for the article code 5419 of RITC group, the Department of Commercial Intelligence and Statistics assumes that rice changes in section 5 excluding article code 5419 are the same as price changes in 5419, but in section 5 of RITC there are nine divisions i.e. 51, 52, 53, 54, 55, 56, 57, 58 and 59 and within these divisions there are different group, to illustrate 512, 513, 514 are the groups in the division 51 etc.

In order to avoid these large variations of price changes, we have assumed in this study that price changes in the item at a four digit level not included in a group are similar to those shown by the items included in the calculation of index number for that particular group. For example, if the quantity data for 5419 are not available, it is assumed that price changes in 5419 are the same as price changes in group 541 excluding 5419. Similarly, for example, if the quantity data are not available for article code 2926, we have assumed that price changes in 2926 are the same as price changes in group 292 excluding 2926.

Whereas in certain groups only one commodity is exported at the four digit level for which the quantity data are not available, one cannot assume that price changes in that commodity are the same as price changes in that particular group, for example in a group 553 only 5530 was exported, hence exports of 5530 are the same as exports of 553. If the quantity data are not available for the article code 5530, the calculation of 5530 or 553 is based on the assumption that price changes in division 55 excluding 5530 is the same as price changes in 5530.

Further in cases, when the quantity data for different commodities are available but unit price is not available on account of absence of exports of that particular commodity in the base year i.e. 1970-71, the adjustments are indispensable to be effected. The adjustment procedure can be elaborated by the following illustration. If the article code 2626 is not exported in the base year (i.e. 1970-71) but it is exported during the other years, then the average price of group 262 is applied to 2626. Whenever unit price is not available at three digit level, then the average price of that particular division is applied to that commodity e.g. article 3320 was exported during other years other than in the base year 1970-71 and this is the only commodity which falls under group 332, in that case an average price of division 33 is applied to article 3320.

Moreover, in case of articles 8971 and 8972, the quantity data were lacking for the period of 1965-66 to 1973-74 but value figures were available. Whereas during the period thereafter (i.e. 1974-75 to 1981-82) the quantity as well as value data were available for these articles. This state of affairs on commodity details created a problem of estimation of quantity and price for these articles during the period of 1965-66 to 1973-74. In order to solve this problem we estimated the rate of average percentage change in price per annum for these articles during the period of 1974-75 to 1981-82. Then the rate of average percentage change in price per annum, so estimated was applied to articles 8971 and 8972 (on the assumption that the same rate of change in prices prevailed during 1965-66 to 1973-74) in order to estimate the prices of these articles in the respective years. Having estimated the prices, we applied them to the value figures to estimate corresponding quantities in the respective years. Thus we could also estimate the base year's price and quantity for these articles.

Quantum Index

Quantum indices are constructed to show movements in the aggregate value of exports after isolating the effects of price changes. The quantum index number is computed according to Laspeyre's formula as furnished below :

$$Q = \frac{\Sigma \text{Po Qn}}{\Sigma \text{Po Qn}}$$

Where, Qo and Qn denote quantity exported in the base year and in the current year respectively and Po refers to unit price of exports in the base year.

References

1. Index Numbers of volume and Prices by R.G.D. Allen in *International Trade Statistics*, ed. by R.G.D. Allend and J.E. Ely., New York, John Wiley & Sons, (1953).
2. Allen, R.G.D., *op.cit.*, pp. 199-202.
3. *Indian Trade Journal*, 31st March, 1976, pp. B820-B821.

4

Price and Quantity Trends

Introduction

The present chapter is designed to examine and analyse the price and quantity trends in Indian exports during the period of 1965-66 to 1981-82 on the basis of price and quantum indices of exports estimated by using the methodology discussed in the preceeding chapter.

With reference to above, the price and quantum indices of various commodity groups of exports viz. consumer goods, Intermediate goods for producing consumer goods, Intermediate goods for producing capital goods, capital goods, primary products and manufactured products are presented in this chapter with a view to examine the price and quantity trends.

However, it is important to note that indices so estimated as mentioned above are utilised to examine the following aspect.

(i) Effects of price and quantity changes on the value of Indian exports by various commodity groups through isolating price effect and quantum effect.

(ii) Relative prices of agricultural and manufactured products.

(iii) Relation of exports prices to domestic prices.

Effects of Price and Quantity on Value of Exports

It is known that the value of exports over time is affected partly by the changes in the quantity of exports and partly by the changes in the unit price of exports. The relative importance of these factors i.e. price and quantity changes can be ascertained with the help of price index and quantum index, the construction of which enables us to seggregate their effects on the value of exports.

It becomes clear from Table 4.1 that the 27.75% fall in the value of total export during the period of 1965-66 to 1970-71 is due to 40.07% fall in the price and 9.65% increase in the quantity of total exports. Further, the value of total exports has increased by 336.89% during 1970-71 to 1981-82 with an increase in price by 110.14% and increase in the quantity by 122.18%. Hence, it becomes intelligible that price has fallen by higher percentage than the quantity during 1965-66 to 1970-71. Whereas during 1970-71 to 1981-82, the quantity has increased by higher percentage then price. In otherwords, during 1965-66 to 1970-71, the price effect has been more powerful than quantum effect on the value of exports, whereas during 1970-71 to 1981-82, quite opposite came to be true.

TABLE 4.1

Change in Value Price and Quantity of Major Commodity Groups of India's Exports (1965-66 to 1981-82)

(Percentage Terms)

Sr. No.	*Name of the Major Commodity Group*	*Period : 1965-66 to 1970-71*			*Period : 1970-71 to 1981-82*		
		Change in			*Change in*		
		Value	*Price*	*Quantity*	*Value*	*Price*	*Quantity*
(1)	(2)	(3)	(4)	(5)	(6)	(7)	(8)
I.	Consumer Goods	↓ 7.10	↓ 24.41	↑ 17.09	↑ 401.19	↑ 102.65	↑ 147.29
II.	Intermediate Goods for Producing consumer Goods	↓ 19.93	↓ 64.01	↑ 36.76	↑ 336.00	↑ 146.71	↑ 76.73
III.	Intermediate Goods for producing capital Goods	↓ 103.50	↓ 74.06	↓ 16.92	↑ 222.00	↑ 113.44	↑ 50.86
IV.	Capital goods	↓ 355.79	↓ 95.66	↓ 132.94	↑ 721.99	↑ 102.37	↑ 306.18
V.	Total Exports	↓ 27.75	↓ 40.07	↑ 9.65	↑ 336.89	↑ 110.14	↑ 122.18

Source : *Appendix Tables 4.1 and 4.2.*

Further, the above table reveals that during 1965-66 to 1970-71 the value of exports of almost all the commodity groups (except the capital goods) has fallen due to fall in prices by higher percentage than quantity indicating price effect being more powerful than quantum effect. Whereas during 1970-71 to 1981-82 the value of exports of intermediate goods for producing consumer goods and capital goods increased due to increase in price by higher percentage than quantity implying price effect being more powerful than quantum effect. While incase of consumer goods and capital goods, the quantum effect on value of exports has been more powerful than price effect.

Hence, it can be conclude from the above analysis that during 1965-66 to 1970-71, the price effect has been more powerful than quantum effect for total exports. Whereas during 1970-71 to 1981-82, the quantum effect has been more powerful than price effect on the value of exports.

Relative Price of Agricultural and Manufactured Products

With references to relative prices of agricultural and manufactured products, there has been a widespread conviction that compared to prices of manufactured products, primary product prices inexorably decline, the idea which continued to be widely accepted despite its contradiction of the classical belief, dating back at least to Robert Torrens, that "the exchange value of manufactured articles compared with the products of agriculture and of mines have as population and industry advance, a certain and decided tendency to fall"[1]

It was Floke Hilgredt who first turned the classical proposition upside down. He argued that in the sixty years before 1938, primary product prices had fallen relative to prices of manufactures and that "general trend of relative movements ..... prices of these two classes of goods can soarcely be doubted"[2] The evidence of this contention consisted of League of Nations indices for primary product and manufactured products prices.

If we examine relative prices of agricultural products and manufactured products within Indian exports for the period 1965-66 to 1981-82, similar results follow.

It becomes evident from Table 4.2 that the price indicies of almost all group of commodity exports reflect an increase during the period 1965-66 to 1981-82. Hence a closer glance at the table is revealing of the fact that as compared to the base year, in the year 1974-75, the price indicies of exports of consumer goods, intermediate goods for producing consumer goods and capital goods show a sharp increase. This state of affairs was purely due to the phenomenon of World wide inflation consequent upon increase in the prices of petroleum products. However, the price indicies of almost all groups of commodity exports show a sharp decline in the year 1978-79 as compared to the previous year because of world wide phenomenon of recession.

TABLE 4.2

Price Indicies of Major Commodity Groups of India's Exports 1965-66 to 1981-82 : (Base Year : 1970-71 = 100)

Year	*Consumer Goods*	*Intermediate Goods for producing Consumer goods*	*Intermediate Goods for producing capital goods*	*Capital Goods*	*Total Exports*
1965-66	79.74	60.97	57.45	51.11	71.39
1966-67	83.08	57.05	72.20	61.31	74.86
1967-68	93.60	71.90	85.33	63.43	87.11
1968-69	84.83	67.05	81.13	34.54	76.78
1969-70	90.49	72.81	89.40	63.35	84.85
1970-71	100.00	100.00	100.00	100.00	100.00
1971-72	102.07	106.94	100.40	95.38	102.30
1972-73	103.70	116.48	105.66	88.10	105.80
1973-74	145.37	130.55	97.82	70.29	126.79
1974-75	174.78	125.93	103.37	175.92	148.08
1975-76	187.25	147.48	143.47	144.42	166.16
1976-77	178.82	145.36	169.80	160.46	168.86
1977-78	190.75	149.76	179.33	200.83	182.28
1978-79	171.34	135.25	155.02	158.48	161.39
1979-80	147.45	192.72	136.91	124.05	149.40
1980-81	141.23	157.70	164.72	151.58	147.07
1981-82	202.65	246.71	213.44	202.37	210.14

Source : *Appendix Table 4.1.*

During the period of 17 years, the price index number of exports of consumer goods has increased by 154.14% or at an average annual rate of 9.07% while the price indices of exports of raw materials and intermediate goods for producing consumer goods and raw materials

products. (3) U.S. exports of manufactures and exports of primary products. (4) U.S. import of manufactures and exports of primary products.

On the basis of this study, he arrived at the conclusion that the imported manufactures declined in prices relative to U.S. agricultural exports but increased compared with total primary product imports and exports and agricultural imports.

TABLE 4.3

Price Indicies of India's Exports of Primary Products and Manufactured Products : 1965-66 to 1981-82

(Base Year : 1970-71 = 100)

Year	*Price Index of Primary Products*	*Price Index of Manufactured Products*
1965-66	74.87	56.80
1966-67	75.65	71.15
1967-68	88.19	82.89
1968-69	79.90	68.38
1969-70	85.16	84.00
1970-71	100.00	100.00
1971-72	103.15	99.20
1972-73	107.08	101.09
1973-74	141.15	89.08
1974-75	160.47	120.42
1975-76	176.50	143.70
1976-77	169.32	167.84
1977-78	181.22	184.92
1978-79	163.51	156.05
1979-80	155.78	131.12
1980-81	144.40	159.06
1981-82	210.43	209.21

Source : *Appendix Tables 4.1.*

Relation of Export Process to Domestic Prices

In order to analyse the shifts in the flow of trade on the balance of payments, one is often interested not in the absolute changes in export prices, but in their relation to domestic prices as it is indicative of relative importance of export goods in the domestic market vis-a-vis world market in terms of relative profitability in the two markets to sellers.

It becomes intelligible from Table 4.4 that the export price (1970-71 = 100) is lower as compared to domestic wholesale price index (1970-71 = 100) for all the years under consideration.[6] Moreover increase in export price index (194.35%) is lower than the increase in the domestic wholesale price index (287.14%). With reference to this type of the result R.E. Lipsey[7] concluded in his study of United States that foreign trade prices compared to domestic prices have declined.

TABLE 4.4

Export Price Index as Percentage of Domestic Wholesale Price Index : 1965-66 to 1981-82

(Base Year : 1970-71 = 100)

Year	*Export Price Index*[1]	*Domestic Wholesale Price Index*[2]	*Export Price Index as Percentage of Domestic Wholesale Price Index*
1965-66	71.39	72.66	98.25
1966-67	74.86	82.77	90.44
1967-68	87.11	92.37	94.30
1968-69	76.78	91.33	84.07
1969-70	84.85	94.75	89.55
1970-71	100.00	100.00	100.00
1971-72	102.30	105.60	97.44
1972-73	105.80	116.20	91.04
1973-74	126.89	139.70	90.76
1974-75	148.08	174.90	84.67
1975-76	166.16	173.00	96.05
1976-77	168.86	176.60	95.62
1977-78	182.88	185.80	98.10
1978-79	161.39	185.80	86.86
1979-80	149.40	217.60	68.66
1980-81	147.07	257.30	57.16
1981-82	210.14	281.30	74.70

Source : 1. Table 4.2

2. *Economic Survey* : 1974-75 and 1984-85

The smaller increase in export price index in relation to increase in domestic prices in the case of India could be in two ways. It is conceivable that there was a considerable divergence between domestic prices and export prices for individual commodities. Alternatively, the commodities that have increased relatively in price might have greater importance in the domestic economy than in the Indian exports. In other words, the relative disparity between domestic prices as reflected by domestic wholesale price index and export prices by export price index is accounted for by (i) rapid growth in domestic demand for exportables leading to increase in domestic consumption resulted in to diversion of exportables to domestic market and reduction in exportables to domestic market and reduction in exportable surplus and (ii) increase in relative profitability of selling exportables in the home market as compared to world market consequent upon inflationary tendencies in the country.

From the persusal of Table 4.5 it is evident that the volume index of total exports increased by 102.63% during the period under consideration. However, the volume indicies of consumer goods, raw materials for producing consumer goods, raw materials for producing capital goods and capital goods have increased by 111.20%, 29.23%, 76.38% and 846.14% respectively during 1965-66 to 1981-82 with fluctuations in different year.

As far as the volume indicies of consumer goods are concerned, the volume index has declined in the years 1966-67 and 1967-68 as the year 1966-67 being drought year resulted in to fall in the volume index of food articles. Further the first year of the Fourth Plan (i.e. 1969-70) which being the year of success of the new agricultural strategy in the country registered a decline in the volume index of consumer goods because the volume index of food articles showed a marginal improvement which was less than compensated for by a greater decline in volume index of non-food articles. Moreover during the year 1972-73, the volume index of consumer goods increased due to increase in volume index of food articles consequent upon increase in agricultural production in the country.

However, during 1973-74 the unprecedented drought has resulted in to fall in the volume index of exports of consumer goods on account of fall in the volume index of food articles. Moreover, in 1976-77 and thereafter, the volume index of consumer goods exports is creased because, the preceding year (i.e. 1975-76) had witnessed a record output of foodgrains (at 120.8 million tonnes). One important feature of the quantity trends of exports of all the major commodity groups and of total exports that is noticeable is that the year 1981-82 shows a decline in the volume indices of exports. This was mainly due to the phenomenon of world recession.

TABLE 4.5

Quantum Indicies of Major Commodity Groups of India's Exports, 1965-66 to 1981-82 : 1965-66 to 1981-82

(Base Year : 1970-71 = 100)

Year	*Consumer Goods*	*Intermediate Goods for producing Consumer goods*	*Intermediate Goods for producing capital goods*	*Capital Goods*	*Total Exports*
1965-66	117.09	136.76	85.53	42.93	109.65
1966-67	107.03	142.33	72.02	33.45	101.50
1967-68	96.16	106.22	74.01	38.61	90.12
1968-69	108.46	138.64	102.61	168.15	115.28
1969-70	99.90	143..51	102.18	116.34	108.58
1970-71	100.00	100.00	100.00	100.00	100.00
1971-72	110.47	105.13	75.55	102.99	101.47
1972-73	120.33	143.46	83.38	127.42	116.45
1973-74	116.57	154.46	107.33	217.24	126.02
1974-75	130.27	179.57	160.05	213.74	149.38
1975-76	138.06	170.13	166.61	235.22	154.71
1976-77	166.14	218.70	211.90	244.00	189.05
1977-78	179.21	180.60	174.39	226.56	182.82
1978-79	198.26	182.86	179.25	330.16	198.17
1979-80	293.58	220.13	175.97	622.26	271.71
1980-81	350.44	278.11	139.31	458.71	297.11
1981-82	247.29	176.73	150.86	406.18	222.18

Source : *Appendix Table 4.2.*

As regards the volume indices of group of raw material for consumer goods it is evident that in the year 1972-73 there has been a sharp increase in the volume index beacause of increase in the volume indicies of exports of chemicals, Tobacco unmanufactured, vegetable oils and fats, Animal oils and fats and Leather manufactures. As against this we find that the volume index of exports of raw materials for producing capital goods has fallen in 1971-72 and 1972-73 on account of recessionary conditions prevailed in this particular group of industries since 1970-71. Moreover, there is a sharp increase in the volume index of export of capital goods in the year 1972-73 on account increase in the volume indices of exports of Machinery and Transport equipment.

(See Appendix Tables from P. 37 to 76)

References

1. Mill John Stuart : *Principles of Political Economy*, New York, 1909, Vol. II, Book IV, Chapter 2, P. 282.
2. League of Nations : *Industrialization and Foreign Trade*, Economic, Financial and Transit Department, U.S.A. 1945, P. 16.
3. Singer H.W. *op.cit.*, pp. 473-485.
4. Morgan Theodore : "The long run terms of trade between agriculture and manufacturing", *Economic Development and Cultural Change*, October, 1959, pp 1-23
5. Lipsey R.E. : *Price and Quantity Trends in Foreign Trade of United States*, 1963, Princeton University Press, Princeton.
6. For similar results for Indian exports during 1961-1974, see Kelker Vijay and Sharma *op.cit.*, pp. 283-311
7. Lipsey R.E. *op.cit.* p. 32

APPENDIX TABLE IV.1 : Price Indices of Exports : 1965-66 to 1981-82 (1970-71 = 100)

Article code No.	1965-66	1966-67	1967-68	1968-69	1969-70	1971-72	1972-73	1973-74
001	122.42	81.90	116.66	41.73	104.00	90.81	106.90	61.94
011	77.67	93.88	85.85	96.18	115.61	74.58	84.98	118.66
012	231.25	158.37	211.11	127.27	103.90	130.63	183.87	183.12
013	325.23	308.86	404.62	349.71	115.85	200.00	242.50	122.73
022	41.28	59.68	69.73	78.10	802.00	94.74	158.63	189..36
023	160.27	76.10	110.22	110.17	0.19	91.44	110.19	142.78
024	–	–	–	100.00	350.00	125.00	–	–
025	–	105.26	75.18	95.95	104.55	100.00	100.00	173.08
031	408.72	103.31	97.03	101.10	111.33	135.64	148.27	178.96
032	85.48	94.73	88.25	754.11	100.71	103.38	133.26	169.37
041	145.16	67.38	142.86	104.42	137.14	117.50	105.44	184.43
042	95.50	90.44	98.36	123.77	115.10	608.52	107.13	293.58
043	78.38	72.22	300.00	67.57	70.59	427.27	97.44	62.75
044	29.11	26.80	–	37.50	115.63	–	43.67	54.32
045	66.67	100.00	100.00	116.67	114.29	100.00	–	–
046	139.78	125.00	107.00	105.10	106.45	120.91	103.86	78.05
047	28.57	–	–	–	–	20.67	90.24	117.65
048	100.21	88.73	95.10	90.49	85.80	152.69	136.66	138.22
049	112.01	90.45	126.92	102.84	96.27	124.67	122.98	173.73
051	81.66	86.53	81.80	92.22	93.41	98.50	101.05	139.24
052	90.30	80.23	104.04	88.94	89.82	91.44	103.78	170.68
053	115.31	116.33	106.93	116.47	92.67	100.10	103.02	142.18
054	94.61	116.55	99.30	108.33	110.07	112.93	129.19	196.25

(Contd.)

APPENDIX TABLE IV.1 (Contd.)

Article code No.	1965-66	1966-67	1967-68	1968-69	1969-70	1971-72	1972-73	1973-74
055	132.02	109.93	122.29	127.33	131.72	104.08	172.66	158.01
061	72.66	59.88	88.82	129.73	131.92	120.53	162.78	216.55
062	87.21	58.94	90.70	88.97	85.57	102.92	167.77	201.02
071	101.69	80.37	71.03	79.72	77.44	79.94	83.38	114.22
072	181.79	129.76	141.13	186.01	0.15	136.68	137.75	126.29
073	68.92	59.18	60.84	57.19	84.77	124.91	108.11	118.16
074	123.16	111.83	119.12	104.75	96.11	1.01	102.46	102.32
075	71.14	66.32	64.14	61.93	100.58	67.64	79.41	109.02
081	105.43	98.11	97.02	94.76	93.24	86.17	117.50	23.19
099	23.02	23.15	30.64	89.46	104.47	1049.55	86.21	107.93
111	4998.20	5580.00	660.00	12666.67	300.00	145.00	257.98	288.89
112	96.46	77.78	57.58	50.00	88.89	43.56	67.37	94.13
121	82.47	87.07	106.23	101.11	91.28	111.73	97.93	1325.35
122	76.54	80.08	85.60	225.29	75.96	100.17	145.42	116.07
211	137.84	145.04	110.38	99.74	124.43	127.98	144.23	273.08
212	193.51	321.89	177.95	303.91	7804.48	74.61	23.46	113.33
221	61.71	72.59	73.88	85.48	96.73	105.25	103.25	177.13
231	126.29	146.81	143.37	112.41	121.57	102.14	109.52	117.95
241	34.78	0.02	210.61	119.57	33.14	23.08	14.29	88.61
242	5.63	77.69	92.49	84.71	96.99	104.25	110.374	151.28

APPENDIX TABLE IV.1 (Contd.)

Article code No.	1974-75	1975-76	1976-77	1977-78	1978-79	1979-80	1980-81	1981-82
001	76.35	256.16	284.92	433.73	348.96	253.73	520.00	417.35
011	91.15	128.29	120.03	128.63	126.03	103.79	92.43	116.35
012	201.72	95.05	63.24	–	33.33	173.68	158.33	166.67
013	114.29	210.00	460.71	800.00	154.70	185.87	208.20	243.87
022	173.16	156.83	153.67	270.31	155.20	321.20	245.82	437.65
023	128.40	165.81	267.63	170.71	249.40	248.44	30.08	254.36
024	–	–	–	–	–	–	–	–
025	274.32	107.65	189.88	178.08	227.76	197.72	159.58	229.12
031	155.27	231.47	311.66	273.58	305.68	338.56	319.80	391.30
032	196.25	140.50	212.20	238.81	249.56	276.09	2.34	205.77
041	438.94	399.31	323.56	126.20	135133.1	135.66	171.55	410.49
042	335.81	247.75	129.12	143.04	228.17	162.17	336.20	274.50
043	62.50	75.97	105.03	110.63	138.89	140.13	162.03	176.17
044	258.33	246.33	130.57	–	500.00	–	–	127.27
045	700.00	596.63	200.00	113.40	120.37	230.77	105.88	254.55
046	–	–	–	181.10	168.96	148.57	164.30	133.33
047	76.00	50.17	131.00	74.15	160.09	151.35	213.58	148.15
048	170.49	194.49	186.04	166.31	213.02	7.30	244.41	307.97
049	1996.06	220.93	205.42	231.05	1.35	7.47	225.37	230.08
051	177.64	161.79	195.29	330.29	254.42	2803.47	380.56	242.85
052	177.85	128.06	154.44	173.01	253.85	275.36	297.81	192.63
053	199.20	396.86	225.40	243.90	279.14	312.62	328.57	269.38
054	186.42	262.93	243.42	164.46	118.67	275.35	308.03	319.43
055	143.21	190.00	152.17	168.20	174.32	214.59	256.65	217.03

(Contd.)

APPENDIX TABLE IV.1 (Contd.)

Article code No.	1974-75	1975-76	1976-77	1977-78	1978-79	1979-80	1980-81	1981-82
061	620.75	499.98	326.03	309.67	231.79	316.63	635.85	407.56
062	195.55	233.28	23.31	226.80	255.51	243.95	344.22	502.61
071	85.09	149.86	314.68	667.89	287.62	334.79	318.70	256.55
072	223.85	228.30	603.33	451.28	406.13	431.76	408.73	347.75
073	157.47	174.96	176.46	310.70	290.97	337.99	393.86	544.67
074	133.95	149.93	161.87	338.49	265.39	242.73	249.49	248.43
075	144.24	150.37	159.64	217.96	182.62	163.58	160.04	152.62
081	183.44	144.83	211.38	248.73	209.05	200.75	236.61	241.40
099	86.99	91.58	72.97	65.45	76.81	70.12	102.16	4.52
111	377.78	390.54	448.94	399.02	633.57	840.32	1439.29	2170.31
112	304.82	127.14	102.61	82.37	73.86	873.79	127.78	94.15
121	162.37	189.90	180.65	191.81	213.55	19.54	239.17	269.03
122	144.99	157.81	165.26	177.23	196.96	206.40	208.25	218.63
211	199.04	301.98	864.26	995.45	387.35	556.02	487.66	806.55
212	135.51	313.46	256.89	254.42	326.42	275.09	224.78	548.48
221	199.67	187.05	205.71	149.00	272.97	138.31	394.52	449.12
231	171.77	168.75	142.61	147.41	211.10	215.77	85.60	278.74
241	137.98	66.76	478.08	293.22	450.00	4357.14	575.60	1098.30
242	130.20	142.69	164.25	158.21	176.53	227.38	151.22	109.04

APPENDIX TABLE IV.1 (Contd.)

Article code No.	1965-66	1966-67	1967-68	1968-69	1969-70	1971-72	1972-73	1973-74
243	34.42	85.71	46.65	52.44	46.59	62.08	40.66	46.26
244	7500.00	2600.00	–	–	83.33	76.79	220.00	–
251	271.28	580.00	130.00	168.57	78.87	103.55	125.00	121.53
261	107.24	107.12	106.29	116.30	99.05	84.58	80.87	210.44
262	153.30	136.00	108.86	97.85	97.20	110.94	143.80	256.58
263	64.74	80.59	76.52	87.18	92.49	117.60	132.74	139.45
264	98.89	106.79	90.04	93.86	107.95	1122.59	104.18	82.39
265	91.48	81.89	87.34	86.89	89.09	97.33	98.49	92.20
266	37.58	34.82	65.31	24.00	28.04	75.81	80.31	46.72
267	107.59	90.33	88.05	84.67	87.98	103.60	115.23	129.02
273	30.99	65.44	254.91	200.25	120.84	114.33	87.51	65.22
274	–	–	–	–	–	1057.89	92.31	102.15
275	200.00	–	26.32	5.05	9.19	4.87	7.71	4.89
276	68.37	137.43	106.38	104.44	101.87	103.35	96.79	91.94
281	97.64	94.62	68.37	101.42	103.31	94.98	96.31	101.05
282	73.93	67.70	77.65	61.60	79.37	51.01	61.92	98.91
283	3085.55	127.47	112.25	107.09	101.18	118.66	128.9[illegible]	219.30
284	122.05	89.58	77.18	76.50	79.68	83.69	103.12	354.14
291	113.32	98.92	119.74	131.75	119.30	100.37	106.61	39.05
292	33.28	31.89	31.31	28.08	35.00	41.41	53.90	53.44
321	98.94	97.94	95.22	83.38	82.33	94.09	108.20	118.24
332	71.59	412.89	95.24	83.33	61.90	127.69	169.61	416.48
341	70.00	100.00	100.00	84.62	65.49	100.00	–	–
411	0.15	84.29	100.00	110.78	125.97	259.48	141.68	154.15
421	100.03	64.43	95.63	83.34	89.46	258.85	122.71	182.41

(Contd.)

APPENDIX TABLE IV.1 (Contd.)

Article code No.	1965-66	1966-67	1967-68	1968-69	1969-70	1971-72	1972-73	1973-74
422	106.70	136.50	97.55	74.62	73.74	92.04	129.10	222.06
431	68.67	58380	90.51	75.36	75.02	98.61	116.63	140.04
512	55.00	59.64	77.46	134.05	60.00	99.99	103.35	135.14
513	66.22	55.56	53.57	79.66	84.70	83.29	86.86	127.11
514	110.77	112.98	135.00	151.23	123.89	101.35	90.77	101.81
521	84.94	89.19	93.19	92.65	98.74	61.30	168.06	366.73
532	153.98	152.42	107.81	104.43	110.70	107.76	124.45	119.30
533	102.20	90.28	92.79	92.05	89.65	104.01	111.58	124.13
534	104.72	81.50	94.27	108.20	111.19	135.90	119.87	168.11
541	24.44	93.24	86.16	71.96	86.26	44.35	64.50	27.27
551	53.17	71.62	73.63	106.74	102.24	82.18	85.03	107.02
553	54.94	43.14	75.76	105.26	102.04	85.47	93.46	104.17
554	120.17	97.13	94.48	95.92	97.46	94.65	117.88	94.91
561	5.35	3.66	0.00	6.29	–	6074.92	9.93	11.39
571	3.10	7.65	22.89	76.17	136.00	62.64	57.59	371.97
581	88.25	90.50	71.23	81.89	94.52	164.98	143.94	165.22
599	19.99	44.73	69.58	65.76	144.61	107.08	38.75	165.97
611	72.40	75.38	67.90	59.97	66.93	62.87	88.53	120.93
612	10.00	56.74	49.16	74.42	80.23	89.36	109.10	138.85
613	1073.33	1225.00	356.67	60.38	71.21	81.28	89.91	102.41
621	130.90	87.21	99.23	128.18	106.83	119.66	155.43	134.86
629	102.77	61.02	42.33	51.29	84.14	100.27	88.89	86.37
631	112.21	119.63	129.14	131.10	110.14	120.53	139.52	142.32
632	122.78	67.77	56.90	73.55	95.67	80.53	85.07	85.59
633	114.47	167.50	184.38	101.79	163.64	227.27	140.98	143.92

APPENDIX TABLE IV.1 (Contd.)

Article code No.	1974-75	1975-76	1976-77	1977-78	1978-79	1979-80	1980-81	1981-82
243	107.52	123.30	76.36	297.67	170.72	189.11	112.98	563.50
244	–	–	590.00	1400.00	566.67	–	–	77.50
251	142.17	194.15	152.77	296.67	755.29	250.00	330.36	133.33
261	139.77	93.59	107.03	133.73	167.15	234.11	158.63	220.07
262	278.77	231.69	270.69	261.72	262.64	247.68	302.68	197.27
263	180.67	179.94	224.97	342.77	282.37	260379	264.38	334.59
264	109.27	120.45	67.14	88.15	84.60	98.88	136.81	127.78
265	126.02	118.70	136..18	179.22	151.37	77.33	301.09	378.84
266	111.28	118.37	135.04	180.47	42.09	25.31	225.00	28.97
267	211.37	240.96	232.07	352.10	434.65	518.18	618.32	430.77
273	68.91	108.28	104.97	103.01	166.03	158.97	152.69	179.45
274	240.34	205.13	191.59	186.52	175.13	326.54	353.54	309.47
275	16.26	32.00	20.45	11.80	8.64	8.29	9.75	8.35
276	95.77	144.26	200.80	102.85	169.88	166.82	2442.04	282.42
281	129.97	169.65	183.57	198.83	196.23	201.69	235.93	266.63
282	221.69	177.34	177.66	112.91	177.70	453.39	166.57	81.85
283	34.33	307.12	333.82	290.69	295.95	274.59	263.79	307.65
284	316.14	714.51	1038.53	660.00	2330.77	529.66	631.47	743.81
291	251.76	232.45	214.92	287.47	185.69	336.56	149.35	237.61
292	73.92	67.25	48.96	60.51	28.99	62.42	84.22	112.08
321	221.04	598.72	352.32	262.04	249.82	233.49	395.11	452.82
332	378.72	48.07	409.22	446.26	381.80	906.56	677.05	592.10
341	–	70.59	–	310.00	312.33	350.00	–	–
411	140.41	360.78	236.55	474.19	430.85	426.97	368.52	303.53
421	198.17	811.06	137.52	296.19	174.84	181.21	313.33	297.01

(Contd.)

APPENDIX TABLE IV.1 (Contd.)

Article code No.	1974-75	1975-76	1976-77	1977-78	1978-79	1979-80	1980-81	1981-82
422	206.89	159.21	143.62	1237.83	395.50	480.78	721.84	555.78
431	164.61	194.16	168.63	237.35	286.15	295.22	302.43	201.48
512	3223.39	312.60	331.14	279.63	318.42	390.95	568.76	617.64
513	119.81	120.76	119.57	150.72	70.40	126.46	191.47	243.60
514	277.84	189.25	158.72	220.57	138.49	192.04	402.27	308.46
521	781.85	339.52	17.21	–	–	–	–	–
532	138.59	175.84	205.25	257.69	222.37	279.31	251.99	273.57
533	210.37	198.83	185.80	215.00	240.53	290.75	325.97	325.20
534	271.78	305.30	385.07	350.44	304.13	340.15	366.35	339.99
541	60.98	178.68	76.94	42.75	33.78	38.44	41.15	42.53
551	230.08	87.09	70.33	136.85	219.16	175.25	145.90	194.34
553	232.56	83.33	113.64	144.15	227.27	129.87	232.56	333.33
554	229.10	226.97	209.71	214.16	245.98	109.06	264.60	369.71
561	–	–	6.88	38.38	–	500.00	18.95	43.37
571	188.43	192.75	222.03	138.96	175.88	159.58	314.00	206.16
581	189.87	214.55	267.58	240.45	348.04	235.05	284.07	514.56
599	199.98	125.34	160.19	196.07	231.66	206.51	289.10	380.40
611	122.04	136.41	190.33	40.43	219.80	319.80	40.37	362.05
612	114.64	158.25	201.04	230.40	295.26	177.49	540.10	571.83
613	106.35	117.74	155.65	38.80	67.88	23.75	79.23	290.09
621	150.44	240.12	213.57	282.85	346.37	294.25	390.82	781.43
629	112.95	109.35	145.72	107.50	155.27	128.42	157.75	175.57
631	181.63	202.83	196.68	344.51	340.39	457.52	387.88	531.71
632	121.63	143.37	148.64	18.62	214.88	225.51	247.64	290.75
633	438.24	168.57	230.30	227.31	741.94	256.93	334.35	306.94

APPENDIX TABLE IV.1 (Contd.)

Article code No.	1965-66	1966-67	1967-68	1968-69	1969-70	1971-72	1972-73	1973-74
641	119.57	94.88	99.07	124.20	93.72	121.43	134.80	206.38
642	78.15	72.64	79.23	73.57	89.55	109.68	105.16	119.81
651	86.28	39.75	79.56	84.73	88.92	110.37	126.95	217.13
653	71.56	60.37	90.86	87.98	90.92	104.34	121.25	126.30
654	110.99	100.95	85.11	78.82	93.03	107.23	97.12	123.22
655	100.30	96.60	94.68	97.18	126.74	103.10	107.57	145.80
656	101.88	76.01	110.88	86.79	103.73	939.73	88.14	171.89
657	93.98	90.97	87.14	91.60	101.90	120.85	115.38	193.66
658	92.01	89.15	85.33	90.25	91.03	110.30	116.11	155.84
659	97.00	99.07	91.04	96.13	103.66	115.49	127.69	119.43
661	134.00	123.76	95.72	91.36	102.34	108.20	124.77	133.69
662	48.33	72.78	78.01	66.65	37.36	86.19	72.85	46.36
663	89.98	106.64	99.40	116.56	107.84	113.06	96.13	9.34
664	68.14	85.08	88.09	97.99	85.06	81.67	104.52	81.20
665	127.51	140.93	154.2	107.58	121.94	130.22	149.58	137.31
666	168.97	71.19	86.19	94.97	72.99	178.16	50.63	229.27
671	100.59	57.99	64.33	56.90	81.22	81.15	76.05	89.97
672	147.37	88.63	84.98	81.67	88.10	124.46	188.11	229.36
673	70.50	65.08	66.45	66.14	77.22	94.20	101.77	183.13
674	171.45	30.01	61.89	63.46	77.73	149.81	74.68	145.58
675	86.57	33.33	205.00	45.45	75.47	89.29	146.67	172.09
676	87.11	59.52	95.64	81.27	99.89	117.92	117.72	151.14
677	53.03	61.32	0.12	60.50	75.75	90.93	96.82	132.62
678	85.87	78.35	83.63	82.67	83.04	106.28	106.57	176.56
679	73.52	8.30	84.49	63.08	99.70	127.96	102.57	123.97

(Contd.)

APPENDIX TABLE IV.1 (Contd.)

Article code No.	1965-66	1966-67	1967-68	1968-69	1969-70	1971-72	1972-73	1973-74
681	75.00	72.09	51.76	80.31	86.42	–	–	293.21
682	55.86	60.66	75.97	89.12	92.67	85.50	748.59	104.95
683	6.24	–	–	229.41	105.98	95.65	–	152.48
684	96.30	71.20	78.86	54.18	72.38	107.53	107.71	130.55
685	9.67	268.00	121.62	114.29	83.33	115.49	211.11	99.44
686	128.07	81.62	72.80	78.49	105.04	347.27	151.59	208.11
687	116.87	110.84	529.41	79.78	53.67	122.31	129.57	111.45
689	37.80	17.67	34.50	0.03	159.88	–	–	250.00
691	109.28	166.64	60.29	62.29	72.21	170.10	184.17	187.87
692	91.62	96.17	82.53	84.08	81.02	77.91	105.44	115.20
693	63.12	107.97	89.51	587.93	90.96	100.39	128.06	157.97
694	101.57	76.58	57.23	68.75	85.04	105.42	120.98	151.13
695	106.24	134.73	144.58	123.41	95.43	97.38	112.07	118.46
696	56.58	69.14	87.59	86.85	94.18	151.95	151.60	172.69
697	59.45	27.75	71.62	75.45	77.28	95.62	99.52	128.71
698	84.32	94.22	96.32	81.75	89.94	124.88	120.77	171.45
711	59.41	62.43	55.31	61.68	86.81	76.17	99.46	81.49
712	76.33	51.36	78.69	28.59	89.84	114.57	74.86	25.91
714	275.52	227.05	175.46	154.24	148.62	110.41	239.07	288.41
715	101.70	90.70	39.27	919.15	80.97	75.19	76.46	7.38
717	34.40	51.61	39.33	75.70	64.46	46.61	19.52	19.55
718	46.25	50.99	45.41	38.19	3.90	49.36	143.04	175.94
719	32.79	74.01	66.07	13.14	86.82	80.51	72.35	101.49
722	26.66	23.14	28.38	85.94	120.89	122.00	151.39	133.97
723	18.20	28.71	60.98	80.67	75.24	81.09	174.91	132.34
724	62.70	19.39	186.43	70.05	99.61	103.37	83.80	58.52

APPENDIX TABLE IV.1 (Contd.)

Article code No.	1974-75	1975-76	1976-77	1977-78	1978-79	1979-80	1980-81	1981-82
641	137.73	376.38	313.65	360.25	364.68	448.86	751.31	379.24
642	215.31	252.31	232.10	211.83	250.09	289.77	365.81	384.84
651	201.87	184.49	194.56	231.85	221.46	289.37	239.37	346.46
653	185.89	186.82	201.08	222.42	213.11	227.63	226.01	230.91
654	196.41	257.66	235.71	189.54	209.83	224.12	209.01	244.53
655	157.68	167.85	176.65	532.24	292378.8	333.14	405.48	518.56
656	207.61	220.30	33.01	182.44	86.25	144.81	75.57	313.87
657	183.28	209.92	225.96	239.57	251.33	274.58	293.27	304.20
658	214.78	195.09	235.32	285.15	246.50	410.39	345.15	438.00
659	199.43	208.63	130.48	142.44	160.23	132.70	145.50	185.10
661	225.78	273.59	277.99	287.87	257.50	297.74	286.12	261.30
662	60.05	116.46	49.18	120.96	122.77	1.01	23.74	41.54
663	6.86	18.25	11.22	19.84	1.12	16.45	9.85	16.43
664	94.16	91.74	143.21	1496.28	121.94	223.82	246.37	247.35
665	190.47	256.98	276.21	13.47	260.02	338.92	338.74	356.27
666	162.96	234.30	143.02	169.42	315.22	495.87	405.95	38.31
671	162.98	179.34	158.30	146.34	169.66	225.16	222.33	36.11
672	260.65	224.93	218.79	2195.34	253.62	33.02	540.93	1055.08
673	266.06	177.70	195.78	176.69	219.48	299.85	305.31	614.93
674	111.99	253.69	138.43	194.00	255.42	284.61	606.09	789.30
675	425.00	4500.00	456.36	141.77	522.86	491.13	454.55	6719.15
676	124.68	357.80	3249.55	315.63	436.19	310.05	537.02	804.76
677	204.52	249.85	172.72	173.60	199.67	241.05	173.91	351.09
678	284.29	227.34	56.92	217.89	179.67	175.54	341.03	356.21
679	221.01	266.27	231.58	278.80	245.92	308.22	337.94	410.47

(Contd.)

APPENDIX TABLE IV.1 (Contd.)

Article code No.	1974-75	1975-76	1976-77	1977-78	1978-79	1979-80	1980-81	1981-82
681	159.86	158.58	171.80	179.75	198.39	251.82	–	–
682	186.08	185.53	153.75	208.14	221.73	163.13	129.37	271.00
683	164.00	168.95	153.54	175.14	42.09	43.92	133.33	18085.11
684	216.50	129.04	110.91	272.56	294.05	481.67	432.20	452.02
685	220.15	98.91	185.55	235.00	453.13	552.17	387.23	1236.84
686	210.03	287.50	702.38	616.82	517.78	472.84	210.78	350.02
687	131.00	259.18	2045.45	220.51	355.10	315.38	232.01	232.80
689	25.58	875.00	222.35	434.23	303.65	68.68	220.03	27.93
691	304.49	286.12	380.47	1044.33	411.60	369.66	508.64	603.48
692	157.79	285.25	204.17	230.76	224.24	437.50	352.68	449.83
693	258.53	269.05	245.52	51.26	219.56	260.30	322.58	251.69
694	209.91	238.89	218.46	177.56	82.40	225.89	278.49	360.07
695	159.11	159.67	199.73	225.60	277.30	285.03	366.84	377.41
696	426.67	285.35	416.70	244.12	226.85	175.53	235.93	376.06
697	209.68	185.47	202.56	235.80	288.11	349.90	250.00	149.91
698	221.60	237.65	238.95	257.90	227.88	269.48	367.12	416.23
711	87.52	86.68	127.85	126.12	124.17	162.22	124.69	147.44
712	181.34	131.34	213.60	202.30	185.01	22.03	241.49	233.94
714	297.15	393.81	195.90	132.15	166.83	174.49	155.94	97.65
715	81.76	46.71	82.87	85.53	72.10	173.55	192.32	258.98
717	316.56	144.82	151.63	128.31	186.68	274.10	232.68	150.57
718	158.51	182.57	126.83	387.35	4.79	17.00	38.60	66.91
719	130.33	143.19	151.39	172.81	160.09	36.28	66.27	137.40
722	167.66	137.77	149.08	335.62	482.45	413.17	389.24	321.50
723	260.46	266.48	424.90	435.37	497.12	399.24	683.99	627.60
724	113.13	86.43	66.46	147.11	86.58	142.99	418.18	360.71

APPENDIX TABLE IV.1 (Contd.)

Article code No.	1965-66	1966-67	1967-68	1968-69	1969-70	1971-72	1972-73	1973-74
725	101.78	91.37	93.04	99.56	99.54	101.69	75.22	105.55
726	100.00	900.00	–	6.74	73.27	67.05	100.81	106.01
729	124.01	121.69	119.59	22.32	33.48	140.01	135.38	91.97
731	446.00	74.54	41.09	60.79	79.36	129.44	188.98	163.49
732	34.65	65.66	63.83	77.67	90.40	128.73	118.04	131.96
733	132.16	85.10	105.71	94.09	102.98	121.49	116.99	139.10
734	43.88	89.86	195.34	39.67	139.27	523.55	47.72	131.46
735	41.86	6.09	57.46	71.56	431.82	90.58	1725.33	481.42
812	68.91	83.08	68.96	89.65	97.47	119.81	111.26	168.11
821	90.53	95.61	117.96	112.57	103.01	91.90	116.05	141.25
831	171.17	125.38	147.25	130.97	144.62	135.26	153.70	256.48
841	75.15	94.49	133.48	84.55	112.75	109.62	108.26	124.04
842	66.67	102.27	81.25	90.91	115.63	101.70	108.61	151.64
851	100.89	88.69	97.45	82.17	84.13	88.00	104.65	110.17
861	16.39	46.01	60.90	49.96	72.23	77.68	458.28	101.37
862	66.56	102.51	28.23	32.18	27.97	138.72	73.85	238.65
863	68.34	56.92	66.69	133.77	82.58	79.97	89.56	91.35
864	94.19	63.93	117.07	109.30	149.25	137.06	95.37	149.60
891	74.58	78.22	104.84	96.54	104.93	111.41	137.01	144.60
892	108.13	86.14	95.90	94.03	108.77	96.23	111.39	110.97
893	112.28	99.03	114.66	103.45	103.18	117.87	137.87	169.53
894	76.60	51.89	71.21	102.94	80.60	99.88	123.09	153.60
895	40.27	30.19	89.18	103.79	134.57	69.90	90.95	95.94
896	93.75	150.83	243.91	76.34	79.36	79.37	59.52	68.49
897	41.99	37.76	44.99	12.24	79.21	12.07	20.72	0.26
899	112.31	91.23	91.78	92.90	76.37	104.23	129.70	140.48

APPENDIX TABLE IV.1 (Contd.)

Article code No.	1974-75	1975-76	1976-77	1977-78	1978-79	1979-80	1980-81	1981-82
725	184.72	177.34	191.62	186.14	154.42	190.00	181.52	172.75
726	106.24	128.90	227.96	142.96	265.73	88.27	29.61	43.63
729	129.21	194.26	176.81	218.37	213.60	190.11	356.66	241.99
731	269.36	261.74	300.98	158.52	371.94	469.60	455.88	963.76
732	159.10	187.81	210.60	215.46	219.61	239.83	285.80	292.44
733	198.40	202.02	20.50	224.26	232.42	267.21	306.19	246.49
734	153.18	46.76	21.49	43.61	13.07	64.34	198.01	312.18
735	316.59	1793.08	3241.37	3946.13	6619.94	17250.73	1538.87	789.77
812	249.04	306.46	221.05	219.46	253.81	293.62	99.45	379.21
821	203.29	235.32	243.43	193.72	38.57	30.69	413.80	396.33
831	285.20	339.11	243.27	220.89	297.66	383.35	512.82	618.52
841	145.24	153.42	157.90	192.82	218.82	78.67	49.29	318.21
842	499.56	139.57	1669.44	192.21	217.39	78.73	49.42	322.76
851	135.10	186.99	192.68	183.01	205.40	287.72	289.28	339.37
861	89.28	190.03	188.01	210.88	281.94	397.26	642.01	386.41
862	105.22	124.99	112.35	78.68	226.88	149.36	26.04	74.06
863	104.12	123.47	129.03	154.75	161.15	161.85	148.52	185.66
864	397.86	200.74	242.53	397.92	396.05	300.15	274.51	283.43
891	163.92	211.81	224.95	275.47	133.43	197.27	228.50	409.06
892	143.27	184.19	190.99	266.82	277.05	270.20	283.30	533.86
893	231.96	222.06	189.12	228.03	23.93	269.75	411.81	326.25
894	204.71	292.47	384.26	580.19	460.22	415.99	479.99	459.88
895	82.77	100.53	62.86	93.07	212.15	196.02	161.27	188.12
896	48.08	74.63	51.81	61.35	34.25	73.53	316.97	107.53
897	41.83	33.72	57.46	134.39	157.24	283.85	120.52	703.71
899	153.40	207.89	190.69	66.55	137.28	201.80	222.57	17.78

Note : Name of the Commodity according to article code number is presented in Appendix *Table IV.3*

Source : Estimates are derived on the basis of the data available in *Monthly Statistics of the Foreign Trade of India, Vol. I, Exports and Re-Exports*, Published by Directorate General of Commercial Intelligence and Statistics Government of India for the years 1965-66 to 1981-82.

Appendix Table IV.2 : Volume Indices of Exports : 1965-66 to 1981-82 (1970-71 = 100)

Article code No.	1965-66	1966-67	1967-68	1968-69	1969-70
001	489.88	582.95	419.94	613.01	28.90
011	26.38	32.79	27.43	20.12	40.49
012	8.65	22.16	9.73	29.73	41.62
013	184.48	272.41	224.14	294.83	141.38
022	43.00	53.68	152.09	44.16	7.22
023	38.22	107.33	71.73	92.67	56701.57
024	–	–	–	50.00	100.00
025	–	82.61	297.83	160.87	47.83
031	8.05	51.88	58.48	72.80	95.50
032	49.32	82.02	83.60	8.67	66.53
041	16.94	77.05	49.73	61.75	38.25
042	8.56	8.04	11.85	20.65	44.68
043	528.57	514.29	14.29	1585.71	728.57
044	790.00	970.00	–	160.00	320.00
045	19.35	3.23	3.23	19.35	22.58
046	5.04	0.59	1.13	4.67	109.14
047	6.60	–	–	–	–
048	92.27	95.19	93.98	105.57	140.61
049	37.86	102.00	12.23	87.48	135.69
051	103.64	102.36	101.26	129.10	117.96
052	120.88	159.12	60.18	149.25	113.50
053	39.24	35.05	54.95	50.94	132.96
054	67.17	60.50	65.70	68.22	85.83
055	44.12	48.84	39.99	58.39	61.68
061	87.59	103.41	63.17	29.29	22.88
062	99.93	112.11	52.09	115.95	73.22
071	79.84	78.50	101.94	89.74	101.05
072	44.71	147.39	127.34	99.03	61057.11
073	46.53	51.30	87.80	120.53	109.06
074	99.06	95.55	102.05	100.79	87.38
075	131.73	113.22	109.45	104.63	88.36
081	91.12	90.49	81.98	91.94	78.62
099	50.36	42.04	47.21	48.39	78.23
111	1518.18	181.82	45.45	27.27	27.27
112	150.67	72.00	88.00	82.67	60.00
121	119.08	78.70	116.47	110.76	114.12
122	279.84	107.13	74.46	22.87	73.04
211	289.62	294.29	177.61	134.16	177.13
212	1233.50	598.50	512.50	448.00	915.50
221	9.99	8.25	40.80	143.56	143.49
231	51.32	12.43	21.96	38.36	80.95

(Contd.)

Appendix Table IV.2 (Contd.)

Article code No.	1965-66	1966-67	1967-68	1968-69	1969-70
241	283.56	277671.2	452.05	63.01	702.74
242	888.32	71.35	76.85	88.01	118.56
243	274.30	3.91	534.08	630.73	491.62
244	4.35	8.70	–	–	391.30
251	1.85	0.05	0.10	0.34	64.92
261	100.07	132.78	112.43	70.52	130.55
262	147.62	115.03	116.87	116.29	100.25
263	132.57	132.47	154.49	110.01	117.08
264	114.48	198.07	70.41	63.41	91.15
265	222.75	273.49	160.66	139.75	94.42

Appendix Table IV.2 (Contd.)

Article code No.	1971-72	1972-73	1973-74	1974-75	1975-76
001	106.94	247.11	363.041	85.55	307.23
011	60.13	113.51	189.71	182.14	263.91
012	60.00	33.51	41..62	31.35	120.00
013	72.41	137.93	37.93	24.14	17.24
022	49.35	352.96	20.35	27.42	40.12
023	984.29	303.14	192.15	42.41	346.07
024	400.00	–	–	–	–
025	19.57	6.52	226.09	321.74	1193.48
031	106.86	126.52	168.64	147.18	200.67
032	64.22	69.06	99.27	49.41	8.88
041	284.15	353803.8	757.92	175.41	1511.48
042	36.37	69.94	45.23	127.23	104.62
043	157.14	557.14	728.57	914.29	2200.00
044	–	38560.00	4050.00	1440.00	8720.00
045	12.90	0.00	–	3.23	287.10
046	36.62	29.34	0.46	–	–
047	196.23	38.68	16.04	23.58	270.75
048	160.25	195.80	110.82	159.54	195.98
049	73.40	50.71	24.89	1.18	22.86
051	118.44	132.25	104.18	125.28	116.06
052	143.72	113.41	127.08	199.60	279.38
053	106.21	165.71	92.49	77.55	75.42
054	41.14	40.25	47.04	55.51	102.88
055	87.38	56.29	78.96	031.75	130.15
061	87.87	28.88	67.57	186.79	324.09
062	64.47	57.00	33.11	33.24	43.88
071	109.98	157.31	160.47	240.39	177.16
072	73.88	96.23	30.50	13.24	12.88
073	76.14	105.72	196.42	66.69	68.35
074	104.67	96.97	95.49	112.79	106.54
075	137.83	94.53	129.76	109.58	121.61
081	86.53	114.12	1317.69	95.48	112.71
099	12.32	169.58	102.59	186.71	389.94
111	545.45	1081.82	81.82	490.91	1345.45
112	517.33	3032.00	704.00	110.67	530.67
121	120.42	198.61	16.44	157.62	156.14
122	243.10	165.35	185.12	110.48	286.84
211	13.04	15.19	13.38	3.86	1.34
212	222.50	948.50	439.00	490.00	52.00
221	107.17	110.50	320.35	246.09	616.14
231	234.66	361.38	3029.89	1293.12	59.26
241	409.59	239.73	108.22	353.42	478.08

(Contd.)

Appendix Table IV.2 (Contd.)

Article code No.	1971-72	1972-73	1973-74	1974-75	1975-76
242	111.61	143.26	189.24	115.35	146.66
243	349.16	1067.60	2344.13	2311.73	3249.16
244	243.48	43.48	–	–	–
251	20.24	1.18	1.42	0.82	2.02
261	83.53	163.90	191.81	57.42	185.92
262	75.59	95.59	65.08	61.80	40.84
263	94.84	113.19	159.83	57.51	150.77
264	27.06	109.54	125.16	381.48	202.14
265	51.72	44.31	50.64	72.91	77.31

Appendix Table IV.2 (Contd.)

Article code No.	1976-77	1977-78	1978-79	1979-80	1980-81	1981-82
001	2919.94	5235.84	3640.75	1684.10	4730.92	3617.63
011	490.11	645.73	903.69	1280.77	1833.05	2156.65
012	36.76	–	1.62	10.27	6.49	4.86
013	48.28	25.86	4015.52	9787.93	34403.45	24868.97
022	240.12	482.11	208.08	119.77	268.98	190.48
023	630.89	927.75	651.83	1614.66	1164.40	1487.96
024	–	–	–	–	–	–
025	9906.52	9691.30	1339.13	7626.09	54263.04	35828.26
031	211.72	230.50	270.80	272.15	245.91	265.47
032	10.56	15.79	13.75	16.83	1695.15	13.99
041	589.07	191187.9	268.31	227787.9	33889.62	750.27
042	94.25	159.38	337.20	1572.51	232.27	2662.77
043	505385.7	116028.5	10285.71	638171.4	83828.57	650671.4
044	1930.00	–	80.00	–	–	440.00
045	12.90	312.90	12222.58	209.68	658.06	70.97
046	–	90.55	852.36	406.18	5.58	0.07
047	1335.85	1726.42	200.94	314.15	326.42	152.83
048	399.94	482.76	598.05	20135.24	442.45	431.57
049	26.63	4.22	498.03	73.41	4.20	4.94
051	108.38	90.93	72.35	94.67	77.15	80.30
052	234.16	370.04	159.34	261.06	483.32	2425.00
053	235.59	233.01	212.85	158.75	232.89	482.81
054	160.35	109.67	271.36	102.99	152.31	160.74
055	228.64	329.45	318.82	288.70	242.95	328.14
061	156.74	20.62	199.88	160.73	21.40	53.43
062	999.66	113.73	90.31	178.40	147.78	51.48
071	144.36	113.73	199.31	194.27	267.66	226.63
072	3.65	137.18	285.66	95.26	175.46	489.31
073	93.72	115.36	95.47	8.72	2.78	47.48
074	122.04	110.66	86.53	102.22	115.05	107.31
075	117.72	162.00	208.92	235.30	179.32	166.76
081	205.82	107.10	118.33	142.22	113.54	009.14
099	301.05	438.52	421.91	500.80	416.97	9815.39
111	4290.91	4618.18	2572.73	563.64	254.55	581.82
112	4756.00	4742.67	9844.00	31986.67	6210.67	7617.33
121	170.34	187.98	165.13	199.71	165.67	242.62
122	303.89	195.63	243.80	469.73	671.28	1200.12
211	0.70	0.70	2.71	2.12	3.18	1.38
212	1092.50	656.00	308.50	273.00	224.00	16.50
221	580.82	48.54	74.39	156.92	257.44	135.68
231	14124.34	13846.56	471.96	365.43	345.50	316.14
241	2112.33	4402.74	287.67	9.59	1610.96	645.21
242	169.61	134.59	132.88	85.97	33.01	32.77

Appendix Table IV.2 (Contd.)

Article code No.	1976-77	1977-78	1978-79	1979-80	1980-81	1981-82
243	14026.26	4586.03	3222.35	1308.38	2577.65	229.61
244	43.48	13.04	91.30	–	–	173.91
251	21.89	1.18	0.84	0.02	11.72	0.30
261	231.35	178.43	328.50	99.25	21.86	77.14
262	58.43	12.24	9.47	10.99	6.60	19.78
263	104.92	6.77	43.29	200.95	408.15	79.98
264	56.36	45.07	38.06	50.69	90.85	228.62
265	226.24	113.08	84.02	101.73	19.11	5.03

Appendix Table IV.2 (Contd.)

Article code No.	1965-66	1966-67	1967-68	1968-69	1969-70
266	322.41	364.43	189.78	536.97	434.59
267	150.88	136.96	107.51	140.22	121.82
273	215.40	53.74	21.05	34.16	41.79
274	–	–	–	–	–
275	1.61	–	20.43	2674.19	333.33
276	153.96	63.26	84.24	80.31	97.89
281	57.90	63.26	64.82	74.32	78.09
282	168.59	210.40	204.13	196.68	162.15
283	3.44	72.83	66.16	86.58	83.14
284	34.17	79.37	99.36	77.27	92.11
291	105.41	145.71	111.78	129.48	114.12
292	233.45	210.89	179.73	226.87	216.43
321	113.13	59.97	47.79	79.70	62.17
332	166.13	29.13	89.77	132.21	140.10
341	12.05	3.61	6.02	15.66	136.14
411	44273.86	29.05	51.04	69.27	75.10
421	195.57	376.51	101.44	204.75	162.90
422	85.64	26.07	56.79	223.08	93.09
431	1678.25	587.50	328.57	458.60	209.25
512	86.53	62.90	38.54	14.90	62.74
513	35.56	19.92	32.43	63.66	55.75
514	33.22	16.79	25.48	42.13	71.00
521	90.03	147.89	163.40	254.07	336.35
532	36.08	40.33	27.20	38.93	33.55
533	24.72	19.75	39.59	57.64	58.75
534	22.15	15.23	13.10	43.30	57.23
541	86.12	47.78	45.63	65.66	81.82
551	181.29	136.13	133.30	107.86	110.81
553	83.35	91.41	61.07	68.65	81.12
554	82.21	66.53	62.64	85.41	91.40
561	2077.78	3944.44	100.00	23855.56	–
571	338.54	989.42	41.81	34.17	6.30
581	26.92	9.95	6.13	69.37	125.58
599	453.98	127.57	102.15	167.96	66.60
611	85.74	114.62	109.48	167.69	168.08
612	624.47	70.52	79.45	144.32	167.38
613	12.10	32.26	24.19	671.77	2562.90
621	37.2	48.36	37.90	47.81	47.88
629	49.08	83.32	105.09	132.31	82.13
631	3.06	7.16	6.39	17.52	48.79
632	37.30	62.70	116.24	73.37	85.03
633	30.40	16.00	25.60	44.80	13.20

(Contd.)

Appendix Table IV.2 (Contd.)

Article code No.	1965-66	1966-67	1967-68	1968-69	1969-70
641	18.60	32.67	57.35	129.71	104.11
642	88.65	69.33	51.37	96.00	78.83
651	79.77	148.58	58.75	83.18	133.46
653	134.68	85.08	55.65	89.38	99.04

Appendix Table IV.2 (Contd.)

Article code No.	1971-72	1972-73	1973-74	1974-75	1975-76
266	78.15	99.58	64.99	18.63	6.86
267	110.34	80.11	57.22	17.92	12.38
273	6.19	4.23	408.14	116.29	12.70
274	6.19	4.23	408.14	116.29	12.70
275	661.83	920.43	956.45	830.11	107.53
276	90.44	107.01	96.31	140.12	91.74
281	93.99	97.20	112.08	105.22	107.45
282	56.28	29.76	42.29	.9.41	59.21
283	67.91	65.35	51.06	499.54	81.57
284	75.92	39.33	16.04	15.50	4.93
291	103.60	102.46	436.49	117.85	72.78
292	267.13	215.80	316.87	355.85	312.13
321	28.28	72.73	64.71	76.66	69.48
332	80.88	90.78	34.35	42.03	458.83
341	12.05	–	–	–	81.93
411	350.21	1683.40	95.02	385.06	363.90
421	164.08	541.10	60.71	99.00	14.12
422	108.98	265.62	200.99	234.51	302.63
431	186.69	358.28	462.99	620.13	1042.86
512	100.56	82.68	117.63	74.76	71.33
513	129.65	175.24	254.49	459.67	335.96
514	66.32	78.12	107.05	115.56	137.16
521	26.36	0.63	4.72	33.99	165.68
532	33.70	42.89	36.31	25.31	46.25
533	60.78	90.72	58.59	97.28	90.82
534	75.67	156.54	196.43	211.35	141.07
541	256.38	189.07	647.72	439.26	146.44
551	125.51	126.08	150.60	106.53	116.39
553	157.58	187.99	156.77	90.98	296.56
554	169.05	158.18	179.17	76.13	211.27
561	3455.56	754111.1	11411.11	–	–
571	297.57	543.83	101.26	315.70	203.86
581	20.86	22.28	29.46	30.95	17.46
599	82.89	217.87	120.64	.74.79	145.03
611	200.28	268.93	191.60	153.21	195.90
612	114.43	193.77	325.47	574.79	300.65
613	288.71	25433.06	22582.26	54787.10	49573.39
621	83.38	38.45	178.72	85.62	63.46
629	111.98	105.73	144.68	170.79	149.55
631	60.65	55.56	226.51	286.61	146.94
632	89.00	84.14	211.38	347.45	559.96
633	8.80	48.80	59.20	13.60	14.00

(Contd.)

Appendix Table IV.2 (Contd.)

Article code No.	1971-72	1972-73	1973-74	1974-75	1975-76
641	29.82	40.27	53.09	71.58	10.94
642	93.89	130.83	146.92	113.33	103.04
651	73.89	84.76	40.39	54.06	35.63
653	107.42	105.92	236.36	117.19	105.84

Appendix Table IV.2 (Contd.)

Article code No.	1976-77	1977-78	1978-79	1979-80	1980-81	1981-82
266	35.57	35.85	283.47	112.32	0.56	1079.97
267	41.93	33.73	17.57	4.92	3.26	1.62
273	1095.50	1436.69	1196.49	1643.12	2695.85	2008.85
274	104.56	86.97	121.82	105.54	41.37	61.89
275	3412.37	6936.56	10253.76	12095.70	4234.41	14035.48
276	77.22	162.96	102.49	115.53	75.83	77.40
281	110.78	100.03	98.69	112.17	101.52	110.81
282	79.01	55.53	22.80	4.48	7.58	13.33
283	84.62	43.62	63.69	69.55	59.10	57.85
284	12.69	8.04	1.00	11.11	3.65	2.68
291	115.33	128.68	108.32	103.32	243.55	132.09
292	503.79	459.74	999.39	518.62	407.17	491.97
321	101.44	187.25	113.16	238.03	160.00	50.73
332	52.41	41.15	42.21	24.27	42.99	48.73
341	–	12.05	263.86	7.23	–	–
411	60.17	77.18	412.86	300.00	254.36	223.65
421	923.67	132.85	118.43	3134.73	0.94	4.18
422	471.58	23.57	48.75	98.99	29.62	45.49
431	1818.18	2842.37	2180.52	5666.56	2347.08	1937.34
512	102.19	110.04	145.73	115.62	72.11	75.82
513	386.74	204.41	1234.56	641.33	468.04	103.47
514	267.68	190.75	329.23	243.41	135.32	260.92
521	53.27	–	–	–	–	–
532	70.55	105.66	112.12	123.84	85.26	71.73
533	106.36	111.41	99.18	110.54	98.77	149.07
534	257.03	282.04	298.69	344.84	401.81	262.77
541	359.55	914.72	1971.76	2688.04	17262.24	3388.27
551	149.52	99.43	63.35	115.88	130.55	106.48
553	342.08	299.44	214.23	511.72	553.83	991.04
554	267.11	272.28	144.78	981.09	1451.39	1687.34
561	15344.44	3155.56	–	122.22	11000.44	8711.11
571	573.89	959.03	1160.96	623.34	149.96	278.00
581	48.80	37.07	19.59	38.43	27.87	21.03
599	259.02	175.11	187.78	399.60	164.90	196.44
611	180.77	178.97	192.30	189.15	959.00	107.95
612	742.91	1236.99	1350.47	4996.96	1883.04	2689.25
613	44109.68	75217.74	9248.39	32240.32	8604.84	366.13
621	134.66	94.07	106.74	100.29	132.39	198.12
629	323.09	260.27	182.57	236.20	233.96	263.64
631	324.16	154.02	171.34	148.74	156.07	147.05
632	764.73	1120.30	1225.78	1263.98	1096.46	985.60
633	52.80	108.40	109.60	109.60	287.60	196.00

(Contd.)

Appendix Table IV.2 (Contd.)

Article code No.	1976-77	1977-78	1978-79	1979-80	1980-81	1981-82
641	12.26	26.71	24.92	12.71	13.31	17.07
642	139.05	103.13	98.34	71.52	52.83	60.37
651	81.19	60.32	47.01	38.04	94.46	40.30
653	161.26	154.31	222.87	199.48	207.07	260.37

Appendix Table IV.2 (Contd.)

Article code No.	1965-66	1966-67	1967-68	1968-69	1969-70
654	67.45	61.18	52.70	109.93	159.36
655	68.87	56.66	71.39	114.50	79.01
656	136.23	76.04	62.52	60.96	129.33
657	88.20	96.75	104.82	108.90	101.39
658	111.15	87.01	95.52	100.00	97.63
659	155.90	132.86	135.60	119.29	104.53
661	21.63	9.25	26.37	107.69	88.05
662	45.91	24.60	23.83	97.97	426.47
663	75.88	74.81	57.09	92.96	117.73
664	36.64	25.89	39.02	71.47	99.72
665	28.36	19.07	21.63	63.92	57.44
666	16.86	68.60	138.95	231.40	101.16
671	19.65	26.99	91.41	133.60	108.77
672	3.69	4.37	93.30	228.86	102.84
673	29.21	56.33	99.44	137.59	120.58
674	19.28	837.80	188.22	117.22	97.03
675	63.21	1.42	9.43	430.66	100.00
676	27.26	14.29	39.04	70.40	120.70
677	23.72	22.85	7802.11	73.90	75.98
678	41.90	57.11	68.09	124.87	142.31
679	54.47	68.80	21.35	24.31	29.28
681	5.26	2569.74	11477.63	54355.26	78645.00
682	19.75	10.33	5.70	50.05	62.58
683	2362.43	0.00	0.00	9.83	67.63
684	10.59	16.08	22.28	316.03	210.71
685	137.24	12.76	18.88	10.71	33.67
686	27.34	32.61	59.95	22.30	28.54
687	21.50	21.50	17.62	23.03	593.26
689	771.04	660.98	505.18	153262.1	311.59
691	0.68	2.23	48.37	87.36	154.13
692	64.16	59.09	90.22	112.62	147.43
693	10.24	19.58	30.48	7.86	91.72
694	20.46	23.72	44.62	83.42	61.10
695	19.29	14.97	23.98	33.98	43.48
696	167.40	57.57	54.58	112.79	93.58
697	113.11	145.99	103.19	124.66	122.12
698	70.69	39.26	51.63	97.96	89.49
711	73.20	48.06	41.72	87.91	81.41
712	25.17	52.91	64.12	311.86	109.93
714	14.27	10.46	33.45	47.59	65.14
715	14.96	21.70	65.74	5.24	112.83
717	48.94	25.78	47.01	39.51	135.50
718	87.71	51.37	39.66	120.75	1159.50
719	71.00	29.03	52.35	441.72	110.68

Appendix Table IV.2 (Contd.)

Article code No.	1971-72	1972-73	1973-74	1974-75	1975-76
654	91.31	103.94	142.22	114.79	164.84
655	76.85	85.95	121.31	126.49	165.03
656	102.36	983.77	155.85	349.74	579.97
657	103.86	146.91	102.97	150.61	149.12
658	93.07	111.96	154.91	102.60	112.03
659	120.51	102.33	99.74	77.64	62.15
661	101.78	173.35	100.79	187.20	301.71
662	73.68	193.88	393.04	757.46	683.40
663	114.65	189.76	3172.51	5422.95	1833.94
664	103.96	169.17	235.77	250.17	357.65
665	62.39	98.56	166.91	165.63	168.96
666	50.58	277.91	190.70	251.16	261.05
671	35.13	78.17	69.93	32.13	32.46
672	0.79	21.43	17.95	44.13	299.43
673	32.32	19.90	9.83	13.34	64.35
674	39.01	175.30	121.87	199.59	212.01
675	13.21	28.30	20.28	16.98	0.47
676	114.66	15.57	34.74	1.06	17.65
677	79.08	41.50	72.13	158.72	138.26
678	95.33	98.40	129.07	160.81	114.18
679	98.47	61.09	114.73	376.17	393.07
681	–	–	25293.42	657955.2	14443.34
682	74.83	9.09	80.52	20.61	10.36
683	26.59	–	58.38	86.71	109.83
684	63.78	64.81	61.45	50.60	198.16
685	115.31	41.33	272.96	68.37	187.24
686	13.19	112.95	118.23	363.55	3.84
687	163.73	77.98	178.76	77.72	12.69
689	–	–	2.44	2308.23	4.88
691	26.44	36.89	26.61	28.83	36.29
692	166.36	202.66	214.76	293.93	226.63
693	98.91	67.35	97.09	196.79	169.11
694	62.37	49.84	87.95	141.11	153.37
695	123.59	135.79	176.71	186.59	253.77
696	68.14	89.39	68.28	38.38	52.88
697	134.39	161.80	190.39	164.82	178.92
698	92.20	109.47	100.38	132.27	147.06
711	133.50	167.98	289.60	554.61	619.38
712	62.76	158.36	968.90	277.19	509.50
714	99.26	47.17	71.74	93.63	59.04
715	120.03	89.91	1649.92	288.85	624.41
717	153.79	325.07	348.16	345.22	207.34
718	222.90	82.64	186.42	220.92	283.16
719	97.77	148.07	171.11	225.79	268.60

Appendix Table IV.2 (Contd.)

Article code No.	1976-77	1977-78	1978-79	1979-80	1980-81	1981-82
654	159.36	159.55	165.94	103.56	131.10	240.80
655	274.38	115.07	160.61	123.41	175.53	180.99
656	3662.81	186.84	926.58	582.43	615.78	176.49
657	215.41	273.72	286.47	356.28	383.51	431.32
658	144.42	110382	93.09	107.74	128.62	101.04
659	80.00	90.72	54.81	132.13	120.45	73.93
661	541.93	260.53	141.95	111.83	78.50	80.69
662	3730.15	2211.17	829.84	52310.37	4953.40	4257.04
663	4846.13	3417.57	35306.25	4391.06	7703.06	5782.54
664	505.31	1135.89	1062.03	621.08	538.15	491.97
665	233.42	6123.46	295.39	223.09	238.86	244.86
666	466.28	1412.79	427.91	520.35	806.98	12547.67
671	156.59	116.85	71.99	28.63	0.75	110.43
672	632.66	77.74	256.08	54.51	14.82	0.40
673	200.01	128.35	82.01	14.96	4.94	1.95
674	676.21	660.38	988.14	398.56	13.04	11.01
675	111.32	1226.42	66.04	191.51	10.38	22.17
676	18.33	51.57	60.11	13.59	1.16	2.22
677	247.28	493.32	720.54	1177.04	914.20	127.79
678	1271.90	297.89	309.05	241.94	141.66	135.98
679	472.90	666.84	420.00	425.32	465.36	565.80
681	1160.18	575336.8	626384.2	11260.53	–	–
682	13.40	6.09	11.86	29.15	63.2	13.51
683	73.41	106.94	4710.98	342.20	183.82	54.34
684	445.92	144.39	61.23	62.74	42.02	37.52
685	310.71	61.22	48.98	35.20	47.96	9.69
686	10.07	25.66	10.79	135.97	562.59	533.57
687	2.85	70.73	12.69	3.37	130.31	322.28
689	699.70	113.11	183.84	1845.73	377.44	923.48
691	61.38	84.71	88.93	96.18	67.51	76.51
692	585.84	565.46	1265.64	533.00	397.25	393.18
693	189.95	1183.42	285.27	218.20	121.47	173.42
694	460.94	576.04	563.71	505.88	299.32	224.67
695	309.35	311.30	329.44	333.62	276.11	267.51
696	34.61	171.07	176.76	214.95	146.65	176.17
697	281.09	274.70	271.47	249.76	360.75	694.63
698	221.04	261.14	425.11	250.38	229.78	272.87
711	486.61	659.59	840.19	801.77	1011.44	1039.11
712	227.13	327.80	616.87	652.83	373.00	883.23
714	61.38	75.48	48.95	33.03	57.28	103.45
715	801.02	662.70	1007.83	522.71	397.50	343.42
717	145.29	122.12	85.62	99.04	118.33	229.04
718	504.82	1207.17	28051.63	8334.29	3732.32	2809.87
719	283.26	335.61	430.51	1911.52	1294.31	747.83

Appendix Table IV.2 (Contd.)

Article code No.	1965-66	1966-67	1967-68	1968-69	1969-70
722	43.62	46.58	69.73	49.51	53.04
723	102.28	72.80	55.29	173.98	146.99
724	23.07	91.75	7.72	74.44	84.80
725	97.68	105.09	102.75	133.45	124.52
726	8.33	0.38	–	84.28	19.13
729	41.36	40.15	36.75	346.43	281.87
731	0.18	39.10	97.42	400.24	37.29
732	25.21	13.83	16.88	35.10	58.90
733	20.64	21.30	29.05	56.21	62.56
734	403.70	564.24	60.14	180.59	105.36
735	47.60	42.44	24.72	81.73	40.59
812	128.72	79.96	97.27	99.89	141.98
821	73.08	45.35	40.19	58.27	68.08
831	12.31	13.73	20.25	22.50	77.80
841	44.32	24.09	21.87	57.69	63.45
842	54.55	800.00	145.45	100.00	290.91
851	71.58	86.49	82.19	97.70	95.91
861	115 59	22.20	42.45	99.33	83.80
862	991.94	106.99	112.37	374.19	684.41
863	64.49	42.73	99.57	37.56	89.83
864	71.43	28.11	37.79	19.82	30.88
891	104.48	109.56	56.54	76.15	90.83
892	92.39	62.33	79.94	88.14	111.79
893	37.84	19.70	30.25	57.89	76.83
894	50.00	67.79	51.22	58.60	83.72
895	75.62	48.34	28.14	48.45	53.08
896	39.55	22.27	17.04	90.53	125.34
897	167.41	133.03	228.68	791.94	129.49
899	46.35	52.24	54.95	65.77	160.15

Appendix Table IV.2 (Contd.)

Article code No.	1971-72	1972-73	1973-74	1974-75	1975-76
722	87.11	83.01	123.67	194.97	270.54
723	186.85	106.74	129.89	160.95	185.94
724	107.11	127.12	289.50	213.17	364.91
725	97.38	262.85	193.95	286.13	291.82
726	244.89	92.99	126.14	642.99	449.97
729	74.63	101.86	202.95	240.83	175.88
731	190.31	74.41	141.39	128.80	185.27
732	55.50	64.80	54.47	90.95	107.78
733	84.95	126.06	149.24	153.54	170.65
734	405.62	417.24	286.97	598.47	896.17
735	153.64	98.34	1369.56	1161.07	247.97
812	108.71	128.66	348.62	270.75	171.58
821	111.89	95.71	186.51	211.87	183.36
831	103.11	241.04	192.84	217.16	306.48
841	113.74	171.29	254.79	309.90	431.03
842	2136.36	1372.73	1109.09	2081.82	15209.09
851	116.82	107.39	106.21	132.46	102.59
861	149.44	147.66	155.79	257.60	170.61
862	143.01	276.34	111.29	411.83	925.27
863	107.05	102.96	104.31	108.63	105.33
864	65.90	99.54	455.30	258.99	687.10
891	108.47	99.14	155.49	166.16	139.80
892	135.39	125.53	190.24	160.48	135.52
893	110.39	94.71	148.14	160.42	170.56
894	160.47	195.67	241.08	325.11	238.06
895	181.02	100.72	207.53	267.02	167.82
896	125.45	202.56	275.40	465.55	302.33
897	600.66	519.35	631.21	671.99	725.22
899	100.96	80.22	75.35	74.02	79.77

Appendix Table IV.2 (Contd.)

Article code No.	1976-77	1977-78	1978-79	1979-80	1980-81	1981-82
722	282.59	140.14	173.24	179.72	155.38	210.41
723	144.20	116.53	90.83	58.06	88.12	177.64
724	547.53	219.87	296.81	157.66	64.06	115.56
725	413.45	416.24	457.97	528.52	701.34	490.99
726	489.77	1143.18	188.45	243.75	3398.86	1276.33
729	294.15	317.32	304.39	552.01	304.93	252.66
731	133.18	141.72	57.56	347.38	182.35	53.55
732	121.14	160.49	167.17	179.31	186.80	214.8.
733	153.36	207.60	194.29	223.42	264.33	333.58
734	1303.96	364.62	308.81	564.75	1097.83	2331.42
735	351.85	207.56	235.06	164.02	159.96	380.44
812	329.23	500.16	398.79	364.32	1411.84	311.76
821	283.59	432.77	2002.44	225.17	181.43	182.68
831	42.65	662.86	761.09	661.38	574.38	620.65
841	680.89	565.59	693.88	2108.76	3798.36	684.78
842	1963.64	9454.55	17046.45	33800.00	3109.09	3754.55
851	134.14	114.79	97.30	102.97	121.08	92.69
861	182.53	189.01	115.21	277.08	320.93	419.79
862	1701.61	113.98	29971.51	1253.7	12833.87	49.77
863	97.83	11.49	130.60	126.20	166.46	147.52
864	469.12	641.47	2135.48	917.97	11.75	4506.91
891	174.63	230.28	605.03	422.44	369.92	353.84
892	168.73	167.71	207.29	194.00	192.42	219.73
893	409.26	361.25	307.13	256.01	174.13	241.22
894	281.43	287.17	363.33	398.92	411.46	436.32
895	243.62	188.59	380.22	212.84	200.38	177.04
896	664.55	736.43	1854.94	1031.99	247.56	907.63
897	562.11	371.50	366.39	308.46	494.92	259.77
899	102.95	313.77	166.86	104.68	96.75	1981.55

Source : Estimates are derived on the basis of the data available in *Monthly Statistics of the Foreign Trade of India, Vol. I, Exports and Re-Exports,* Published by Directorate General of Comercial Intelligence and Statistics, Government of India for the Years 1965-66 to 1981-82.

Appendix Table IV.3

Name of the Commodity According to Article Code Number According to RITC 1965 Group

Article Code No.	*Name of the Articles*
1	2
001	Live Animals
011	Meat, fresh, chilled or frozen
012	Meat, dried, salted, or smoked whether or not in airtight containers
013	Meat in airtight containers, n.e.s., and Meat preparations whether or not in airtight containers
022	Milk and cream
023	Butter
024	Cheese and curd
025	Eggs
031	Fish, fresh and simply preserved
032	Fish in airtight containers, n.e.s. in fish preparations whether or not in airtight containers including crustacea and Molucss)
041	Wheat (including spelt) and meslin unmilled
042	Rice
043	Barley, unmilled
044	Maize (corn), unmilled
045	Cereals unmilled, other than wheat, rice, barley and maize
046	Meal and flour of wheat or of meslin
047	Meal and flour of cereals, except meal and flour of wheat or of meslin
048	Cereals preparations and preparations of flour and starch of fruits and vegetables
049	Pulses and flour thereof
051	Fruits, fresh and nuts (not including oil nuts, fresh or dried)

(Contd.)

1	2
052	Dried fruits (including artificially dehydrated)
053	Fruits preserved and fruit preparations
054	Vegetables, fresh, frozen or simply preserved (excluding dried leguminous vegetables), roots tubers and other edible products, n.e.s. fresh or dried
055	Vegetables, roots and tubers, preserved or prepared, n.e.s., whether or not in airtight containers
061	Sugar and honey
062	Sugar confectionery and other sugar preparations (except, chocolate confectionery)
071	Coffee
072	Cocoa
073	Chocolate and other food preparations containing Cocoa or chocolates n.e.s.
074	Tea and mate
075	Spices
081	Feeding stuff for animals (not including unmilled cereals)
091	Margarine and shortening
099	Food preparations, n.e.s.
111	Non-alcoholic beverages, n.e.s.
112	Alocholic beverages
121	Tobacco unmanufactured
122	Tobacco manufactured
211	Hides and skins (except fur skin) undressed
212	Furskins undressed
221	Oilseeds, oilnuts and oil kernels
231	Crude rubber (including synthetic and reclaimed)
241	Fuelwood and charcoal
242	Wood in the rough or roughly squared
243	Wood shaped or simply worked

(Contd.)

1	2
244	Cork, raw and waste
251	Pulp and waste papers
261	Silk
262	Wool and other animal hair (except human hair)
263	Cotton
264	Jute
265	Vegetable fibres except cotton and Jute
266	Synthetic and regenerated fibres (man made fibres)
267	Waste materials from textile fabrics (including rags)
271	Fertilizers, crude
273	Stone, and gravel
274	Sulphur and unroasted pyrites
275	Natural abrasive (including industrial diamonds)
276	Other crude minerals
281	Iron oil and concentrates
282	Iron and steel scrap
283	Ores and concentrates of non-ferrous base metals
284	Non-ferrous metal scrap
285	Silver and platinum ores
286	Ores and concentrates of uranium and thorium
291	Crude animal material, n.e.s.
292	Crude Vegetable materials, n.e.s.
321	Coal, Coke and briquettes
331	Petroleum, Crude and partly refined for further refining (excluding natural gas) (excluding natural gas)
332	Petroleum products
341	Gas, Natural and manufactured
351	Electric energy
411	Animal oils and fats

(Contd.)

1	2
421	Fixed Vegetable oils soft
422	Other fixed vegetable oils
431	Animal and Vegetable oils and fats, processed and waxes of animal or of vegetable origin
512	Organic chemicals
513	Inorganic chemicals, elements, Oxides, and halogen salt
514	Other inorganic chemicals
515	Radio-active and associated materials
521	Mineral tar and crude chemicals from coal petroleum and natural gas
532	Dyeing and tanning extracts and synthetic tanning materials
533	Pigments, paints, varnishes and related materials
534	Synthetic organic dyestuff, natural indigo and colour lakes
541	Medicinal and pharmaceutical products
551	Essential oils, perfumes and flavour materials
553	Perfumery and cosmetics, dentifrices and other toilet preparations (except soap)
554	Soaps, cleansing and polishing preparations
561	Fertilizers, manufactured
571	Explosives and pyrotechnic products
581	Plastic materials, requenerated cellulose and artificial resins
599	Chemical materials and products, n.e.s.
611	Leather
612	Manufactures of leather or of artificial or reconstituted leather, n.e.s.
613	Furskins, tanned or dressed (including dyed)
621	Materials of rubber
629	Articles of rubber
631	Veeners, plywoodboards, "improved" reconstituted wood and other wood worked, n.e.s.

(Contd.)

1	2
632	Wood manufactures, n.e.s.
633	Cork manufactures
641	Paper and paper board
642	Articles made of paper, pulp of paper or of paper board
651	Textile yarn and thread
653	Textile fabrics woven (not including narrow or special fabrics) other than cotton and jute fabrics
654	Tulle, luce, embraoidery ribbons, trimmings and other small wares except of cotton and jute
655	Special textile fabrics and related products except of cotton and jute
656	Made up articles, wholly or chiefly of textile materials, n.e.s.
657	Floor coverings, tapestries etc. other than of cotton and jute
658	Cotton manufactures excluding, yarn, thread and clothing
659	Jute Manufactures excluding, twist and yarn
661	Lime, cement and, fabricated building materials except glass and clay materials
662	Clay construction materials and refractory construction materials
663	Mineral manufactures, n.e.s.
664	Glass
665	Glassware
666	Pottery
667	Pearls and precious and semi-precious tones unworked or worked
671	Pig-iron, Spiegeleisem, sponage iron, iron and steel powders and shot and ferro-alloys
672	Ignots an other primary forms (including blanks for tubes and pipes) of iron and steel
673	Iron and steel bars, rods, angles, shapes and sections (including sheet pilings)

(Contd.)

1	2
674	Universal plates and sheets of iron or steel
675	Hoops and strips of iron or steel
676	Rails and railway track construction materials of iron or steel
677	Iron and steel wire (excluding wire rod)
678	Tubes, pipes, and fittings of iron or steel
679	Iron and steel casting and forgings unworked, n.e.s.
681	Silver, platinum and other metals of the platinum group
682	Copper
683	Nickel
684	Aluminium
685	Lead
686	Zinc
687	Tin
688	Uranium and thorium and their alloys
689	Miscellaneous, non-ferrous base metals employed in metallurgy
691	Finished structural parts and structures, n.e.s.
692	Metal containers for storage and transport
693	Wire products (excluding electric) and fencing grills
694	Nails, screws, nuts, bolts, rivets and similar articles of iron, steel or of copper
695	Tools for use in the hand or in machine
696	Cutlery
697	Household equipments of base metals
698	Manufactures of metal, n.e.s.
711	Power generating machinery other than electric
712	Agricultural machinery and implements
713	Office machines
715	Metal working machinery

(Contd.)

1	2
717	Textile and leather machinery
718	Machines for special industries
719	Machinery and appliances (other than electrical) and machine parts.
722	Electrical power machinery and switchgear
723	Equipments for distributing electricity
724	Tele-communication apparatus
725	Domestic electric equipment
726	Electric apparatus for medical purposes and radiological apparatus
729	Other electrical machinery and apparatus
731	Railway Vehicles
733	Road vehicles other than motor vehicles
734	Aircraft
735	Ships and boats
812	Sanitary, plumbing, heating and lighting fixtures and fitting
821	Furniture
831	Travel goods, hand bags and similar articles
841	Clothing (except fur clothings)
842	Fur-clothing (not including headgear) and other articles made of furskins, artificial fur and articles thereof
851	Footwear
861	Scientific, medical, optical, measuring and controlling instruments and apparatus
862	Photographic and cinematographic supplies
863	Developed cinematographic films
864	Watches and clocks
891	Musical instruments sound recorders and reproducer and parts and accessories there of
892	Printed matter

(Contd.)

1	2
893	Articles of artificial plastic materials, n.e.s.
894	Perambulators, games, and sporting goods
895	Office and stationery supplies, n.e.s.
896	Works of art collectors pieces and antiques
897	Jewellery and goldsmith's and silversmith's ware
899	Manufactured articles, n.e.s.
911	Postal packages not classified according to kind
931	Special transactions not classified according to kind
941	Animals n.e.s. (including Zoo animals, dogs and cats)
951	Firearms of war and ammunitions thereof
961	Coins (other than gold coins) not being legal tender.

Source : Revised Indian Trade Classification, 1995 Central Statistical Organization, Government of India, New Delhi.

5

Structure of Indian Exports -I

Introduction

Foreign trade accupies a place of strategic importance in general and in the Indian economy in particular as it indicates through imports what types of goods a country lacks and how much of them it needs or is able to buy. Further, exports of a country is an indicator of the potential markets abroad for domestically produced goods and of capacity to import through export earnings. As far as the developing country like India is concerned, the potentiality of export earnings is significantly very important, as its capacity to import in general is contigent upon potentiality of export earnings.

As an economy gets an exposure to the path of economic development, its magnitude and structure of foreign trade is bound to undergo a spectacular change on account of variations in relative demand and supply conditions overtime. In the context of Indian economy, it has been the matter of historical experience, that until 1947, India had a pattern of trade which was substantially of that of colonial and agricultural country. However, with an inception of 'Economic Planning' for industrial development since Independence, India's foreign trade has undergone a fundamental change and is no longer confined to a few countries and few commodities. In view of these changes, it is imperative as well as interesting to examine the extent to which is magnitude of exports and the structure of exports have undergone a change overtime.

Magnitude of Exports

As regards the magnitude of exports, it is important to note that the use of current price figure or constant price figure is not a matter of indifference for analytical purpose. In fact, if the figures of exports of different commodity groups at one point of time are compared with those of another, the use of current price figure is bound to conceal the true picture because the current price figure would involve the effects of inter-commodity variation in the price movements over time.

In the context of undertaking an analysis of magnitude of exports, it is pertinent to note that the analysis should be carried out at current prices as well as at constant prices. As evident from Tables 5.1 that the total exports at current prices turns out to be Rs. 118021.34 lakhs in 1965-66, while the same turns out to be Rs. 766114.57 lakhs in 1981-82. Thus, Indian exports have increased by 32.30% per year on an average. Further, it should be noted that the year 1973-74 is a urning point because the total exports at current prices in the year 1973-74 have increased by slightly more than double (i.e. 109.11%) as compared to the year 1965-66. This state of affairs can be viewed from the fact that the total exports increased from Rs. 118021.34 lakhs in 1965-66 to Rs. 246800.75 lakhs in 1973-74. Whereas during 1973-74 to 1981-82 the total exports have increased by 210.42%. Thus we can see that over a period of 1965-66 to 1981-82, the total exports have increased by five and a half times. However, the total exports at (1970-71 price level) constant prices display a less impressive magnitudinal change over period of 1965-66 to 1981-82. As evident from Table 5.2 that the total exports at (1970-71 price level) constant prices increased from Rs. 162052.99 lakhs in 1965-66 to Rs. 328363.21 lakhs (i.e. 102.63%) in 1981-82. It becomes evident from the above analysis that the total exports at current prices as well as at (1970-71 price level) constant prices display a rising trend with marked differences in magnitudnal change over the period under consideration.

Apart from the above analysis, it must be emphasized that the trends in total exports of a country are the consequences of trends in the exports of different commodities. The total exports consists of four major commodity groups i.e. [1] Consumer goods [2] Intermediate goods and raw materials for producing consumer goods [3] Intermediate goods and raw-materials for producing capital goods and [4] Capital goods.

TABLE - 5.1

Magnitude of Indian Exports by Major Commodity Groups at Current Prices : 1965-66 to 1981-82

(Rupees in Lakhs)

Year	*Consumer Goods*	*Intermediate Goods for producing consumer Goods*	*Intermediate Goods for producing Capital Goods*	*Capital Goods*	*Total Exports*
1965-66	77264.34	23057.53	16051.54	1647.93	118021.34
1966-67	73577.96	22501.43	16984.58	1540.47	114604.44
1967-68	74483.33	22025.44	20629.00	1914.25	119052.02
1968-69	76140.56	27589.75	27191.91	4362.70	135284.92
1969-70	74804.12	30176.64	29840.06	5535.65	140356.47
1970-71	82748.75	29051.31	32664.44	7510.94	151975.44
1971-72	93305.01	33104.70	24774.99	7377.63	158562.33
1972-73	103257.12	49398.46	28777.84	8431.51	189864.93
1973-74	140227.41	60810.21	34293.96	11469.17	246800.75
1974-75	188406.22	65713.37	54040.22	28242.92	336402.73
1975-76	213926.72	74680.27	78077.24	25515.30	392199.53
1976-77	245805.82	103282.12	117525.12	29407.53	496020.59
1977-78	282875.16	121826.11	102150.48	40209.36	547601.11
1978-79	281096.26	132552.22	90764.63	39299.32	543712.43
1979-80	358202.96	157372.65	78248.56	57977.95	651802.12
1980-81	409550.75	169237.66	74951.05	52225.53	705964.99
1981-82	414684.79	184510.56	105180.20	61739.02	766114.57

Source : Appendix Table V.1.

It becomes intelligible from table 5.1 and 5.2 that the exports of consumer goods have increased by Rs. 337420.45 lakhs i.e. by 436.71% in money terms whereas the same increased by Rs. 107747.17 lakhs i.e. 111.21% in real terms. In case of intermediate goods and raw materials, for producing consumer goods, the exports have increased by Rs. 161453.03 lakhs i.e. 700.22% in money terms whereas the same increased by Rs. 9938.60 lakhs i.e. 29.23% in real terms. Similarly, the exports of intermediate goods and raw materials for producing capital goods have increased by Rs. 89128.66 lakhs i.e. 555.26% in money terms whereas the same increased by Rs. 21340.88 lakhs i.e. by 76.38% in real terms over the period under consideration. However, the exports of capital goods have increased by Rs. 60091.09 lakhs i.e. 3646.46% in money terms whereas the same increased by Rs. 27283.57 lakhs i.e. 846.16% in real terms. Thus it becomes clear that the exports of capital goods registerd a highest percentage increase in money terms as well as in real terms as compared to the percentage change in exports of other major commodity groups over the period under consideration.

TABLE - 5.2

Magnitude of Indian Exports by Major Commodity Groups at Constant (1970-71) Prices : 1965-66 to 1981-82

(*Rupees in Lakhs*)

Year	*Consumer Goods*	*Intermediate Goods for producing consumer Goods*	*Intermediate Goods for producing Capital Goods*	*Capital Goods*	*Total Exports*
1965-66	9688.76	34001.50	27938.33	3224.40	162052.99
1966-67	88556.80	35389.30	23524.73	2512.45	149983.28
1967-68	79574.93	26408.96	24176.57	3018.06	13178.52
1968-69	89751.72	34470.42	33514.63	12629.85	170366.62
1969-70	82663.82	35682.86	33378.71	8737.66	160463.05
1970-71	82748.75	24863.44	32664.44	7510.94	147787.57
1971-72	914111.14	26138.32	24675.97	7735.36	149960.79
1972-73	99568.52	35719.16	27235.76	9570.38	172093.82
1973-74	96458.74	38405.70	35058.82	16315.82	186239.08
1974-75	107794.36	44646.61	52277.55	16054.73	220773.25
1975-76	114247.16	42299.92	54421.02	17667.78	228635.88
1976-77	137477.72	54375.63	39214.28	18326.89	279394.52
1977-78	148298.01	44902.14	56962.73	20021.19	270184.07
1978-79	164055.09	45466.13	58550.19	24798.08	292869.49
1979-80	242926.95	54729.83	57154.58	46735.51	401546.87
1980-81	289982.87	69145.07	45503.04	34453.37	439084.35
1981-82	204635.93	43940.10	49279.21	30507.97	328363.21

Source : Appendix Table V.1.

As regards an analysis of the magnitude of other individual items belonging to the different groups of commodity exports both in real terms and money terms seems redundent since, Appendix Table V.1 and V.2 are self explanatory.

From the above analysis it can be concluded that the trends in magnitude of exports both in real terms as well as in money terms display a rising trend with marked differences in magnitudenal change over the period under consideration.

Macro and Micro Aspects of Structural Changes

The structure of exports can be visualized from the following two aspects :

[i] Macro (aggregated) and [ii] Micro (disaggregated)[1]

Macro Aspects of structural changes

Under macro analysis the prominent features of exports and changes in them can be examined in terms of the following parameters :

[i] Share of exports of NNP

[ii] Share of exports in world exports

[iii] Growth rates of exports

[iv] Instability co-efficients of exports

Share of Exports to NNP

The parameter, share of exports to NNP is of a paramount importance for the economy as it indicates primarily the degree of outward orientation or openness of the economy in regard to the trade activity and also reflects in a broad way the nature of trade strategies adopted in the economy. Further this ratio of exports to NNP could be interpreted also to mean the supply capability of the economy in regard to exports. Moreover, the behaviour of this ratio is of prime importance to the economy as it is also indicative of presence or abscence of tendency to have a comparative advantage over a period of time. With reference to this, Simon Kuznets[2] stated that 'Given the tendency of small nations to concentrate economic production a limited range of activities, the second general proposition follows. Foreign trade is of greater weight in the economic activity of small nations than in that of large units. This is particularly true of nations that have developed and attained fairly high levels of per capita output and consumption. For at these levels, the variety of goods demanded by ultimate consumers is far wider than that of domestic output of final goods. But it is likely to be true even of underdeveloped countries, for they tend to have some comparative advantages, some resources that permit exports to world markets - whether jute, bananas, oil, coffee or copra'.

In the context of Indian economy, the total exports and NNP at current prices have reflected a close correspondence with each other over the period under consideration, as is evident from table 5.3. The total exports have increased from Rs. 1180 crores in 1965-66 to Rs. 7661 crores in 1981-82 i.e., increased by 6481 crores. Whereas NNP has increased from Rs. 20637 crores in 1965-66 to Rs. 121243 crores in 1981-82 i.e. increased by Rs. 100606 crores. In other words, the total exports have increased by 549.24% while NNP has increased by 487.50% over the period under consideration. A closer glance at the table reveals that the proportion of exports to NNP which was 5.72% in 1965-66 remained stagnant around 4.58% on an average during 1966-67 to 1973-74 but thereafter reflected an increasing trend. However, the average proportion of exports to NNP during the period of Annual Plan (i.e. 1966-67 to 1968-69) and Fourth Plan (i.e. 1969-70 to 1973-74) was 4.58% increased to 6.67% during the Firth Plan period and thereafter further increased to 6.78% during the first three years of the Sixth Plan period. This means that the average proportion of exports to NNP showed an increasing trend over the period under consideration.

Similarly, it becomes clear from Table 5.4 that the total exports and NNP at constant prices (1970-71 price level) have also shown a close correspondence in their movements over a period of 1965-66 to 1981-82. The total exports have increased from Rs. 1621 crores in 1965-66 to Rs. 3284 crores in 1981-82 i.e. increased by Rs. 1663 crores. While NNP has increased from Rs. 27103 crores in 1965-66 to Rs. 49887 crores in 1981-82 i.e. increased by Rs. 22784 crores. In other words, at constant prices, the total exports have increased by 102.60% whereas NNP has increased by 84.06%. Now it becomes clear that exports have increased by larger percentage than NNP at current prices as well as at constant prices. Therefore, this enables us to se clearly from Table 5.4 that the ratio of exports of NNP at constant prices has increased over a period under consideration. The proportion of exports to NNP which was 5.98% in 1965-66 declined to 4.92% on an average during the period of Annual

Plan and Fourth Plan. However, this average proportion of exports to NNP increased from 4.92% during 1966-67 to 1973-74 to 6.23% during the Fifth Plan period which further increased to 8.32% during the first three years of the Sixth Plan. This is indicative of the fact that the proportion of exports to NNP has increased at constant prices during the period under consideration.

TABLE - 5.3

Proportion of India's Total Exports in Net National Product at Current Prices : 1965-66 to 1981-82

Year	*Total Exports At current Prices*[1] [Rs. in Crores]	*N.N.P. At Current Prices*[2] [Rs. in Crores]	*Proportion of Total Exports in N.N.P.* [In Percentages]
1965-66	1180	20637	5.72
1966-67	1146	23848	4.81
1967-68	1190	28054	4.24
1968-69	1353	28607	4.73
1969-70	1404	31606	4.44
1970-71	1520	34235	4.44
1971-72	1586	36573	4.34
1972-73	1899	40270	4.72
1973-74	2468	50424	4.89
1974-75	3364	59446	5.66
1975-76	3922	62069	6.32
1976-77	4960	66754	7.43
1977-78	5476	75536	7.25
1978-79	5437	81123	6.70
1979-80	6518	88672	7.38
1980-81	7060	106539	6.63
1981-82	7661	121243	6.32

Source : 1. *Appendix Table V.1*

2. *National Account Statistics* : (1970-71 - 1981-82).February 1983. Central Statistical Organisation. Department of Statistics. Ministry of Planning. Government of India. Appendix pp. 150-153.

TABLE - 5.4

Proportion of India's Total Exports in Net National Product at Constant (1970-71) Prices : 1965-66 to 1981-82

Year	*Total Exports 1970.71 Prices*[1] [Rs. in Crores]	*N.N.P. 1970-71 Prices*[2] [Rs. in Crores]	*Proportion of Total Exports in N.N.P.* [In Percentages]
1965-66	1621	27103	5.98
1966-67	1500	27298	5.19
1967-68	1332	29715	4.48
1968-69	1704	30513	5.58
1969-70	1605	32408	4.95
1970-71	1478	34235	4.32
1971-72	1500	34715	4.32
1972-73	1721	34191	5.03
1973-74	1862	35967	5.18
1974-75	2208	36502	6.05
1975-76	2286	40064	5.70
1976-77	2794	40271	6.94
1977-78	2702	43951	6.15
1978-79	2929	46386	6.31
1979-80	4015	43922	9.14
1980-81	4391	47490	9.25
1981-82	3284	49887	6.58

Source : 1. *Appendix Table V.2*

2. *National Account Statistics* : (1970-71 - 1980-81) February 1983, Central Statistical Organization, Department of Statistics, Ministry of Planning, Government of India, Appendix A-I pp. 150-153.

Hence, it can be concluded from the above discussion that the increasing trend of the ratio of exports to NNP is mainly due to increasing tendency to have comparative advantage over a period of time. This result is in consonance with the view expressed by Simon Kuznets.[3]

As regards, the proportion of exports to NNP, it is commonly held belief that as the rate of economic development accelerates, the ratio of exports to NNP tends to increase over a period of time.[4] Therefore, to ascertain the relation between them, we have run a simple regression of the form : Y = a + bx to the time series (1965-66 to 1981-82) data at current prices as well as at constant prices of the proportion of exports to NNP (Y) and per capita income†(X). Where per capita income is considered as a rough indicator of the level of economic development of a country. Accordingly, the following regression results were obtained for India.

(i) At Current Prices :

$$Y = 0.0362058 + 0.0000220\,X \qquad R^2 = 0.5648$$
$$(7.276)^* \qquad (4.418)^*$$

(ii) At Constant Prices :

$$Y = 0.0354393 + 0.0000263\,X \qquad R^2 = 0.5352$$
$$(5.620)^* \qquad (4.168)^*$$

(Where * : t – Values of regression coefficients are significant at 1% level)

It becomes evident from the above regression results that the proportion of exports to NNP has increased over a period of time with the level of economic development and both are positively correlated at current prices as well as at constant prices. In case of equation (i) changes in the level of per capita income explains about 56.48% variations in the proportion of exports to NNP whereas in equation (ii) it explains 53.52% variations in the dependent variables.

National Income and Exports : An Inter Country Analysis

In the context of the Indian economy, we have already seen that the proportion of exports to national income has increased both in real terms and in money terms over a period of time. In other words, the proportion of exports to national income has a rising tendency with the process of economic development of a country. Therefore, in the light of this proposition, this study has attempted to examine the same with respect to different countries of the world at a point of time. This proposition is examined for alternate years following the year 1965 to 1981 by considering those countries for which data on value of exports at f.o.b.

† For per Capita N.N.P at Current and Constant (1970-71) prices see appendix Table : V.7

and exports inclusive of non-factor services and national income at market prices are available. Thus, we have calculated the proportion of exports to national income in two ways : One excludes the non-factor services whereas the other includes it. In doing so, we have excluded some of the countries[@] on account of the following reasons :

(i) Non-availability of data either on exports or national income or both.

(ii) Differences in time of reporting data on exports and national income (Exports figures are reported as per calender year, whereas national income figures are reported at financial year, year ending 30th June and 30th September as the case may be).

(iii) Differences in units of currency (i.e. exports figures are expressed in millions of U.S.$, whereas national income figures are expressed in the currency units of the respective countries). However, the present study has attempted to estimate the proportion of exports to national income during different years only for those countries for which value figures of exports f.o.b. and value figures of exports inclusive of non-factor services and national income at market prices are available in terms of single currency with uniformity in regard to time of reporting. This is done with a new to examine the trend behaviour of the proportion of exports to national income for different groups of the countries of the world over a period under consideration.

In can be readily visualized from table 5.5A showing proportion of exports to national income (where exports refer to exports of goods only) that from among the highly developed countries, the proportion of exports to national income was lowest for the U.S.A., while it was highest for Belgium during the period under consideration. Similarly, within the group of intermediate countries, the proportion of exports to national income was lowest for Spain, whereas highest for Libya during the 1965, 1967, 1969, 1971,1973, 1975 and 1977. However, during years, 1979 and 1981, the proportion of exports to national income was highest for Ireland but lowest for Panama in the year 1981. Moreover, in case of underdeveloped countries, the proportion of exports to national income came to be lowest for Brazil but highest for Zambia in the year 1965 only. Whereas after 1965 it remained lowest for Turkey but highest for Zambia except for the years 1975 and 1981.

@ For list of the excluded countries. see Appendix Table V.8

In the year 1975 the highest proportion of exports to national income was represented by Iraq (64.44) while lowest proportion was represented by Turkey (3.97). Whereas the year 1981 differs from the earlier years in the sense that the highest proportion of exports to national income was represented by Korea (34.43) while lowest proportion was represented by Paraguay (5.94).

TABLE 5.5A

Proportion of Exports to National Income for Different Countries of the World

(Percentage)

Sr. No	*Countries*	*1965*	*1967*	*1969*	*1971*	*1973*
1	2	3	4	5	6	7
1.	Australia	14.65	14.64	14.44	14.24	15.5
2.	Austria	19.27	18.87	21.34	21.45	21.35
3.	Belgium	41.57	40.01	48	48.53	53.38
4.	Brazil	5.24	5.31	6.01	7	8.33
5.	Canada	18.75	20.24	21.63	22.09	24
6.	Colombia	9.13	7.98	10.23	8.74	10.86
7.	Costa Rica	20.42	22.4	24.04	22.47	24.6
8.	Cyprus	18.79	17.95	19.69	18.36	17.69
9.	Denmark	25.02	22.41	22.65	22.47	23.49
10.	Dominican Republic	14.18	15.09	14.83	15.8	20.78
11.	El Salvador	25.15	24.81	22.54	23.89	28.48
12.	Fiji	35.65	31.76	37.17	32.13	23.35
13.	Finland	20.14	19.59	24.14	23.33	23.35
14.	France	11.42	11.1	12.33	14.5	16
15.	Germany	17.27	19.64	21.04	20.17	21.64
16.	Ghana	0	0	18.4	21.52	22.43
17.	Greece	5.64	7.12	6.46	6.24	9.17
18.	Guyana	52.72	53.52	59.06	60.65	49.91
19.	Hondruas	27	28.45	27.34	26.76	29.5
20.	Hungary	0	0	0	34.47	42.89
21.	Iceland	29.42	18.94	32.88	27.29	30.5
22.	Iraq	34.19	29.45	31.73	35.28	40.51
23.	Ireland	24.26	27.41	27.63	31.23	34.75

(Contd.)

1	2	3	4	5	6	7
52.	U.S.A.	4.33	4.31	4.4	4.5	5.9
53.	Venezuela	35	32.58	28.71	28.42	32.61
54.	Zaire	0	0	45.53	37.71	39.87
55.	Zambia	61.45	55.62	66.36	49.82	57.34
56.	Highly Developed Countries	20.2	19.92	22.11	22.29	23.86
57.	Intermediate Countries	22.23	22.47	23.35	24	25.58
58.	Underdeveloped Countries	19.73	18.65	18.82	18.41	21.77

TABLE 5.5A (Contd.)

(Percentage)

Sr. No.	*Countries*	*1975*	*1977*	*1979*	*1981*	*1983*
1	2	3	4	5	6	7
31.	Morocco	17.23	11.95	12.58	16.26	0
32.	Netherlands	46.74	42.69	44.6	53.98	55.63
33.	Nicaragua	26.12	33.11	41.92	21.53	12.29
34.	Norway	30.17	30.35	35.61	38.75	39.81
35.	Panama	16.56	13.25	11.92	9.32	0
36.	Papua New Gunea	38.97	45.48	42.33	38.48	0
37.	Peraguay	12.24	14.74	9.95	5.94	0
38.	Philippines	16.13	16.88	16.81	16.34	16.16
39.	Portugal	13.78	13.18	0	0	0
40.	South Africa	28.75	31.47	40.07	31.97	29.41
41.	Spain	8.07	9.33	10.3	12.27	14.14
42.	Sri Lanka	15.47	18.71	29.46	27.82	0
43.	Suriname	62.18	49.5	56.04	0	0
44.	Sweden	26.56	26.06	28.88	29.13	0
45.	Switzerland	25.83	30.91	29.68	30.22	0
46.	Tanzania	15.31	14.73	11.7	11.6	0
47.	Thailand	16.21	19.64	21.44	21.7	17.66
48.	Togo	22.16	24.59	23.21	0	0
49.	Tunisia	21.75	19.88	27.05	32.93	0
50.	Turkey	3.97	3.8	3.64	0	0

(Contd.)

1	2	3	4	5	6	7
51.	U.K.	20.63	24.79	23.45	22.8	0
52.	U.S.A.	7.78	7.04	8.42	8.89	6.85
53.	Venezuela	33.97	28.31	32	32.28	0
54.	Zaire	26.53	23.97	22.78	12.74	0
55.	Zambia	41.06	45.44	50.05	31.47	0
56.	Highly Developed Countries	24.95	25.66	27.58	30.09	29.7
57.	Intermediate Countries	27.91	28.89	27.96	28.94	20.22
58.	Underdeveloped Countries	22.42	21.54	22.98	21.34	14.54

Note : (i) Exports refer to goods only (ii) For List of Countries excluded See, *Appendix Table V.8* (iii) For Countries grouped by the level of economic development, see. *Appendix Table V.9*

Source : Calculated on the basis of information available in *International Financial Statistics*, Year Book 1984, International Monetary Fund.

In global sense of the phenomenon, about 47 countries out of the total of 55 countries of the world, reflected a rising trend of the proportion of exports to national income, while remaining 8 countries : Panama, Portugal, Venezuela, Nicaragua, Paraguay, Tanzania, Turkey and Zambia reflected a falling tendency. Thus about 85.45% of the total number of countries showed a rising trend of the proportion of exports to national income over a period under consideration.

As regards, the trend behaviour of proportion of exports to national income for different groups of the countries of the world, it becomes evident that the trend behaviour of proportion of exports to national income reflected a rising trend. The proportion of exports to national income for highly developed countries** increased from 20.20 in 1965 to 30.09 in the year 1981 which indicated an increase of about 9.89 percent points. Similarly, the same for intermediate countries increased from 22.23 in 1965 to 28.94 in the year 1981 which represented an increase of 6.71 percent points. While for underdeveloped countries it increased from 19.73 in 1965 to 21.34 in the year 1981. Which showed an increase of 1.61 percent points. Thus, it becomes evident that the increase in the proportion of exports to national income was the lowest for underdeveloped countries, while it was highest for highly developed countries.

**—For countries grouped by level of economic development, see Appendix Table V.9.

Further, it can be seen from table 5.5-B, showing proportion of exports to national income (where exports refer to exports of goods and non factor services), that within the group of highly developed countries, the proportion of exports to national income was lowest for the U.S.A., while it was highest for Kuwait during the period under consideration except in the year 1981. However, it should be noted that the year 1981 differs from earlier years in the sense that the proportion of exports to national income was not highest for Kuwait, but it was highest for Netherlands (64.75). Similarly, in the case of intermediate countries, Libya represented the highest proportion of exports to national income i.e. 69.53, 67.03, 75.33, 74.08, 68.28, 63.84 and 68.64 during the years 1965, 1967, 1969, 1971, 1973, 1975 and 1977 respectively. While during 1979 and 1981, the highest proportion of exports to national income was shown by Ireland (i.e. 58.35 and 57.80 in 1979 and 1981 respectively). As regards, the lowest proportion of exports to national income, there are marked differences in terms of countries during the period under consideration. Spain represented the lowest proportion of exports to national income (i.e. 6.62, 7.15, 14.64, 15.92 and 16.45 during the years 1965, 1967, 1975, 1977 and 1979 respectively). While Greece represented the lowest proportion of exports to national income of 10.07 in 1969 and Uraguay represented the lowest proportion i.e. 10.08, 14.48 and 15.56 during 1971, 1973 and 1981 respectively. From among the underdeveloped countries, India represented the lowest proportion of exports to national income i.e. 4.09 and 4.95 during the years 1965 and 1967 respectively. Similarly, Yemen Arab Republic also represented the lowest proportion of exports to national income i.e. 2.13, 1.93, 2.76, 4.25, 4.24, 4.54 and 6.17 during 1969, 1971, 1973, 1975, 1977, 1979 and 1981 respectively. As regards, the highest proportion of exports to national income, there are marked differences in terms of countries during the period under consideration. Zambia showed the highest proportion of exports to national income i.e. 60.26, 56.21, 74.72, 60.27, 48.66 and 56.87 in years 1965, 1967, 1969, 1973, 1977 and 1979 respectively. In a similar way, Iraq represented the highest proportion of exports to national income i.e. 52.32 and 61.25 in 1971 and 1975 respectively. Jordon, for the first time in 1981 showed the highest proportion of exports to national income of 44.40.

TABLE 5.5B

Proportion of Exports to National Income for Different Countries of the World

(Percentage)

Sr. No.	*Countries*	*1965*	*1967*	*1969*	*1971*	*1973*
1	2	3	4	5	6	7
1.	Australia	16.82	16.88	16.51	16.29	17.22
2.	Austria	29.26	29.89	33.76	36.33	.36.85
3.	Belgium	39.79	39.77	45.96	47.65	51.9
4.	Bolivia	22.39	24.09	22.77	18.4	24.58
5.	Brazil	7.14	6.17	6.53	6.94	8.81
6.	Cameroon [J]	–	–	21.34	26.66	21.64
7.	Canada	22	24.22	25.28	25.29	26.79
8.	Chile	–	–	–	–	22.22
9.	China People's Rep.	–	–	–	–	–
10.	Costa Rica	24.69	27.45	29.13	29.28	33.97
11.	Denmark	33.48	29.77	29.45	29.76	30.84
12.	Dominican Republic	16.36	18.08	18.31	19	24.12
13.	Ecuador	17.15	16.93	14.14	16.76	29.1
14.	El Salvador	28.2	27.15	24.8	26.17	31.72
15.	Finland	23	22.59	27.61	28.21	29.65
16.	France	13.9	13.86	14.91	17.56	18.91
17.	Germany	21.01	24.03	25.46	25.18	26.32
18.	Ghana	–	–	24.68	23.31	23.04
19.	Greece	9.23	11.02	10.07	10.7	14.77
20.	Haiti [S]	–	11.34	12.85	13.93	11.89
21.	Hondruas	30.17	31.14	30.35	29.36	32.67
22.	Hungary	–	–	–	34.47	42.88
23.	India [F]	4.09	4.95	4.7	4.4	5.09
24.	Indonesia	–	9.44	9.77	15.74	22.31
25.	Iraq	46.38	40.23	44.58	52.32	49.65
26.	Ireland	36.79	40.19	39.95	38.78	41.02
27.	Israel	22.94	27.21	32.77	36.31	36.71
28.	Italy	15.11	15.41	17.16	17.62	18.49
29.	Ivory Coast	31.88	34.77	38.67	38.76	41.9
30.	Japan	12.64	11.66	12.71	14.25	12.52

(Contd.)

1	2	3	4	5	6	7
31.	Jordon	16.39	15.27	10.86	9.29	22.47
32.	Korea	9.08	12.04	14.26	16.3	31.85
33.	Kuwait [F]	98.09	75	74.49	87.08	97.3
34.	Libya	69.53	67.03	75.33	74.08	68.28
35.	Morocco	21.09	20.76	19.31	17.94	21.9
36.	Nicaragua	31.15	28.2	26.22	28.45	31.18
37.	Netherlands	49.24	46.57	48.8	52.12	53.86
38.	New Zeland [F]	23.63	22.76	27.3	24.86	26.46
39.	Norway	47.46	49.46	49.5	47.14	51.05
40.	Pakistan [J]	6.45	6.11	–	8.3	15.76

TABLE 5.5B (Contd.)

(Percentage)

Sr. No.	*Countries*	*1975*	*1977*	*1979*	*1981*
1	2	3	4	5	6
1.	Australia	16.82	17.25	19.39	17.07
2.	Austria	38.38	39.28	42.53	47.17
3.	Belgium	50.4	57.23	61.89	71.56
4.	Bolivia	23.07	24.49	21.57	–
5.	Brazil	7.94	7.79	7.39	9.89
6.	Cameroon [J]	25.82	23.22	19.47	–
7.	Canada	26.37	27.45	32.16	32.41
8.	Chile	31.14	24.05	26.79	19.06
9.	China People's Rep.	–	5.28	6.32	9.47
10.	Costa Rica	33.22	33.7	29.59	51.42
11.	Denmark	33.06	31.77	32.62	41.73
12.	Dominican Republic	30.85	21.9	22.77	23.31
13.	Ecuador	29.29	27.96	29.76	25.37
14.	El Salvador	35.15	40.06	38.84	28.34
15.	Finland	28.19	34.49	37.63	40.4
16.	France	20.74	22.57	23.11	25.19
17.	Germany	29.96	.31	30.92	36.44
18.	Ghana	20.8	–	–	–

(Contd.)

1	2	3	4	5	6
19.	Greece	17.59	17.61	18.35	21.46
20.	Haiti [S]	23.69	26.33	28.29	27.46
21.	Hondruas	32.44	37.54	41.56	36.61
22.	Hungary	46.58	46.6	47.23	43.8
23.	India [F]	6.89	7.87	8.32	7.44
24.	Indonesia	25.31	26.12	33.84	30.72
25.	Iraq	61.25	–	–	–
26.	Ireland	46.35	55.7	58.35	57.8
27.	Israel	38.91	52.98	–	–
28.	Italy	23.51	26.8	27.97	27.42
29.	Ivory Coast	41.08	46.55	40.66	–
30.	Japan	15.76	15.95	14.69	19.25
31.	Jordon	32.71	35.46	38.12	44.4
32.	Korea	29.13	33.74	29.56	40.06
33.	Kuwait [F]	77.56	65.59	71.43	–
34.	Libya	63.87	68.64	–	–
35.	Morocco	23.27	19.17	17.88	22.28
36.	Nicaragua	30.93	37.24	48.76	23.06
37.	Netherlands	57.84	52.06	54.16	64.75
38.	New Zeland [F]	25.25	29.67	31.29	30.92
39.	Norway	49.47	48.97	54.77	58.09
40.	Pakistan [J]	12.14	9.48	10.78	12.31

TABLE 5.5B (Contd.)

(Percentage)

Sr. No.	*Countries*	*1965*	*1967*	*1969*	*1971*	*1973*
1	2	3	4	5	6	7
41.	Panama	40.83	42.52	43.52	40.13	39.58
42.	Peraguay	16.12	13.36	14.84	14.37	16.06
43.	Peru	19.32	19.22	21.67	17.2	15.79
44.	Philippines	18.71	18.46	14.19	20.6	24.45
45.	Portugal	27.1	27.69	25.34	25.52	26.91
46.	South Africa	30.49	29.13	27.01	24.81	29.43
47.	Spain	6.62	7.15	15.08	15.79	15.79

(Contd.)

1	2	3	4	5	6	7
48.	Sri Lanka	27.08	21.39	19.86	27.83	28.24
49.	Sudan [J]	18.84	18.85	18.64	17.93	17.59
50.	Sweden	24.14	23.42	25.19	27.44	30.34
51.	Switzerland	31.47	31.88	35.61	34.07	33.7
52.	Thailand	19.23	20.85	18.65	18.91	21.12
53.	Tanzania	27.85	28.49	26.29	25.68	24.13
54.	Togo	26.06	28.51	34.66	29.85	22.39
55.	Tunisia	19.68	22.7	23.66	25.18	27.12
56.	Turkey	5.82	6.17	5.46	7.21	8.61
57.	United Kingdom	20.06	19.83	23.37	24.52	25.33
58.	United States	5.27	5.33	5.37	5.69	7.23
59.	Uruguay	20	14.81	13.69	10.08	14.48
60.	Venezuela	37.31	34.72	32.56	30.05	32.94
61.	Yeman Arab Rep.	–	–	2.13	1.93	2.76
62.	Zambia	60.26	56.21	74.72	51.44	60.27
63.	Highly Developed	29.7	28.48	30.9	31.38	33.89
64.	Intermediate	28.91	28.92	30.22	29.82	31.26
65.	Under Developed	21.87	20.77	21.31	21	23.94

TABLE 5.5B (Contd.)

(Percentage)

Sr. No.	*Countries*	*1975*	*1977*	*1979*	*1981*
1	2	3	4	5	6
41.	Panama	50.03	48.6	44.28	46.37
42.	Peraguay	16.37	21.42	18.06	12.36
43.	Peru	13.81	17.99	33.3	21.64
44.	Philippines	20.66	21.37	20.68	21.18
45.	Portugal	20.7	18.83	–	–
46.	South Africa	32.31	37.95	43.35	35.63
47.	Spain	14.64	15.92	16.45	19.52
48.	Sri Lanka	32.56	41.44	35.53	33.18
49.	Sudan [J]	13.29	–	–	–
50.	Sweden	31.23	30.82	34.34	34.73
51.	Switzerland	34	39.29	37.71	39.62

(Contd.)

1	2	3	4	5	6
52.	Thailand	20.54	22.68	26.12	27.76
53.	Tanzania	19.18	18.88	14.65	13.58
54.	Togo	29.26	28.3	26.9	–
55.	Tunisia	33.21	32.4	42.4	45.1
56.	Turkey	6.27	5.53	5.76	–
57.	United Kingdom	28.45	33.7	31.66	30.42
58.	United States	9.29	8.69	10.02	10.78
59.	Uruguay	16.76	20.24	17.3	15.56
60.	Venezuela	35.41	30.04	33.34	33.49
61.	Yeman Arab Rep.	4.25	4.24	4.54	6.17
62.	Zambia	45.31	48.66	56.87	33.22
63.	Highly Developed	33.72	35.26	36.11	36.89
64.	Intermediate	33.61	34.57	33.8	34.89
65.	Under Developed	24.88	24.75	26.02	24.13

Note : (i) [F] : Financial Year, [J] : Year ending 30th June
[S] : Year ending 30th September
(ii) Exports refer to exports of goods and non-factor services
(iii) For list of countries excluded, See, *Appendix Table V.8*
(vi) For Countries grouped by the level of economic development, see *Appendix Table V.9*

Source : Calculated on the basis of information available in *International Financial Statistics* Year Book 1984 and 1985, International Monetary Fund, Geneva.

If we view, the trend behaviour of exports to national income in aggregate terms, then we can visualize that out of about 62 countries of the world under examination, 52 countries reflected a rising trend of the same, while remaining 10 countries : Kuwait, Chile, Portugal, Venezuela, Cameroon, Ghana, Nicaragua, Sudan, Tanzania and Zambia reflected a falling tendency. Thus, about 83.87% of the total number of countries showed a rising trend of the proportion of exports to national income over a period under consideration.

As regards, the trend behaviour of the proportion of exports to national income for different groups of countries, it becomes clear that it showed a rising trend. The proportion of exports to national income for highly developed countries increased from 29.70 in 1965 to 36.89 in 1981 which indicated an increase of 7.9 percent points. Similarly, for intermediate countries, the same increased from 28.91 in 1965 to 34.89 in 1981 represented an increase of 5.98 percent point while for underdeveloped countries, it increased from 21.87 in 1965 to 24.13 in 1981 indicated an increase of 2.26 percent points. Thus it becomes evident that, the proportion of exports to national income for underdeveloped countries remained lower than that of for highly developed countries over a period under consideration.

Moreover, it can be discerned from the above analysis that regardless of whichever the definition of exports (i.e. exports referring to exports of goods only or exports of goods and non-factor services) adopted for estimating proportion of exports to national income, for various countries of the world, we can observe that for majority of the countries, the proportion of exports to national income has shown a rising trend in terms of cross-section analysis. This supports the view that the proportion of exports to national income is positively related to the process of economic development of a country. This signifies that as the economic development acclerates, a country tends to have an increase in tendency for comparative advantage leading to an increase in the proportion of exports to national income over a period of time.[5]

Indian Exports and World Exports

In order to ascertain the outward orientation of Indian exports, it is imperative to examine the magnitude of Indian exports in relation to world exports in terms of its percentage share in world exports and rate of growth over a period of time. With reference to this, Table 5.6 reveals that world exports have increased from 170.5 billions of U.S. Dollars in 1965 to 1662.9 billions of U.S. Dollars in 1983 represented an increase of 875.31%. As against this, Indian exports have increased from 1.687 billions of U.S. Dollars in 1965 to 8.512 billions of U.S. Dollars in 1983 reflected an increase of 404.56%. Further in terms of average percentage rate of growth of exports per annum, world exports have grown at the rate of 14.54% per annum, whereas Indian exports have grown at the rate of 10.27% per annum. As regards, the percentage share of Indian exports in world exports, it has declined from 0.99% in 1965 to 0.51 in 1983. This precipitous decline in India's share in world exports over a period of 17 years is a manifestation of stagnation in Indian exports which was also empirically evidenced for the period of 1951 to 1961 by Benjamin Cohen[6].

TABLE - 5.6

Indian Exports and World Total Exports : 1965 to 1983

Year	*Indian Exports* (Billions of Dollars)	*World Total Exports* (Billions of U.S. Dollars)	*Percentage Share of* Indian Exports in World Total Exports
1965	1.687	170.5	0.99
1966	1.954	187.2	1.04
1967	1.613	195.8	0.82
1968	1.761	218.3	0.81
1969	1.835	249.9	0.73
1970	2.026	286.8	0.71
1971	2.034	321.8	0.63
1972	2.448	383.4	0.64
1973	2.917	534.6	0.54
1974	3.926	791.3	0.50
1975	4.355	812.4	0.54
1976	5.549	923.1	0.60
1977	6.378	1048.8	0.61
1978	6.671	1026.3	0.55
1979	7.806	1531.5	0.51
1980	8.242	1876.4	0.44
1981	7.300	1844.8	0.39
1982	9.358	1704.1	0.55
1983	8.512	1662.9	0.51

Source : *International Financial Statistics*, Year Book 1983 pp. 72-75 and Volume XXXVII, Number 12, December 1984 p. 70, *International Monetary* Fund.

Growth Rates of Indian Exports

While considering the structure of exports at macro level, the growth rate of different commodity exports is also one of the important parameters that requires to be examined and it is therefore, in this study, an attempt is made to estimate continuous compound rate of growth of exports. In other words, for estimating the growth rates we have fitted a semilogarithmic function to the exports of different commodity groups at constant prices for the period of 1965-66 to 1981-82.

Algebraically, it may be stated as :

$$Y = ad^{bt}$$

Where Y, t and b denote the exports of different commodities, time and the growth coefficients respectively.

In the above formula, b measures the rate of growth of exports. Thus, this model has been used to measure constant rate of growth of exports of different commodities over time.

In this present study, an attempt is made to estimate, the constant rate of growth of exports only in real terms because the trend of exports in money terms as well as in real terms tend to diverge from each other over time and as a result, there is bound to be a divergence between trend rate of growth of exports in real terms and money terms.

In the context of above Table 5.7 throws light on the growth parametric structure of Indian exports in terms of continuously compounded rate of growth for major commodity groups of exports and principal commodity groups of exports. From among the major commodity groups of exports, the rate of growth of capital goods exports being highest was 15.75% whereas the lowest growth rate was registered by exports of intermediate goods for producing consumer goods which was 4.15%. However, the rate of growth of exports of consumer goods and intermediate goods for producing capital goods was 6.96% and 5.82% respectively. In an aggregate terms, the rate of growth of total exports was 6.76%.

Similarly, from among 20 principal commodities of exports, for 5 commodities viz., Sugar and Honey, Gums, Resins and Lac, Vegetable Oils and Fats, Textile Fibre Yarn and Thread and Petroleum and Petroleum products, the growth rates being -3.61%, -2.81%, -1.53%, -2.57 and -3.81% respectively, indicated that the trend rates of growth of exports had declined. There are two commodities viz., Fruits, Nuts and Vegetables and Tea and Mate for which growth rate was less than 1% i.e. 0.35% and 0.71% respectively. However, the export of Footwear showed a growth rate of 1.79%. From among the rest of 12 commodities, the highest growth rate of 16.24% was registered by machinery followed by 14.20% growth rate for Transport Equipment which belong to the group of capital goods. Moreover, Food Articles and Non-food consumer Articles which belong to the group of consumer goods showed the growth rates of 5.44% and 7.72% respectively. Further, the growth rates of rest of the commodities, viz. Coffee, Spices, Chemicals, Dyeing, Tanning and Colouring Materials, Tobacco unmanufactured, Leather and Manufactures were 6.71%, 3.91%, 10.31%, 13.74%, 3.78%, 5.39%,

12.68% and 8.96% respectively.

TABLE 5.7

Growth Rates of Indian Exports : 1965-66 to 1981-82

Sr. No.	*Name of the Commodity*	*Growth rates* (in Percentage)*
[A]	**Major Commodity Groups of Exports :**	
I.	Consumer Goods	6.96
II.	Intermediate Goods for producing Consumer Goods	4.15
III.	Intermediate Goods for producing Capital Goods	5.82
IV.	Capital Goods	15.75
V.	Total Exports	6.76
[B]	**Principal Commodities of Exports :**	
1.	Food Articles	5.44
2.	Non-Food Consumer Articles	7.72
3.	Fruits, Nuts and Vegetables	0.35
4.	Sugar and Honey	-3.61
5.	Coffee	6.71
6.	Tea and Mate	0.71
7.	Spices	3.91
8.	Chemicals	10.31
9.	Dyeing, Tanning & Colouring Materials	13.74
10.	Gums, Resins and Lac	-2.81
11.	Tobacco Unmanufactured	3.78
12.	Vegetables Oils and Fats	-1.53
13.	Leather and Manufactures thereof	5.39
14.	Textile Fibre Yarn and Thread	-2.57
15.	Iron and Steal.	12.68
16.	Footwear	1.79
17.	Petroleum and Petroleum Products	-3.81
18.	Rubber and Rubber Manufactures	8.96
19.	Machinery	16.24
20.	Transport Equipment	14.20

* Exponential growth rates derived by fitting a Semi-log function to the time series data of exports for the period 1965-66 to 1981-82.

Source : Appendix Table : V.2

Instability in Indian Exports

Exports instability is defined here as short term fluctuations in export receipts corrected for trend. However, some form of trend corrections is a necessary expedient in order to avoid an interpretation of a constant year to year variations (i.e. increase or dicrease) as indicating instability.

Broadly speaking, there are four main different methods for estimating instability index as enumerated below :

1. The average of percentage deviations from the least square trend line through the actual values.
2. The UN measure of the average annual percentage changes dividing always by the higher figure.[7]
3. Mac Bean measure of the average annual deviations from a five year moving averages.[8]
4. Coppock's Log Variance method.[9]

As regards, the second method, it is important to metnion that it has some deficiences. That means a steady increase of 10 per cent per year in the values of a series such as 100, 110, 121 etc. would according to the United Nations Systems, yield fractions like 10/110, 11/121 etc. which when averaged would be less than the conventional 10 per cent, but the resulting percentage would show considerable instability, wherein reality there would be none at all.[10]

The third method viz., Mac Bean's measure, it suffers from the disadvantage of losing two years from the begining and end of the time series.[11] The first method involves constant absolute changes from year to year, while Coppock's method involves constant percentage trend.

The method that involves a constant percentage changes from year-to-year is a better measure than the constant absolute changes from year-to-year and it is for this reason that we have adopted here, the Coppock's method known as 'Log-Variance' method to estimate instability index of Indian exports.

According to Coppock, the instability index equals the antilog of the square root of the logarithmic Variance of the series is given in algebraic terms as :

$$V \log = \frac{1}{N-1} . \Sigma \left[\log X_{t+1} - \log X_t - \frac{1}{N-1} . \Sigma (\log X_{t+1} - \log X_t) \right]^2$$

or

$$V \log = \frac{\left(\log \frac{X_{t+1}}{X_t} - m\right)^2}{N-1}$$

Where N and X is the number of years and value of exports receipts respectively and subscripts indicate the date. Further m refers to the mean value of the logarithmic first differences.

The process of estimating this index is as follows[12] :

1. Logarithms are obtained for each annual value of a variable, for example total exports for Year 1, Year 2 etc.
2. The logarithms of the value for year 1 is subtracted from the logarithms of the value for year 2 etc. in order to get first differences of logarithms.
3. The arithmetic mean of the logarithmic first differences is then obtained.
4. The logarithmic mean is subtracted from each year to year logarithmic first difference in order to obtain the logarithmic difference between the actual and average (trend) year to year logarithmic differences.
5. These logarithmic differences from trend some positive and some negative are then squared, summed up and divided by the number of years minus one. The resulting number is termed as 'log variance'.
6. The next step is to take the square root of the log variance and obtain the antilog of the square root value. Unity is then substracted from antilog and decimal moved two places to the right. The resulting "instability index" is a close approximation of the average year to year percentage variation adjusted for trend.

TABLE - 5.8

Instability of Indian Exports of Different Commodities : 1965-66 to 1981-82

Sr., No.	*Name of the Commodity*	*Instability Index of Indian Exports of Different Commodities*					
		Period 1965-66 to 1981-82		*Period 1965-66 to 1970-71*		*Period 1970-71 to 1981-82*	
		At Current Prices	*At Constant Prices*	*At Current Prices*	*At Constant Prices*	*At Current Prices*	*At Constant Prices*
(1)	(2)	(3)	(4)	(5)	(6)	(7)	(8)
[A]	**Major Commodity Groups of Exports :**						
I.	Consumer Goods	11.39	17.66	5.76	9.92	10.59	19.47
II.	Intermediate Goods for producing Consumer Goods	12.73	26.18	11.90	29.69	11.26	24.94
III.	Intermediate Goods for producing Capital Goods	24.58	21.85	9.52	19.96	29.96	23.73
IV.	Capital Goods	34.28	55.13	38.26	108.53	33.63	30.92
V.	Total Exports	10.18	16.63	5.99	16.12	10.26	16.66
[B]	**Principal Commodities of Exports :**						
1.	Food Articles	20.08	16.77	9.11	11.70	23.67	18.94
2.	Non-Food Consumer Articles	18.67	27.16	9.24	11.18	19.16	31.38
3.	Fruits, Nuts and Vegetables	20.66	13.40	18.89	14.16	22.13	13.79
4.	Sugar and Honey	212.65	228.14	89.76	142.01	280.38	282.98
5.	Coffee	31.84	29.82	20.78	16.07	36.21	35.65

6.	Tea and Mate	30.26	12.81	25.38	11.10	33.59	14.09
7.	Spices	31.18	24.34	23.12	12.41	35.27	28.26
8.	Chemicals	42.17	55.95	43.52	61.42	44.09	56.30
9.	Dyeing, Tanning and Colouring Materials	41.41	35.73	49.87	41.44	39.49	31.31
10.	Gums, Resins and Lac	28.90	16.09	6.94	15.55	36.01	17.07
11.	Tobacco Unmanufactured	27.34	27.53	42.18	33.62	18.40	25.10
12.	Vegetables Oils and Fats	109.74	204.80	133.05	162.80	100.12	238.43
13.	Leather and Manufactures there of	30.32	59.80	25.36	42.85	33.57	69.55
14.	Textile Fibre Yarn and Thread	62.50	78.89	22.92	71.22	78.32	86.71
15.	Iron and Steal	31.61	28.69	40.98	31.39	28.62	27.45
16.	Footwear	18.70	18.59	9.11	11.57	22.30	21.19
17.	Petroleum and Petroleum Products	117.53	241.95	134.56	128.49	119.04	307.43
18.	Rubber and Rubber Manufactures	38.93	37.01	28.15	43.67	44.90	36.12
19.	Machinery	40.52	66.44	35.68	131.47	40.20	38.71
20.	Transport Equipment	41.81	36.77	53.98	67.60	34.77	17.99

Source : Calculated from Appendix Table : V.1 and V.2.

The instability index for different groups for commodity export from India is estimated here both in money terms and in real terms. It becomes evident from Table 5.8 *(see p. 104)* the total exports are more stable at current prices with an instability index of 10.18 than at constant prices with an instability index of 16.63. Similarly, the consumer goods, intermediate goods for producing consumer goods and capital goods are more stable at current prices with an instability index of 11.39, 12.73 and 34.28 respectively than at constant prices with an instability index of 17.66, 26.18 and 55.13 respectively. However, the intermediate goods for producing capital goods are more stable at constant prices with an instability index of 21.85 than at current prices with an instability index of 24.58. In short, majority of major commodity groups of exports and total exports, there was greater stability at current prices than at constant prices. Conversely, it means that Indian exports are more unstable at constant prices. But one important thing that is noticeable is that capital goods are more unstable both at current prices as well as at constant prices as compared to consumer goods and intermediate goods.

From among the principal commodities of exports, Sugar and Honey, Vegetable Oils and Fats, and Petroleum and Petroleum products are more unstable at current prices and at constant prices with an instability index of 212.65, 109.74, 117.53 and 228.14, 204.80 and 241.95 respectively as compared to other commodities. However, at current prices, the instability index varies between 18.67 for non-food consumer articles to 212.65 for Sugar and Honey and at constant prices, it varies from 13.40 for Fruits, nuts and Vegetables to 241.95 for Petroleum and petroleum products. Out of the total 20 commodities of principal exports, 11 commodities are more stable at constant prices. These commodities are Food articles, Fruits, nuts, and vegetables, Coffee, Tea and Mate, Spices, Dyeing. Tanning and Coluring materials, Gums, resins and lac, Tobacco unmanufactured, Iron and Steel, Footwear, Rubber and Rubber manufactures and Transport equipment, conversely, these commodities are unstable at current prices.

Similarly, rest of the commodities viz. Sugar and Honey, Chemicals, Tobacco unmanufactured, Vegetable and thread. Petroleum and petroleum products and Machinery are more stable at current prices but unstable at constant prices. It is significant to note here that whatever are the differences in instability index of commodity exports at current prices and at constant prices, they are mainly accounted for by fluctuations in the variation of unit price of commodity exports.

In order to estimate instability index for primary commodities of exports and manufactured products of exports, we have regrouped the consumer goods and intermediate goods for producing consumer goods as primary commodity group and intermediate goods for producing capital goods and capital goods as manufactured products. Accordingly, primary commodity exports show an instability index of 11.22 at current prices and 18.30 at constant prices while manufactured products show an instability index of 21.96 at current prices and 24.20 at constant prices during the period under consideration. Thus, it is found that the manufactured products are more unstable at constant prices than at current prices as compared to primary commodities of exports. This result is in consonance with the empirical findings by J.D. Coppock. He has calculated instability indices of total value of world trade in primary commodities and in manufacturing commodities (1948 to 1958). These show manufactures to have been more unstable with an index of 6.8 compared with an index of 3.8 for other commodities.

As regards, the instability index for primary commodities, the Crawford, Report States, "Primary Commodity markets clearly continued to be permeated by a degree of instability appreciably greater than is evident in markets for other products".[13] However, in case of India, the instability index at current prices and at constant for primary commodities of exports being evidenced as lower than that of for manufactured products provides an evidence conflicting to the hypothesis maintained in the Crowford Report.

Micro Aspects of Structural Changes

Apart from the macro level analysis of structural changes in Indian exports, the micro level analysis of structural changes is of a paramount importance. The micro level aspects would mainly refer to commodity composition of exports.

With reference to structural changes in the commodity composition, the following questions need to be analysed :

(i) What is the degree of concentration in the commodity composition of exports ? Has there been any change in the degree of concentration over time ?

(ii) Is there any shift in the shares of the consumer goods, intermediate goods and capital goods in the total exports of a country ?

Commodity Concentration Index

This index is useful to ascertain as to what extent the economic fortune of a country depends on one or few commodities. As per Michaely Michael[14] commodity concentration index is defined as

$$C = \sqrt{\Sigma(Xi/X)^2} \cdot 100.$$

Where xi refers to exports of ith item from India and Z refers to total exports from India in some specified year. The value of commodity concentration index will be lower, more evenly exports are distributed over the various possible categories and vice versa. According to Michaely, the value of - concentration index depends in an important way on what commodity classification scheme is employed[15]. Further, the concentration index will be higher, greater the level of aggregation over the commodities, for at higher level of aggregation, products which are relatively dissimilar are classified together. Massell[16] has estimated commodity concentration index at one digit level and three digit level of SITC groups for different countries of the world and he has also come to the conclusion that concentration index is higher at one digit level than at three digit level of SITC group.

In this present study, we have made an attempt to estimate commodity concentration index both at current prices as well as at constant prices at the three digit level of RITC 1965 group.

It would be interesting to examine the trends in the commodity concentration index both in money terms and in real terms. A closer scrutiny of data representing concentration index in money terms and in real terms in Table 5.9 indicates that there is no clear-cut relationship between these two i.e. we cannot conclude that the concentration is greater or smaller in current rupee rather than the in constant rupee.

For the years 1965-66, to 1969-70, 1971-72 to 1972-73, 1974-75 to 1975-76, 1977-78 and 1981-82, the commodity concentration index at constant prices being lower than that of at current prices reflect that exports are more diversified in real terms than in money terms. Whereas for the years, 1970-71, 1973-74, 1976-77 and 1978-79 to 1980-81, the commodity concentration index at current prices being lower than that of at constant prices indicates that exports are more diversified in money terms rather than in real terms.

It can be concluded from the above discussion that, even though the commodity concentration index involves fluctuations both at current prices as well as at constant prices, it reflects a fair increase in the diversification of exports over a period of 17 years. It becomes clear from Table 5.9 that exports are more diversified in money terms than in real terms over the period under consideration, as the same index in money terms has declined by 35.87% while it has declined by 32.46% in real terms over a period of 17 years.

TABLE - 5.9

Commodity Concentration Index of Indian Exports in Money Terms and in Real Terms : 1965-66 to 1981-82

Year	*Commodity concentration Index of Indian Exports By 3-Digit Level Commodity Groups*	
	In Money Terms	*In Real Terms*
1	2	3
1965-66	30.22	27.57
1966-67	29.23	27.00
1967-68	28.31	26.86
1968-69	24.52	22.80
1969-70	22.46	21.76
1970-71	21.67	22.10
1971-72	24.02	23.77
1972-73	21.93	21.80
1973-74	20.90	31.82
1974-75	20.03	18.82
1975-76	20.45	18.56
1976-77	17.90	18.21
1977-78	20.43	17.95
1978-79	24.46	25.96
1979-80	19.31	22.13
1980-81	20.12	35.23
1981-82	19.38	18.62

Source : Estimated on the basis of the data available in *Monthly Statistics of the Foreign Trade of India, Vol. I. Exports and Re-exports* Published by Directorate General of Commercial Intelligence and Statistics, Calcutta, Government of India.

Commodity Composition of Exports

Prior to an examination of commodity composition of exports, one important point which needs due attention is regarding trends in relative prices of different commodities because divergence in relative prices of different commodity groups could result in to shifts in commodity shares in total exports. Therefore, it becomes very pertinent to inquire about the share of commodity groups in total exports both in the money and terms as well as in real terms.

It becomes evident from table 5.10 and 5.11 that the share of consumer goods has declined in money terms from 64.84% in the biennium 1965-66 to 1966-67 to 56.49% in the biennium 1979-80 to 1980-81 i.e. it has declined by 12.88% while in real terms, it has increased from 59.42% during the biennial average of 1965-66 to 1966-67 to 63.27% during the biennial average of 1979-80 to 1980-81 i.e. it has increased by 6.48%. Thus, it can be seen that the share of consumer goods exports to total exports has declined in current rupee while reverse is the case in constant rupee.

TABLE 5.10

Biennial Average of the Percentage Share of Export of Different Commodity Groups to Total Exports At Current Prices.

Biennium	*Consumer Goods*	*Intermediate Goods for producing Consumer Goods*	*Intermediate Goods for producing Consumer Goods*	*Capital Goods*
1965-66 to 1966-67	64.84	19.59	14.21	1.37
1967-68 to 1968-69	59.42	19.44	18.72	2.42
1969-70 to 1970-71	53.88	20.21	21.38	4.44
1971-72 to 1972-73	56.61	23.45	15.40	4.55
1973-74 to 1974-75	56.42	20.08	14.98	6.53
1975-76 to 1976-77	52.06	19.93	21.80	6.22
1977-78 to 1978-79	51.68	23.32	17.67	7.34
1979-80 to 1980-81	56.49	24.06	11.31	8.15

Source : Appendix Table V-1.

TABLE 5.11

Biennial Average of the Percentage Share of Exports of Different Commodity Groups to Total Exports At Constant (1970-71) Prices

Biennium	*Consumer Goods*	*Intermediate goods for producing Consumer Goods*	*Intermediate Goods for producing Consumer Goods*	*Capital Goods*
1965-66 to 1966-67	59.42	22.29	16.46	1.84
1967-68 to 1968-69	56.22	20.03	18.91	4.85
1969-70 to 1970-71	53.76	19.53	21.45	5.26
1971-72 to 1972-73	59.41	19.09	16.14	5.36
1973-74 to 1974-75	50.31	20.42	21.26	8.02
1975-76 to 1976-77	49.59	18.98	24.29	7.15
1977-78 to 1978-79	55.46	16.07	20.54	7.94
1979-80 to 1980-81	63.27	14.69	12.30	9.75

Source : Appendix Table V-2.

Further, the share of intermediate for producing consumer goods has increased by 22.82% in money terms while the same has declined by 34.10% in real terms. Whereas the share of intermediate goods for producing capital goods has declined by 20.41% and 25.27% in money terms and in real terms respectively during the period under consideration. However the share of capital goods exports in total exports has increased by 494.89% and 428.89% both in money terms and real terms respectively. Thus, it becomes evident that the share of intermediate goods for producing capital goods has declined in current and constant rupee while the reverse is true in case of the share of capital goods.

It can be concluded that the diversification emerges with respect to consumer goods exports and intermediate goods for producing capital goods as for the former, its share has declined in money terms, whereas for the latter the share has declined both in money terms and in real terms over the period under consideration.

Relation Between Indian Exports and Economic Development

It is argued that the development of the economy generally affects its structure of foreign trade in general and exports in particular. However, it is our interest in the present study to ascertain whether there is or not a relationship between the share of different commodity exports to total exports and the level of development of a country. In view of this inquiry to be pursued, we have fitted a bivariate linear regression model of the form Y = a + bx (where Y and X indicate the percentage share of commodity exports to total exports and per capita income respectively) to the times series data for the years 1965-66 to 1981-82 on current year basis and constant year basis for different groups of commodity exports i.e. consumer goods, intermediate goods for producing consumer goods, Intermediate goods for producing capital goods and capital goods and food articles. The prime objective of carrying out the bivariate analysis is to ascertain the total explanation of the dependent variable (percentage share of exports of different commodity groups to total exports) by the explanatory variable (per capita income).

Regression Results

[1] Consumer Goods :

Y = 06153584 - 0.0000569 X, R^2 = 0.2630
ta = 25.0377 Significant at 1 per cent level
tb = 2.3136 Significant at 5 per cent level

[2] Intermediate Goods for producing Consumer Goods :

Y = 0.1855502 + 0.0000338 X, R^2 = 0.3117
ta = 14.29.7 Significant at 1 per cent level
tb = 2.6015 Significant at 5 per cent level

[3] Intermediate Goods for producing Capital Goods :

Y = 0.1959333 - 0.0000309 X, R^2 = 0.1134
ta = 8.7892
tb = 1.3852

[4] Capital Goods :

Y = 0.0032499 + 0.0000539 X, R^2 = 0.7523
ta = 0.4063
tb = 6.7346 Significant at 1 per cent level

[5] Food Articles :

$Y = 0.24828773 - 0.0000145\ X,$ $R^2 = 0.0456$
ta = 14.5552
tb = 0.8494

At Constant Prices

[1] Consumer Goods :

$Y = 04712071 + 0.0001445\ X,$ $R^2 = 0.215$
ta = 2.9405
tb = 0.5748

[2] Intermediate Goods for producing Consumer Goods :

$Y = 0.4930407 - 0.0004837\ X,$ $R^2 = 0.7152$
ta = 9.8134 Significant at 1 per cent level
tb = 601373 Significant at 5 per cent level

[3] Intermediate Goods for producing Capital Goods :

$Y = 0.2180114 - 0.0000490\ X,$ $R^2 = 0.0042$
ta = 1.7608
tb = 0.2523

[4] Capital Goods :

$Y = 0.1822596 - 0.0003882\ X,$ $R^2 = 0.5487$
ta = 3.1451 Significant at 1 per cent level
tb = 4.2704 Significant at 1 per cent level

[5] Food Articles :

$Y = 0.3410404 - 0.0002021\ X,$ $R^2 = 0.1088$
ta = 3.5817
tb = 1.3530

Note : These regression equations have been estimated on the basis of information available in Appendix Table V : 5, 6 and 7

Out of 10 regression equations, only three turn out to be significant, on current year basis, consumer goods. Intermediate goods for producing consumer goods and capital goods and two on constant year basis, intermediate goods for producing consumer goods and capital goods. The consumer goods turns out be significant at 5 per cent level with R^2 0.2630 and negative sign of the slope coefficient on current year basis indicating a negative relationship between its share in total exports and per capita income while on constant year basis it turns out to be insignificant. Further, the intermediate goods for producing consumer goods turns out to be significant at 5 per cent level with R^2 0.3117 and positive sign of the slope coefficient on current year basis implying a positive relationship between its share in total exports and per capita income while on constant year basis, it turns out to be significant at 1 per cent level with R^2 0.7152 and negative sign of the slope coefficient reflecting negative relationship between its share in total exports and per capita income. However, capital goods turns out to be significant at 1 per cent level on current year basis and constant year basis with R^2 0.7523 and 0.5487 respectively and positive sign of the slope coefficient showing a positive relationship between its share in total exports and per capita income.

From the above, analysis, it becomes evident that the share of capital goods in total exports being positively related to per capital goods in total exports being positively related to per capita income indicates that as economic development of a country takes place, the share of capital goods in total exports tends to rise over a period of time, the result which is inconsonance with our development takes place, the capital base of the country tends to improve remarkably which gets reflected into increased production and exports of capital goods.

India's Exports of Principal Commodities : A Percentage Share Analysis

It becomes evident from tables 5.12 and 5.13 that during the period of 1965-66 to 1981-82 the share of different commodities in total exports reflect different trends behaviour. There are some commodities whose shares in total exports have increased at current prices as well as at constant prices. These commodities are coffee, Dyeing Tanning and Colouring materials, Tobacco unmanufactured, iron and Steel, Petroleum and Petroleum products, Machinery and Transport equipments. While there are some other commodities whose shares have declined at current prices as well as at constant prices. These commodities are Fruits, Nuts and Vegetable Oils and Fats, Textile Fibre Yarn and Thread, Gums, Resins and Lac and Footwear. Moreover, the shares of Food Articles and Non-Food Articles have declined at current prices but increased at constant prices, whereas the share of chemicals and Leather and Manufactures thereof has increased at current prices but declined at constant prices.

TABLE - 5.12

India's Exports of Principal Commodities : (Percentage Distribution) at Current Prices

Year	Food Articles	Non-Food Consumer Articles	Fruits Nuts & Vegetables	Sugar & Honey	Coffee	Tea & Mate	Spices	Chemicals	Dying Tanning & Colouring Materials	Gums Resins & Lac
1	2	3	4	5	6	7	8	9	10	11
1965-66	21.82	43.65	4.44	1.58	1.73	9.73	3.08	0.35	0.16	0.61
1966-67	26.03	38.17	4.8	1.58	1.8	13.63	21.54	0.23	0.11	0.67
1967-68	26.48	36.08	4.33	1.38	1.53	15.14	2.29	0.26	0.17	0.62
1968-69	23.12	33.16	5.36	0.76	1.33	11.57	1.85	0.34	0.27	0.6
1969-70	21.54	31.76	5.01	0.63	1.4	8.87	2.46	0.4	0.29	0.64
1970-71	23.27	31.17	4.28	1.93	1.65	9.75	2.55	0.6	0.48	0.68
1971-72	23.92	34.93	4.44	1.96	1.39	9.86	2.28	0.52	0.34	0.75
1972-73	23.31	31.07	4.27	0.72	1.73	7.76	1.53	0.46	0.49	0.6
1973-74	19.7	37.12	3.65	1.74	1.86	7.87	2.23	0.68	0.46	0.83
1974-75	27.05	28.95	4	10.1	1.53	6.66	1.82	1.08	0.69	0.97
1975-76	29.15	25.4	3.34	12.1	1.7	6.04	1.81	0.62	0.48	0.47
1976-77	20.39	29.17	3.19	3.02	2.3	5.9	1.47	0.73	0.67	0.34
1977-78	25.15	26.51	3.58	0.34	3.48	10.14	2.5	0.57	0.65	0.32
1978-79	24.11	27.59	2.63	2.54	2.65	6.26	2.72	0.91	0.62	0.4
1979-80	23.31	31.64	2.78	2.29	2.51	5.64	2.29	0.81	0.67	0.36
1980-81	19.29	38.73	3.11	0.56	3.03	6.03	1.58	0.72	0.72	0.33
1981-82	21.71	32.41	2.44	0.83	1.91	5.16	1.29	0.66	0.57	0.4

(Contd.)

TABLE - 5.12 (Contd.)

Year	*Tobacco Articles*	*Vegetable Consumer Articles*	*Leather Fibre Yarn & Manufactures Thereof*	*Textile Fibre yarn & Thread*	*Iron & Steel*	*Foot-wear*	*Petroleum & Petroleum Products*	*Rubber & Rubber Manufactures*	*Machinery*	*Transport Equipment*
	12	13	14	15	16	17	18	19	20	21
1965-66	2.61	0.56	3.8	1.83	0.6	0.7	0.16	0.29	1.06	0.33
1966-67	1.88	0.25	5.42	2.63	0.48	0.77	1.03	0.3	0.96	0.38
1967-68	3.26	0.33	4.49	2.12	0.91	0.77	0.76	0.25	1.14	0.47
1968-69	2.6	0.86	5.37	2.07	1.26	0.68	0.89	0.34	2.01	1.21
1969-70	2.33	0.35	5.79	2.16	1.69	0.66	0.8	0.34	2.75	1.19
1970-71	2.06	0.46	4.75	2.72	1.83	0.75	0.64	0.45	2.9	2.04
1971-72	2.66	0.48	5.72	3.01	1.53	0.74	0.67	0.49	2.7	1.95
1972-73	3.22	1.3	9.04	2.73	1.58	0.68	1.52	0.34	2.78	1.66
1973-74	2.77	1.25	6.86	2.19	1.56	0.54	0.5	0.42	3.02	1.63
1974-75	2.39	1	4.09	1.74	2.02	0.61	0.49	0.41	6.48	1.91
1975-76	2.37	0.85	4.95	1.5	2.07	0.56	0.64	0.28	4.38	2.12
1976-77	1.95	0.98	5.15	1.32	2.64	0.6	0.37	0.62	4.05	1.87
1977-78	2.07	0.38	4.46	0.61	3.93	0.44	0.29	0.49	5.22	2.12
1978-79	2.04	0.25	6	0.7	3.43	0.42	0.25	0.37	4.96	2.27
1979-80	1.57	0.64	7.43	1.48	3.04	0.52	0.29	0.32	4.59	4.31
1980-81	1.76	0.21	4.76	3.22	2.59	0.57	0.35	0.37	4.63	2.77
1981-82	2.67	0.23	4.82	0.97	2.82	0.47	2.88	0.4	5.3	2.76

Source : *Calculated from Appendix Table V.1*

TABLE - 5.13

India's Exports of Principal Commodities : (Percentage Distribution) at Constant (1970-71) Prices

Year	*Food Articles*	*Non-Food Consumer Articles*	*Fruits Nuts & Vegetables*	*Sugar & Honey*	*Coffee*	*Tea & Mate*	*Spices*	*Chemicals*	*Dying Tanning & Colouring Materials*	*Gums Resins & Lac*
1	2	3	4	5	6	7	8	9	10	11
1965-66	19.47	4.032	3.87	1.58	1.24	9.06	3.15	0.62	0.11	0.79
1966-67	21.49	37.55	4.11	2.02	1.31	9.44	2.93	0.3	0.09	0.64
1967-68	24.21	35.54	4.61	1.39	1.92	11.36	3.19	0.29	0.16	0.73
1968-69	23.35	29.33	4.53	4.69	1.32	8.77	2.38	0.29	0.22	0.63
1969-70	23.16	28.36	4.6	4.18	1.58	8.07	2.14	0.36	0.26	0.65
1970-71	23.93	32.06	4.4	1.98	1.7	10.03	2.63	0.61	0.49	0.7
1971-72	24.89	36.06	4.73	1.72	1.84	10.35	3.57	0.57	0.31	0.71
1972-73	24.66	33.19	4.58	0.49	2.29	8.35	2.13	0.63	0.46	0.43
1973-74	20.25	31.54	3.39	1.06	2.16	7.6	2.7	0.7	0.4	0.34
1974-75	20.8	28.02	3.44	2.48	2.73	7.57	1.93	0.86	0.43	0.35
1975-76	21.75	28.22	3.26	4.15	1.94	6.91	2.06	0.62	0.33	0.3
1976-77	17.22	31.98	2.81	1.64	1.3	6.48	1.63	0.75	0.4	0.24
1977-78	17.51	37.37	2.49	0.22	1.06	6.07	2.33	0.54	0.45	0.24
1978-79	18.71	37.3	2.31	2	1.71	4.38	2.77	1.36	0.41	0.27
1979-80	19.78	40.72	1.66	1.17	1.14	3.77	2.27	0.69	0.34	0.2
1980-81	14.48	51.56	1.41	0.14	1.53	3.88	1.58	0.39	0.33	0.19
1981-82	25.76	36.56	2.26	0.48	1.73	4.84	1.97	0.41	0.4	0.25

(Contd.)

TABLE - 5.13 (Contd.)

Year	*Tobacco Articles*	*Vegetable Consumer Articles*	*Leather Fibre Yarn & Manufactures Thereof*	*Textile Fibre yarn & Thread*	*Iron & Steel*	*Foot-wear*	*Petroleum & Petroleum Products*	*Rubber & Rubber Manufactures*	*Machinery*	*Transport Equipment*
	12	13	14	15	16	17	18	19	20	21
1965-66	2.31	0.38	4.01	2.17	0.58	0.51	0.94	0.21	1.55	0.44
1966-67	1.65	0.16	5.5	4.3	0.58	0.66	0.28	0.37	1.28	0.4
1967-68	2.75	0.31	5.92	2.47	1.03	0.71	0.72	0.53	1.64	0.63
1968-69	2.04	0.92	7.1	1.93	1.26	0.66	0.83	0.52	6.08	1.34
1969-70	2.23	0.41	7.56	3.43	1.87	0.68	0.99	0.35	4.33	1.12
1970-71	2.12	0.48	4.88	2.8	1.88	0.77	0.66	0.47	2.99	2.09
1971-72	2.52	0.52	2.94	2.76	1.44	0.89	0.48	0.51	3.6	1.56
1972-73	3.62	1.11	5.44	2.35	1.4	0.71	0.98	0.42	4.11	1.45
1973-74	2.77	0.75	7.47	2.21	1.44	0.65	0.16	0.61	7.31	1.45
1974-75	2.24	0.74	5.12	1.62	1.45	0.69	0.18	0.54	5.7	1.57
1975-76	0.21	0.91	6.21	1.61	1.59	0.51	1.8	0.44	5.95	1.78
1976-77	1.91	1.21	4.79	1.22	1.99	0.55	0.18	0.58	5.08	1.47
1977-78	2.18	0.07	5	0.51	3.22	0.49	0.13	0.83	5.46	1.95
1978-79	1.77	0.12	4.97	0.48	2.59	0.38	0.12	0.43	6.74	1.73
1979-80	1.56	0.29	4.09	0.9	1.68	0.29	0.05	0.4	10.05	1.59
1980-81	1.18	0.05	6.77	1.96	1.2	0.32	0.08	0.36	6.39	1.46
1981-82	2.32	0.1	2.83	0.8	2	0.32	1.14	0.35	7.09	2.2

Source : Calculated from *Appendix Table V.2*

Thus, it can be concluded from the above analysis that the divergence in relative price movements has resulted in to a shift in the commodity shares and shares of different commodity groups in total exports. When the impact of price change is remove, it shows an entirely reverse trend of shares of some of the commodity groups to total exports.

(See Appendix Tables from P. 120 to 154)

References

1. V.R. Panchmukhi suggests to distinguish the macro and micro aspects of trade structure and in its changes, vide, Panchmukhi V.R. : *Trade Policies of India, A Quantitative Analysis*, P. 20, Concept Publishing Co. Delhi 1978.
2. Kuznets Simon : '*Economic Growth of Small Nations*' in Robinson E.A.G. (ed) : *Economic Consequences of the Size of Nations*, p. 18 Macmillan & Co. Ltd., New York, St. Martin press, 1963.
3. Kuznets Simon, *op. cit.*, P. 18.
4. W.A. Lewis : *The Theory of Economic Growth*, George Allen & Unwin Ltd. 1955 P. 342
5. W.A. Lewis, *op.Cit.*, p. 342
6. Cohen Benjamin I. : *Op.Cit.*, pp. 590-604
7. United Nations Secretariat : *Instability in exports Markets of Underdeveloped Countries*, U.N. Department of Economic Affaris 1952.
8. Mac Bean A.I. : *Exports Instability and Economic Development*, p. 34. George Allen & Unwin Ltd, London, 1966.
9. Coppock J.D. : *International Economic Instability*, P. 24.. McGraw-Hill Book Co., New York, 1962.
10. Coppock J.D. : *Op.Cit.*, P. 24
11. Mac Bean A.I. : *Op.Cit.* p. 34
12. Coppock J.D. : *Op.Cit.* P. 24
13. United Nations Secretariat : *Instability in Exports Market of Underdeveloped Countries*, United Nations, Dept. of Economics Affairs, 1952.
14. Michaely Michael, "Concentration of Exports and Imports, An International Comparision", *The Economic Journal*, Dec. 1958, pp. 722-736
15. Michaely Michael : *Op.Cit.* pp. 722-736
16. Massell Benton F., "Exports concentration and fluctuations in Export Earnings : A cross-section analysis", *American Economic Review*, March 1964, pp. 47-63.

APPENDIX TABLE-V.1 (Contd.)

Post-Devaluation (Rupees in Lakhs)

Sr. No.	Name of the Commodity	1973-74	1974-75	1975-76	1976-77
		11	12	13	14
I.	**Consumer Goods :**	140227.41	188406.22	213926.72	245805.82
1.	*Food Articles* :	48618.48	91012.4	114315.02	101116.1
[a]	Cereals	696.29	2167.97	1442.55	1021.34
[b]	Dairy Products	7.91	4.34	15.32	57.82
[c]	Fruits, Nuts & Vegetables	9019.95	13489.14	13120.58	15824.09
[d]	Sugar and Honey	4286.64	33970.56	47475.1	14972.42
[e]	Coffee	4601.3	5135.51	6665.26	11404.97
[f]	Tea	14484.9	22398.51	23681.43	29286.99
[g]	Spices	5489.58	6133.3	7096.19	7292.33
[h]	Other Food Articles	10031.91	7713.07	14818.59	21256.14
2.	*Non-Food Consumer Articles*	91608.93	97393.82	99611.7	144689.72
[a]	Beverages and Tobacco Manufactured	255.28	190.97	537.58	642.22
[b]	Medicinal & Pharmaceutical Products	1494.92	2267.43	2214.94	2341.79
[c]	Paper and paper board	690.35	747.22	544.65	626.31
[d]	Travel Goods	306.6	383.93	644.27	643.39
[e]	Clothing	9545.45	13603.56	19991.92	32502.11
[f]	Footwear	1338.59	2047.26	2194.54	2956.99
[g]	Scientific, medical, optical measuring and photographic Instruments	787.62	997.62	1244.32	1262.92
[h]	Watches & Clocks	14.78	22.36	29.93	24.69
[i]	Textile Fabrics :	524.27	680.35	670.15	764.13
	(i) Cotton Fabrics	30.01	63.56	43.17	12.07
	(ii) Silken Fabrics	285.26	450.63	479.55	585.4
	(iii) Woollen Fabrics	209	166.16	147.43	166.66
[j]	*Others*	76651.07	76453.12	71539.4	102925.17
II.	*Raw-Materials & Intermediate Goods for Producing Consumer Goods*	60810.21 (50138.72)	65713.37 (56223.14)	74680.27 (62385.94)	103282.12 (79038.62)

(Contd.)

APPENDIX TABLE-V.1 (Contd.)

Post-Devaluation (Rupees in Lakhs)

Sr. No	Name of the Commodity	1977-78	1978-79	1979-80	1980-81	1981-82
.		15	16	17	18	19
I.	**Consumer Goods**:	282875.16	281096.26	358202.96	409550.75	414684.79
1.	*Food Articles* :	137720	13100.65	151944.84	136157.22	166357.7
[a]	Cereals	5656.3	10562.02	19113.41	5090324	37637.5
[b]	Dairy Products	120.57	53.44	103.29	52.52	158.48
[c]	Fruits. Nuts & Vegetables	19633.48	14298397	18123.64	21931.61	18677.62
[d]	Sugar and Honey	1870.78	13573.61	14910.23	3985.87	6379.99
[e]	Coffee	19069.49	14391.59	16327.89	21415.66	14596.48
[f]	Tea	555531.7	34045.26	36783.96	42550.39	39520.41
[g]	Spices	13702.22	14805.57	14936.36	11136.68	9876.41
[h]	Other Food Articles	22138.46	29370.19	31645..96	29994.25	39510.81
2.	*Non-Food Consumer Articles*	145155.16	149995.61	206258.12	273393.53	248327.09
[a]	Beverages and Tobacco Manufactured	453.05	631.27	1344.06	1690.35	3151.08
[b]	Medicinal & Pharma-ceutical Products	3309.74	5637.74	8746.96	60129.79	12197.79
[c]	Paper and paper board	700.28	719.72	529.58	678.15	596.74
[d]	Travel Goods	907.66	1404.38	1571.71	1825.96	2379.69
[e]	Clothing	32952.25	45891.09	50123.78	56537.83	65814.42
[f]	Footwear	2403.46	2286.36	3389.5	4007.22	3598.77
[g]	Scientific, medical, optical measuring and photographic Instruments	1646.33	2959.51	2796.38	4439.87	3990.2
[h]	Watches & Clocks	55.39	183.53	59.79	98.99	277.19
[i]	Textile Fabrics :	1064.42	1398.18	1712.66	1843.32	2910.04
	(i) Cotton Fabrics	24.8	20.81	4.7	14.78	21.97
	(ii) Silken Fabrics	875.66	1114.27	1385.99	1504.98	2430.11
	(iii) Woollen Fabrics	163.96	263.1	321.97	323.56	457.96
[j]	*Others*	101662.58	88883.83	135983.7	.142142.05	153411.17
II.	*Raw-Materials & Intermediate Goods for Producing Consumer Goods*	121826.11	132552.22	157372.65	169237.66	184510.56
		(67246.01)	(61493.4)	(105477.85)	(109045.2)	(108403.65)

APPENDIX TABLE-V.1 (Contd.)

Sr. No.	Name of the Commodity	1965-66	1966-67	1967-68	1968-69	1969-70
1	2	3	4	5	6	7
1.	**Chemicals**	409.14	264.36	307.98	464.16	560.48
	[a] Organic & In-organic	298.1	194.54	221.02	329.03	442.65
	[b] Chemical Materials & Products	111.04	69.82	86.96	135.13	117.83
2.	Copra & Coconut Kernel	–	1.24	0.53	–	–
3.	Dyeing, Tanning &	188.97	131.61	205.33	365.91	403.4
4.	Fertilizers	0.1	0.13	0	1.35	0
5.	Gums, resins & Lac	721.94	769.33	739.36	809.85	903.78
6.	Hides & Skins undressed	1504.39	1608.55	738.81	504.3	830.57
7.	Tobacco Unmanufactured	3083.21	2151.52	3884.96	3516.36	3270.55
8.	Vegetable Oils & Fats	659.21	283.37	396.23	1171.18	495.07
9.	Animal Oils & Fats	1.59	0.59	1.23	2.57	2.28
10.	Leather & Manufactures thereof	4480.11	6208.5	5344.3	7261.94	8131.18
11.	Furskins, Tanned or dressed	1.61	4.9	1.07	5.03	22.63
12.	*Textile, Fibres, Yarn & Thread*	2160.95	3012.29	2522.88	2804	3034.63
	[a] Silk Yarn & Thread	1.51	3.61	2.67	3.74	5.6
	[b] Cotton raw	971.86	1110.44	1475.06	1110.49	1469.04
	[c] Cotton twist yarn & thread	697.09	977.06	763.12	1431.82	1104.44
	[d] Jute	485.57	907.16	271.9	255.26	422.01
	[e] Silk	0.22	0.89	1.52	0.97	23.64
	[f] Synthetic fibre Yarn & Thread	3.59	0.55	8.1	0.52	3.91
	[g] Wool and Wool tops	0.07	11.27	0.08	–	5.92
	[h] Woollen yarn & knitting wool	1.04	1.31	0.43	1.2	0.07
13.	*Others*	9846.31 (7520.33)	8065.04 (5752.32)	7882.76 (4845.3)	10683.1 (6207.09)	12522.37 (8325.65)
III.	*Raw-Materials & Intermediate Goods for Producing Capital Goods*	16051.54	16984.58	20629	27191.91	29840.06

(Contd.)

APPENDIX TABLE-V.1 (Contd.)

Sr. No.	*Name of the Commodity*	*1970-71*	*1971-72*	*1972-73*	*1973-74*
		8	9	10	11
1.	**Chemicals**	906.29	826.25	867.63	1683.36
	[a] Organic & In-organic	786.94	717.66	764.35	1442.82
	[b] Chemical Materials & Products	122.358	108.57	103.28	240.54
2.	Copra & Coconut Kernel	–	–	0.05	0.55
3.	Dyeing, Tanning &	725.98	545.06	926.51	1138.39
4.	Fertilizers	0.93	188.93	67.37	1.16
5.	Gums, resins & Lac	1031.74	1183.71	1139.46	2053.47
6.	Hides & Skins undressed	376.85	62.7	82.54	137.74
7.	Tobacco Unmanufactured	3139.76	4224.61	6106.98	6841.46
8.	Vegetable Oils & Fats	703.2	757.32	2462.75	3084.83
9.	Animal Oils & Fats	2.41	21.9	57.48	3.53
10.	Leather & Manufactures thereof	7216.92	9073.64	17167.48	16931.03
11.	Furskins, Tanned or dressed	1.24	2.91	283.55	286.78
12.	*Textile, Fibres, Yarn & Thread*	4131.77	4769.25	5189.35	5396.74
	[a] Silk Yarn & Thread	13.43	8.63	50.91	22.78
	[b] Cotton raw	1395.37	1664.27	2157.61	3239.95
	[c] Cotton twist yarn & thread	2216.52	1768	2467.53	1597.3
	[d] Jute	428.9	1303.1	489.47	442.3
	[e] Silk	1.43	1.79	2.26	8.9
	[f] Synthetic fibre Yarn & Thread	76.12	19.75	15.27	77.37
	[g] Wool and Wool tops	–	1.02	0.01	–
	[h] Woollen yarn & knitting wool	–	2.69	6.29	8.14
13.	*Others*	10814.02 (6626.15)	11448.22 (6296.76)	15047.29 (7254.36)	23251.17 (12579.68)
III.	*Raw-Materials & Intermediate Goods for Producing Capital Goods*	32664.44	24774.99	28777.84	34293.96

(Contd.)

APPENDIX TABLE-V.I (Contd.)

Sr. No.	Name of the Commodity	1974-75	1975-76	1976-77	1977-78
		12	13	14	15
1.	**Chemicals**	3621.05	2424.3	3626.06	3121.95
	[a] Organic & In-organic	2704.04	2201.89	3118.39	2701.87
	[b] Chemical Materials & Products	917.02	222.41	507.67	420.08
2.	Copra & Coconut Kernel	0.52	3 79	14.36	13.37
3.	Dyeing, Tanning &	2317.86	1879.21	3325.41	3555.13
4.	Fertilizers	–	–	0.95	1.09
5.	Gums, resins & Lac	3271.43	1827.93	1673.18	1769.42
6.	Hides & Skins undressed	28.94	15.28	22.73	26.28
7.	Tobacco Unmanufactured	8035.51	9309.55	9661.81	11320.91
8.	Vegetable Oils & Fats	3365.49	3329.28	4857.71	2068.28
9.	Animal Oils & Fats	13.03	31.64	3.43	8.82
10.	Leather & Manufactures thereof	13773.33	19406.13	25570.15	24434.02
11.	Furskins, Tanned or dressed	722.53	723.77	851.37	361.9
12	*Textile, Fibres, Yarn & Thread*	5859.48	5877.14	6566.81	3316.16
	[a] Silk Yarn & Thread	5.99	9.83	37.14	24.03
	[b] Cotton raw				
	[c] Cotton twist yarn & thread	1521.74	3924.156	2699.34	70.15
	[d] Jute	2517.12	887.96	3613.37	3020.31
	[e] Silk	1787.89	1044.24	162.3	170.42
	[f] Synthetic fibre Yarn & Thread	21.87	3.1	32.04	23.27
	[g] Wool and Wool tops	–	–	–	2.74
	[h] Woollen yarn & knitting wool	3.78	4.12	19.22	4.94
13.	*Others*	24704.19 (15213.96)	29852.25 (17557.92)	47107.82 (22864.32)	71828.78 (17248.68)
III.	*Raw-Materials & Intermediate Goods for Producing Capital Goods*	54040.22	78077.24	117525.12	102150.48

(Contd.)

APPENDIX TABLE-V.I (Contd.)

Sr. No.	Name of the Commodity	1978-79	1979-80	1980-81	1981-82
		16	17	18	19
1.	**Chemicals**	4948.21	5300.54	5100	5019.41
	[a] Organic & In-organic	4415.96	4290.88	4516.74	4105.13
	[b] Chemical Materials & Products	532.25	1009.66	583.26	914.28
2.	Copra & Coconut Kernel	201.68	820.47	87.02	983.32
3.	Dyeing, Tanning &	3350.04	4394.21	5071.88	4403.78
4.	Fertilizers	–	0.55	187.64	3.4
5.	Gums, resins & Lac	2188.01	2358.93	2353.96	3063.38
6.	Hides & Skins undressed	39.51	44.37	58.47	41.86
7.	Tobacco Unmanufactured	11072.06	10225.01	12441.12	20493.41
8.	Vegetable Oils & Fats	1358.06	4179.8	1469.65	1739.51
9.	Animal Oils & Fats	42.87	30.87	22.59	16.36
10.	Leather & Manufactures thereof	32547.5	48460.77	33628.8	36921.76
11.	Furskins, Tanned or dressed	77.84	94.93	84.54	13.17
12.	*Textile, Fibres, Yarn & Thread*	3820.75	9633.16	22744.26	7440.15
	[a] Silk Yarn & Thread	11.58	10.45	10.82	24.05
	[b] Cotton raw	1601.02	7509.82	16487.55	3631.52
	[c] Cotton twist yarn & thread	1799.54	1799.28	5622.25	2447.4
	[d] Jute	138.15	214.97	533.08	1252.99
	[e] Silk	20.11	–	0.78	2.22
	[f] Synthetic fibre Yarn & Thread	47.38	79.33	61.26	72.19
	[g] Wool and Wool tops	1.02	–	–	0.11
	[h] Woollen yarn & knitting wool	23.95	19.31	28.52	9.67
13.	*Others*	72905.69 (1846.87)	71829.04 (19934.24)	85987.73 (25795.27)	104371.05 (28264.14)
III.	*Raw-Materials & Intermediate Goods for Producing Capital Goods*	90764.63	78248.56	74951.05	105180.2

APPENDIX TABLE-V.I (Contd.)

Sr. No.	Name of the Commodity	1974-75	1975-76	1976-77	1977-78
		12	13	14	15
1.	*Metal & Metal Manufactures*	15668.9	26956.23	30902.21	31469.86
	[a] Iron & Steel	6804.66	8139.02	13094.84	21539.19
	[b] Non-Ferrous Metal	8864.24	18817.21	17807.37	9930.67
	(i) Aluminium	542.11	1265.41	2447.62	1947.61
	(ii) Copper	267.92	134.34	143.89	88.5
	(iii) Tin	3.93	1.27	2.25	6.02
	(iv) Zinc	31.84	0.46	2.95	6.6
	(v) Others	8018.44	17415.73	15210.66	7881.94
2.	*Petroleum & Petroleum Products*	1664.03	2526.23	1846.51	1571.92
3.	*Rubber & Rubber Manufactured*	1386.94	1121.61	3064.71	2685.72
	[a] Natural, Reclaimed & Synthetic	83.96	3.78	761.42	771.54
	[b] Rubber Manufactured	1302.98	1117.83	2303.29	1914.18
4.	*Others*	35320.35	474783.17	81711.69	66422.98
IV.	Capital Goods	28242.92	25515.3	29407.53	40209.36
1.	*Machinery*	21807.48	17197.11	20122.72	28587.34
	[a] Electrical	5628.74	6396.98	8285.95	8665.58
	[b] Non-Electrical	16178.74	10800.13	11836.77	19921.76
2.	*Transport Equipment*	6435.44	8318.19	9284.81	11622.02
	[a] Railway Locomotives and Wagons	977.42	1366.14	1129.33	632.92
	[b] Road & Moton Vehicles	3024.68	4231.16	5332.71	7227.97
	[c] Bicycles	352.24	611.69	624.28	797.03
	[d] Aircraft	71.78	32.81	21.94	12.45
	[e] Others	2009.32	2076.39	2176.55	2951.65
V.	Total Exports : (I + II + III + IV)	336402.73	392199.53	496020.59	547601.11
		(3269112.5)	(379905.2)	(471777.09)	(492481.01)

(contd.)

APPENDIX TABLE-V.I (Contd.)

Sr. No.	Name of the Commodity	1978-79	1979-80	1980-81	1981-82
		16	17	18	19
1.	*Metal & Metal Manufactures*	29206.85	21936.36	19846.09	22787.59
	[a] Iron & Steel	18626.83	19817.93	18279.75	21573.13
	[b] Non-Ferrous Metal	10580.02	2118.43	1566.34	1214.46
	(i) Aluminium	891.03	1495.49	898.72	839.25
	(ii) Copper	183.66	332.22	571.38	255.85
	(iii) Tin	1.74	0.41	11.67	28.96
	(iv) Zinc	2.33	26.81	49.45	77.88
	(v) Others	9501.26	263.5	36.12	12.52
2.	*Petroleum & Petroleum Products*	1379.65	1883.57	2491.48	22093.25
3.	*Rubber & Rubber Manufactured*	2008	2106.89	2587.86	3092.17
	[a] Natural, Reclaimed & Synthetic	37.66	29.56	11.18	33.31
	[b] Rubber Manufactured	1907.34	2077.33	2576.68	3058.86
4.	*Others*	58170.13	52321.74	50025.62	57207.19
IV.	Capital Goods	39299.32	57977.95	52225.53	61739.02
1.	*Machinery*	26970.29	29916.6	32675.82	40583.69
	[a] Electrical	9595.03	10237.57	11673.22	14588.2
	[b] Non-Electrical	17375.26	19679.03	21002.5	25995.49
2.	*Transport Equipment*	12329.03	28061.35	19549.71	21155.33
	[a] Railway Locomotives and Wagons	603.18	4595.88	2341.94	1454.03
	[b] Road & Moton Vehicles	7673.94	8988.78	11159.15	13132.06
	[c] Bicycles	847.96	964.13	2078.25	1789.18
	[d] Aircraft	3.16	28.45	170.21	569.89
	[e] Others	3200.79	4807.11	3800.13	4210.17
V.	Total Exports : (I + II + III + IV)	543712.43	651802.12	705964.99	766114.57
		(472653.61)	(599907.32)	(645772.53)	(690007.66)

Note : (i) The Value figures of total exports are exclusive of re-exports as the percentage share of exports in total exports formed less than one percent. *See Appendix Table V.3*

(ii) The Value figures of exports given in the brackets are exclusive of the value figures of exports of RITC 1965 Commodity Group 667 - Pearls and precious and semiprecious stones worked or unworked. These bracketed figures are used for computation of price and quantum indicies of exports as for this

(Contd.)

group, the quantity date are not available.

(iii) With effect from 6th June 1966, Government of India has devalued the rupee by 36.5% by reducing its par value from 0.186621 gramme of gold to 0.118489 gramme of gold. As a result export value has been multiplied by 1.575 in order to make comparable export value before and after June 1966 (i.e. for April 1965 to May 1966).

Source : Estimates are derived on the basis of information available in *Monthly Statistics of the Foreign Trade of India, Vol. 1, Exports and Re-Export* Published by Directorate General of Commercial Intelligence and Statistics Government of India for the Year 1965-66 to 1981-82.

APPENDIX TABLE-V.2

Indian Exports at Constant (1970-71) Prices : 1965 to 1981-82

(Rupees in Lakhs)

Sr. No.	*Name of the Commodity*	*1965-66*	*1966-67*	*1967-68*	*1968-69*
1	2	3	4	5	6
I.	**Consumer Goods:**	96888.76	88556.8	79574.93	89751.72
1.	*Food Articles* :	31547.43	32232.38	32242.24	39778,93
[a]	Cereals	44.62	43.22	60.54	106.35
[b]	Dairy Products	3.72	5.77	11.91	4.84
[c]	Fruits, Nuts & Vegetables	6272.1	6170.69	6144.71	7720.4
[d]	Sugar and Honey	2566.17	3029.65	1850.81	7996.1
[e]	Coffee	2004.28	1970.65	2559.31	2252.96
[f]	Tea	14685.41	14164.48	15127.96	14941.33
[g]	Spices	5111.91	4393.55	4247.43	4060.02
[h]	Other Food Articles	859.22	2454.37	2239.57	2696.93
2.	*Non-Food Consumer Articles* :	65341.33	56324.42	47332.69	49972.79
[a]	Beverages and Tobacco Manufactured	328.45	125.41	87.36	27.58
[b]	Medicinal & Pharmaceutical Products	729.06	404.45	386.26	555.81
[c]	Paper and paper board	203.69	230.65	331.34	651.9
[d]	Travel Goods	7.63	8.51	12.55	13.95
[e]	Clothing	1337.91	728.34	660.58	1742.28
[f]	Footwear	818.95	989.46	940.24	1117.74
[g]	Scientific, Medical, Optical Measuring and Photographic Instruments	560.59	283.84	645.7	368.23
[h]	Watches & Clocks	1.55	0.61	0.82	0.43
[i]	Textile Fabrics :	262.87	230.67	288.22	373.58
	(i) Cotton Fabrics	37.01	19.1	28.43	60.12
	(ii) Silken Fabrics	34.01	45.85	74.9	86.79
	(iii) Woollen Fabrics	191.85	165.72	184.89	226.67
[j]	Others	61090.63	53322.48	43979,62	45121.29
II.	*Raw-Materials & Intermediate Goods for Producing Consumer Goods*	34001.5	35389.3	26408.96	34470.42
1.	*Chemicals :*	997.01	446.56	381.65	488.09
	[a] Organic & In-Organic	441.56	290.48	256.67	282.59
	[b] Chemical Materials and Products	555.45	156.08	124.98	205.5

(Contd.)

APPENDIX TABLE-V.2 (Contd.)

(Rupees in Lakhs)

Sr. No.	*Name of the Commodity*	*1969-70*	*1970-71*	*1971-72*	*1972-73*
		7	8	9	10
I.	**Consumer Goods**:	82663.82	82748.75	91411.14	99568.52
1	*Food Articles* :	37161.7	35370.96	37329.7	42446.21
[a]	Cereals	226.39	50548	188.36	6865.49
[b]	Dairy Products	6.83	8.86	22.31	30.25
[c]	Fruits, Nuts & Vegetables	7377.1	6501.74	7090.74	7881.47
[d]	Sugar and Honey	6704.48	2929.83	2574.4	846.21
[e]	Coffee	2536.93	2510.5	2760.93	3949.17
[f]	Tea	12953.91	14824.7	15517.6	14376.18
[g]	Spices	3428.96	3880.53	5348.54	3668.16
[h]	Other Food Articles	3927.1	4209.32	3826.82	4829.28
2.	*Non-Food Consumer Articles* :	45502.12	47377.79	54081.44	57122.31
[a]	Beverages and Tobacco Manufactured	85.48	117.23	287.38	192.42
[b]	Medicinal & Pharmaceutical Products	692.55	846.48	2170.18	1600.44
[c]	Paper and paper board	525.85	540.83	255.57	351.05
[d]	Travel Goods	48.23	61.99	63.92	149.42
[e]	Clothing	1916.48	3019.84	3436.96	5174.14
[f]	Footwear	1097.23	1144.04	1336.52	1228.61
[g]	Scientific, Medical, Optical Measuring and Photographic Instruments	658.07	729.83	842.23	818.21
[h]	Watches & Clocks	0.67	2.17	1.43	2.16
[i]	Textile Fabrics :	411.06	675.98	397.95	292.61
	(i) Cotton Fabrics	61.04	66.28	66.14	23.77
	(ii) Silken Fabrics	122.86	310.5	79.05	78.87
	(iii) Woollen Fabrics	227.16	299.2	252.76	189.97
[j]	*Others*	40066.5	40239.4	45289.3	47313.25
II.	*Raw-Materials & Intermediate Goods for Producing Consumer Goods*	35682.86	24863.44	26138.32	35719.16
1.	*Chemicals* :	580.68	906.29	859.55	1085.56
	[a] Organic & In-Organic	499.2	783.94	758.14	819
	[b] Chemical Materials and Products	81.48	122.35	101.41	266.56

(Contd.)

APPENDIX TABLE-V.2 (Contd.)

(Rupees in Lakhs)

Sr. No.	*Name of the Commodity*	*1973-74*	*1974-75*	*1975-76*	*1976-77*
		11	12	13	14
I.	**Consumer Goods**:	96458.74	107794.36	114247.16	137477.72
1.	*Food Articles* :	37718.39	45927.63	49733.6	48124.13
[a]	Cereals	246.03	645.45	565.2	840.73
[b]	Dairy Products	5.08	2.71	9.39	28.69
[c]	Fruits, Nuts & Vegetables	6315.48	7599.53	7444.46	7855.11
[d]	Sugar and Honey	1979.54	5472.54	9495.41	4592.33
[e]	Coffee	4028.52	6035.11	4447.63	3624.27
[f]	Tea	14155.95	16721.5	15794.79	18092.37
[g]	Spices	5035.19	4252.17	4719.2	4568.1
[h]	Other Food Articles	5952.6	5198.62	7257.52	8522.53
2.	*Non-Food Consumer Articles* :	58740.35	61866.73	64513.56	89353.59
[a]	Beverages and Tobacco Manufactured	215.42	128.56	339.25	394.02
[b]	Medicinal & Pharmaceutical Products	5482.8	3718.25	1239.58	3043.52
[c]	Paper and paper board	425.19	448.58	194.69	252.89
[d]	Travel Goods	119.54	134.62	189.99	264.48
[e]	Clothing	7695.31	9360.39	13032.68	20563.32
[f]	Footwear	1215.04	1515.39	1173.63	1534.65
[g]	Scientific, Medical, Optical Measuring and Photographic Instruments	84.6	1010.28	876.83	864.25
[h]	Watches & Clocks	9.88	5.62	14.91	10.18
[i]	Textile Fabrics :	288.52	219.29	188.57	193.27
	(i) Cotton Fabrics	21.86	26.35	20	4.82
	(ii) Silken Fabrics	101.64	81.81	79.94	87.78
	(iii) Woollen Fabrics	165.02	111.31	88.63	100.67
[j]	*Others*	42454.05	45325.75	47263.43	62233.01
II.	*Raw-Materials & Intermediate Goods for Producing Consumer Goods*	38405.7	44646.61	42299.92	54375.63
1.	*Chemicals*:	1312.58	1907.90	1426.76	2102.2
	[a] Organic & In-Organic	1164.98	1449.36	1249.31	1785.29
	[b] Chemical Materials and Products	147.6	458.56	177.45	316.91

(Contd.)

APPENDIX TABLE-V.2 (Contd.)

(Rupees in Lakhs)

Sr. No	*Name of the Commodity*	*1977-78*	*1978-79*	*1979-80*	*1980-81*	*1981-82*
		15	16	17	18	19
I.	**Consumer Goods**:	148298.01	164055.09	242926.95	289982.87	204635.93
1.	*Food Articles* :	47318.55	54803.55	79418.34	63576.23	84572.85
[a]	Cereals	4382.87	1746.73	12528.12	11849.6	13867.85
[b]	Dairy Products	48.13	26.87	39.13	40.84	41.62
[c]	Fruits, Nuts & Vegetables	6739.01	6766.11	6676.88	6174.29	7413.36
[d]	Sugar and Honey	604.13	5856.04	4709.1	626.86	1565.42
[e]	Coffee	2855.2	5003.7	4577.06	6719.63	5689.45
[f]	Tea	16405.48	12828.28	15154.13	17055.14	15908.32
[g]	Spices	6286.64	8107.27	9130.79	6958.74	6471.12
[h]	Other Food Articles	9997.09	14468.55	26603.13	14151.1	33615.71
2.	*Non-Food Consumer Articles :*	100979.46	109251.54	163508.61	226406.64	120063.08
[a]	Beverages and Tobacco Manufactured	268.31	360.37	787.14	828.04	1454.35
[b]	Medicinal & Pharma-ceutical Products	7742.89	16690.59	22753.74	146121.38	28681.04
[c]	Paper and paper board	256.91	242.83	155.29	130.14	156.03
[d]	Travel Goods	410.91	471.8	409.99	356.06	384.74
[e]	Clothing	17089.63	20972.03	63716.11	14704.06	20682.63
[f]	Footwear	1313.27	1113.14	1178.07	1385.25	1060.42
[g]	Scientific, Medical, Optical Measuring and Photographic Instruments	981.14	1486.3	1156.56	1670.14	1578.99
[h]	Watches & Clocks	13.92	46.34	19.92	36.06	97.8
[i]	Textile Fabrics :	206.88	275.98	322.42	326.85	480.12
	(i) Cotton Fabrics	10.8	5.89	1.01	4.57	4.97
	(ii) Silken Fabrics	122.3	146.49	179.74	179.91	277.28
	(iii) Woollen Fabrics	73.78	123.6	141.67	142.37	197.87
[j]	*Others*	72695.6	67592.16	73009.37	60848.66	65486.96
II.	*Raw-Materials & Intermediate Goods for Producing Consumer Goods*	44902.14	45466.13	54729.83	69145.07	43940.1
1.	*Chemicals :*	1469.3	3988.37	2758.65	1709.38	1362.48
	[a] Organic & In-Organic	1255.05	3758.62	2269.74	1507.63	1122.13
	[b] Chemical Materials and Products	214.25	229.75	488.91	201.75	240.35

APPENDIX TABLE-V.2 (Contd.)

Sr. No.	Name of the Commodity	1965-66	1966-67	1967-68	1968-69	1969-70
1	2	3	4	5	6	7
2.	Copra & Coconut Kernel	–	0.6	0.25	–	–
3.	Dyeing, Tanning & Colouring Materials	177.22	139.69	219.25	377.39	414.07
4.	Fertilizers	1.87	3.55	–	21.47	–
5.	Gums, resins & Lac	1281.07	961.52	976.42	1074.43	1037.52
6.	Hides & Skins Undressed	1091.43	1109.05	669.33	505.59	667.51
7.	Tobacco Unmanufactured	3738.75	2471.04	3657	3477.69	3538.14
8.	Vegetable Oils & Fats	619.8	239.42	406.5	1565.75	665.78
9.	Animal Oils & Fats	1.67	0.7	1023	2.32	1.84
10.	Leather & Manufactures thereof	6500.96	8246.31	7883.81	12088.43	12129.98
11.	Furskins, Tanned or dressed	0.15	0.41	0.3	8.33	31.78
12.	Textile, Fibres, Yarn & Thread :	3516.88	6435.25	3288.41	3292.04	5503.93
	[a] Silk	0.76	1.34	0.91	0.83	2.29
	[b] Cotton raw	1547.85	1443.68	1939.81	1232.62	1526.49
	[c] Cotton twist yarn & thread	1365.51	4127.06	1037.6	1784.13	3506.72
	[d] Jute	491.01	849.52	301.97	271.95	390.94
	[e] Silk	1.37	1.11	0.9	0.71	31.53
	[f] Synthetic fibre Yarn & Thread	109.7	0.34	6.62	0.39	3.22
	[g] Wool and Wool tops	0.07	11.6	0.06	--	6.71
	[h] Woollen yarn & knitting wool	0.81	0.6	0.54	1.41	0.03
13.	Others	16074.69	15335.21	8924.72	11568.89	11066.63

(Contd.)

APPENDIX TABLE-V.2 (Contd.)

Sr. No.	Name of the Commodity	1970-71	1971-72	1972-73	1973-74
		8	9	10	11
2.	Copra & Coconut Kernel	–	–	0.02	0.31
3.	Dyeing, Tanning & Colouring Materials	725.98	467.71	800.59	749.83
4.	Fertilizers	0.93	3.11	678.77	10.27
5.	Gums, resins & Lac	1031.94	1065.91	735.97	642.27
6.	Hides & Skins Undressed	376.85	49.15	57.23	50.44
7.	Tobacco Unmanufactured	3139.76	3781.04	6235.93	5162.2
8.	Vegetable Oils & Fats	703.2	775.17	19113.91	1390.92
9.	Animal Oils & Fats	2.41	8.44	40.57	2.29
10.	Leather & Manufactures thereof	7216.92	4404.29	9364.56	13905.13
11.	Furskins, Tanned or dressed	1.24	3.58	315.37	280.02
12.	Textile, Fibres, Yarn & Thread :	4131.77	4142.26	4037.48	4111.36
	[a] Silk	13.43	5.11	7.55	4.22
	[b] Cotton raw	1395.37	1395.47	1650.98	2383.34
	[c] Cotton twist yarn & thread	2216.52	1554.74	1876.03	1120.83
	[d] Jute	428.9	1163.08	469.82	536.83
	[e] Silk	1.43	1.42	2.38	5.81
	[f] Synthetic fibre Yarn & Thread	76.12	19.99	24.29	56.45
	[g] Wool and Wool tops	–	–	1.46	0.01
	[h] Woollen yarn & knitting wool	–	2.45	4.97	3.74
13.	Others	6626.15	10578.11	10455.27	10788.08

(Contd.)

APPENDIX TABLE-V.2 (Contd.)

Sr. No.	*Name of the Commodity*	*1974-75*	*1975-76*	*1976-77*	*1977-78*
		12	13	14	15
2.	Copra & Coconut Kernel	0.18	2.01	0.67	6.37
3.	Dyeing, Tanning & Colouring Materials	956.1	764.94	1122.83	1218.04
4.	Fertilizers	–	–	13.81	2.84
5.	Gums, resins & Lac	772.18	679.18	665.07	640.12
6.	Hides & Skins Undressed	14.54	5.06	2.63	2.64
7.	Tobacco Unmanufactured	4948.91	4902.3	5348.23	5902.24
8.	Vegetable Oils & Fats	1627.38	2081.91	3388.51	183.27
9.	Animal Oils & Fats	9.28	8.77	1.45	1.86
10.	Leather & Manufactures thereof	11302.52	14198.57	13372.75	13531.16
11.	Furskins, Tanned or dressed	679.36	614.71	546.96	932.7
12.	Textile, Fibres, Yarn & Thread :	3578.08	3670.17	3460.6	1365.36
	[a] Silk	1.35	3.93	15.13	6.6
	[b] Cotton raw	868.89	2257.62	1329.65	14.29
	[c] Cotton twist yarn & thread	1058.02	506.91	1764.73	1132.72
	[d] Jute	1636.15	866.97	241.73	193.32
	[e] Silk	0.68	30.42	24.59	2.08
	[f] Synthetic fibre Yarn & Thread	10.38	2.18	25.88	11.99
	[g] Wool and Wool tops	–	–	–	3.55
	[h] Woollen yarn & knitting wool	2.61	2.14	5.06	1.01
13.	Others	18850.26	18357.61	24403.92	19646.24

(Contd.)

APPENDIX TABLE-V.2 (Contd.)

Sr. No.	Name of the Commodity	1978-79	1979-80	1980-81	1981-82
		16	17	18	19
2.	Copra & Coconut Kernel	75.59	276.67	34.81	236.16
3.	Dyeing, Tanning & Colouring Materials	1205.58	1317.82	1442.69	1329.34
4.	Fertilizers	–	0.11	990.04	7.84
5.	Gums, resins & Lac	783.64	788.97	832.69	829.18
6.	Hides & Skins Undressed	10.2	7.98	11.99	5.19
7.	Tobacco Unmanufactured	5184.76	6270.56	5201.73	7617.53
8.	Vegetable Oils & Fats	353.96	1182.08	203.67	313.29
9.	Animal Oils & Fats	9.95	7.23	6.13	5.39
10.	Leather & Manufactures thereof	14551.59	1644.37	29747.76	9291.92
11.	Furskins, Tanned or dressed	114.68	399.78	106.7	4.54
12.	Textile, Fibres, Yarn & Thread :	1412.44	3631.99	8611.42	2618.96
	[a] Silk	10.26	3.09	2.88	11.9
	[b] Cotton raw	513.46	2850.32	5717.88	1028.79
	[c] Cotton twist yarn & thread	630.54	530.32	2480.09	572.82
	[d] Jute	163.26	217.4	389.66	980.57
	[e] Silk	61.03	–	0.36	1.83
	[f] Synthetic fibre Yarn & Thread	21.93	28.05	17.66	20.15
	[g] Wool and Wool tops	1.18	–	–	0.06
	[h] Woollen yarn & knitting wool	10.78	2.81	2.89	2.84
13.	Others	17775.57	21587.62	20246.06	20318.37

APPENDIX TABLE-V.2 (Contd.)

Sr. No.	*Name of the Commodity*	*1965-66*	*1966-67*	*1967-68*	*1968-69*	*1969-70*
1	2	3	4	5	6	7
III.	Raw-Materials & Intermediate Goods for Producing Consumer Goods	27938.33	23524.73	24176.57	33514.63	33378.71
1.	Metal & Metal Manufactures	1195.73	1059.9	1639.76	4484.96	5107.67
	[a] Iron & Steel	934.44	864.16	1376.22	2150.75	2993.59
•	[b] Non-ferrous Metals	261.29	195.43	263.54	2334.21	2114.08
	(i) Aluminium	52.41	79.59	110.25	1563.95	1042.77
	(ii) Copper	138.02	72.2	39.83	349.69	437.24
	(iii) Tin	0.83	0.83	6.79	0.89	22.9
	(iv) Zinc	1.14	4.36	2.5	0.93	1.19
	(v) Others	68.89	41.45	104.17	418.75	609.98
2.	Petroleum & Petroleum Products	1524.34	417.14	953.84	1420.08	1580.88
3.	Rubber & Rubber Manfactured	334.83	560.99	700.65	882.54	555.64
	[a] Natural, reclaimed & synthetic	1.94	0.47	0.83	1.45	364
	[b] Rubber manufactured	332.89	560.52	699.82	881.09	552.58
4.	Others	24883.43	21487.01	20882.32	26727.05	26134.52
IV.	Capital Goods	3224.4	2512.45	3018.06	12629.85	8737.66
1.	Machinery	2516.23	1915.49	2180.81	10351.02	6944.83
	[a] Electrical	929.04	1029.4	827.05	2549.06	2237.72
	[b] Non-Electrical	1587.19	886.09	1353.76	7801.96	4707.11
2.	Transport Equipments	708.17	596.96	837.25	2278.83	1792.83
	[a] Railway Locomotives & Wagons	0.5	110.16	274.45	1127.61	105.05
	[b] Road & Motor Vehicles	526.94	289.16	352.85	733.65	1231.15
	[c] Bicycles	63.95	50.93	100.1	151.02	159.76
	[d] Aircrafts	31.61	44.18	2.36	14.14	8.25
	[e] Others	85.17	102.53	107.49	252.41	288.62
V.	Total Exports : (I+II+III+IV)	162052.99	149983.28	133178.52	170366.62	160463.05

(Contd.)

APPENDIX TABLE-V.2 (Contd.)

Sr. No.	*Name of the Commodity*	*1970-71*	*1971-72*	*1972-73*	*1973-74*
		8	9	10	11
III.	Raw-Materials & Intermediate Goods for Producing Consumer Goods	32664.44	24675.97	27235.76	35058.82
1.	Metal & Metal Manufactures	3993.7	3008.66	2803.41	3769.19
	[a] Iron & Steel	2784.39	2160.6	2410.55	2692.04
	[b] Non-ferrous Metals	1209.31	848.06	392.86	1077.15
	(i) Aluminium	494.88	315.63	320.73	304.1
	(ii) Copper	698.67	522.84	63.51	562.55
	(iii) Tin	3.86	6.32	3.01	6.91
	(iv) Zinc	4.17	0.55	4.71	4.93
	(v) Others	7.73	2.72	0.9	198.66
2.	Petroleum & Petroleum Products	969.52	722.29	1699.45	299.42
3.	Rubber & Rubber Manfactured	689.45	767.82	717.86	1144.06
	[a] Natural, reclaimed & synthetic	3.78	8.87	13.67	114.53
	[b] Rubber manufactured	685.67	758.95	704.19	1029.53
4.	Others	27011.77	20177.2	22015.04	29846.15
IV.	Capital Goods	7510.94	7735.36	9570.38	16315.82
1.	Machinery	4415.86	5395.78	7073.46	13622.88
	[a] Electrical	1608.09	1788.27	1889.96	2864.68
	[b] Non-Electrical	2807.77	3607.51	5183.5	10758.2
2.	Transport Equipments	3095.08	2339.58	2496.92	2692.94
	[a] Railway Locomotives & Wagons	281.27	536.17	209.64	398.33
	[b] Road & Motor Vehicles	2090.27	1160.19	1354.46	1138.56
	[c] Bicycles	243.88	153.68	260.09	207.17
	[d] Aircrafts	7.83	31.76	32.67	22.47
	[e] Others	471.37	457.78	640.06	926.41
V.	Total Exports : (I+II+III+IV)	147787.57	149960.79	172093.82	186239.08

(Contd.)

APPENDIX TABLE-V.2 (Contd.)

Sr. No.	Name of the Commodity	1974-75	1975-76	1976-77	1977-78
		12	13	14	15
III.	Raw-Materials & Intermediate Goods for Producing Consumer Goods	52277.55	54421.02	69214.28	56962.73
1.	Metal & Metal Manufactures	8684.06	15684.09	16719.37	13841.69
	[a] Iron & Steel	3192.51	3647.69	5571.07	8701.5
	[b] Non-ferrous Metals	5491.55	12036.4	11148.3	5140.19
	(i) Aluminium	250.1	980.67	2206.76	714.56
	(ii) Copper	143.98	72.41	93.59	42.52
	(iii) Tin	2.99	0.49	1.09	2.73
	(iv) Zinc	15.16	0.16	0.42	1.07
	(v) Others	5079.02	10982.67	8846.44	4379.31
2.	Petroleum & Petroleum Products	398.34	4115.94	509.11	352.24
3.	Rubber & Rubber Manfactured	1193.66	1001.08	1614.68	2256.72
	[a] Natural, reclaimed & synthetic	48.88	2.24	53.39	523.4
	[b] Rubber manufactured	1144.78	998.84	1561.29	1733.32
4.	Others	42001.49	33619.91	50371.12	40512.08
IV.	Capital Goods	16054.73	17667.78	18326.89	20021.19
1.	Machinery	12591.1	13598.04	14209.68	14753.91
	[a] Electrical	3400.14	3992.9	5024.85	3529.74
	[b] Non-Electrical	9190.96	9605.14	9184.83	11224.17
2.	Transport Equipments	3463.63	4069.74	4117.21	5267.28
	[a] Railway Locomotives & Wagons	362.87	521.95	375.22	399.28
	[b] Road & Motor Vehicles	1901.11	2252.86	2532.2	3354.61
	[c] Bicycles	186.88	362.57	324.78	394.55
	[d] Aircrafts	46.86	70.17	102.1	28.55
	[e] Others	965.91	862.19	782.91	1090.29
V.	Total Exports : (I+II+III+IV)	220773.25	228635.88	279394.52	270184.07

(Contd.)

APPENDIX TABLE-V.2 (Contd.)

Sr. No.	*Name of the Commodity*	*1978-79*	*1979-80*	*1980-81*	*1981-82*
		16	17	18	19
III.	Raw-Materials & Intermediate Goods for Producing Consumer Goods	58550.19	57154.58	45503.04	49279.21
1.	Metal & Metal Manufactures	12820.52	7435.09	5963.93	6890.57
	[a] Iron & Steel	7584.71	6762.65	5269.32	6544.38
	[b] Non-ferrous Metals	5235.81	672.65	694.61	346.19
	(i) Aluminium	303.02	310.65	207.94	185.67
	(ii) Copper	82.83	203.65	441.67	94.41
	(iii) Tin	0.49	0.13	5.03	12.44
	(iv) Zinc	0.45	5.67	23.46	22.25
	(v) Others	4849.02	152.72	16.51	31.42
2.	Petroleum & Petroleum Products	361.35	207.77	367.99	3753.12
3.	Rubber & Rubber Manufactured	1246.26	1519.34	1585.89	1799.45
[a]	Natural, reclaimed & synthetic	17.84	13.7	13.06	11.95
	[b] Rubber manufactured	1228.42	1577.64	1572.83	1787.5
4.	Others	44122.06	47920.38	37585.23	36836.07
IV.	Capital Goods	24798.08	46735.51	34453.37	30507.97
1.	Machinery	19725.5	40369.82	28064.18	23295.6
	[a] Electrical	3760.28	4333.99	3592.87	3661.89
	[b] Non-Electrical	15965.22	36035.83	24471.31	19633.71
2.	Transport Equipments	5072.58	6365.69	6389.19	7212.37
	[a] Railway Locomotives & Wagons	162.17	978.67	513.73	150.87
	[b] Road & Motor Vehicles	3494.35	3748	3904.24	4490.48
	[c] Bicycles	398.94	426.57	821.61	742.56
	[d] Aircrafts	24.18	44.22	85.96	182.55
	[e] Others	992.94	1168.23	1063.32	1645.91
V.	Total Exports : (I+II+III+IV)	292869.49	401546.87	439084.35	328363.21

Note : (i) The Value figures of exports are exclusive of re-exports

(ii) The value figures of exports of raw materials and intermediate goods for producing consumer goods are exclusive of RITC 1965 commodity group 667-Pearls & Precious Stones unworked or worked, as for this commodity group quantity date are not available.

Source : Estimate are derived on the basis of information available in *Monthly Statistics of India, Vol. I, Exports & Re-Exports*, published by Directorate General of Commercial Intelligence and Statistics, Government of India for the years, 1965-66 to 1981-82.

APPENDIX TABLE-V.3

Percentage Share of Re-Exports in India's Total Exports 1965-66 to 1981-82

Year	*Value of Re-Exports* (*In `100 Rs.*)	*Value of Total Exports* (*In `100 Rs.*)	*Percentage Share of Re-Exports in Total* (*In '% age*)
1	2	3	4
1965-66*	39,898	126,87,566	0.31
1966-67*	56,157	115,28,769	0.48
1967-68	58,666	119,28,027	0.49
1968-69	36,811	135,63,413	0.27
1969-70	45,74.	140,86,381	0.32
1970-71	1,07,742	152,43,876	0.70
1971-72	50,707	156,35,442	0.32
1972-73	64,403	195,44,505	0.32
1973-74	50,603	247,81,595	0.20
1974-75	55,193	329,86,218	0.16
1975-76	1,03,058	393,12,792	0.26
1976-77	1,36,474	512,90,640	0.26
1977-78	1,03,641	536,31,833	0.19
1978-79	1,80,316	570,65,968	0.31
1979-80	1,60,404	638,86,331	0.25
1980-81	1,73,250	669,33,804	0.25
1981-82	76,056	779,82,989	0.09

* Note : The value figures of exports and re-exports are adjusted for Devaluation of Rupee undertaken by Govt. of India on 6th June 1966 by raising value figures by 57.5% in order to establish comparability.

Source : Various Issues of March 1966 to 1982 of *Monthly Statistics of the Foreign trade of India, Vol. I Exports and Re-Exports. Published by Directorate General of Commercial Intelligence and statistics, Calcutta, Government of India.*

APPENDIX TABLE-V.4

Classification of Commodities of Exports into Different Commodity Groups*

	Name of the Commodity Groups	*Article Code Numbers of RITC 1965 group*
I.	**Consumer Goods :**	
1.	**Food Articles :**	
[a]	Cereals	041, 042, 043, 044 and 045
[b]	Dairy products	022, 023 and 024
[c]	Fruits, nuts and Vegetables	051, 052, 053, 054 and 055
[d]	Sugar and honey	061
[e]	Coffee	071
[f]	Tea	0741
[g]	Spices	075
[h]	Other food items	001, 011, 012, 013, 025, 031, 032, 046, 047, 048, 062, 072, 073, 091 & 099
2.	**Non-Food Consumer Articles :**	
[a]	Beverages & Tobacco manufactured	111, 112 & 122
[b]	Medicinal and pharamaceutical products	541
[c]	Paper, paperboard and manufactures thereof	641 & 642
[d]	Travel goods	831
[e]	Clothing	841 & 842
[f]	Footwear	851
[g]	Scientific, medical, optical Measuring photographic instruments	861, 862 and 863
[h]	Watches and clocks	864
i]	Textile fabrics :	
	(i) Cotton fabrics	6585219, 6585229, 6585239, 6585259, 6585300, 6585603
	(ii) Silken fabrics	6531103, 6531105 to 6531107, 6531111, 6531201, 65321202 and 6531300
	(iii) Woollen fabrics	6532
[j]	Others*	081, 551, 553, 554, 653*, 654, 655, 656, 657, 658*, 659, 665, 666, 821, 891, 892, 893, 894, 895, 896, 897 and 899

* [*Note* :(i) 653 excludes silken and woollen fabrics, (ii) 658 excludes cotton fabrics)

II. Raw-Materials and Intermediate Goods for Producing Consumer Goods :

1. Chemicals :

   [a] Organic and In-organic - 512, 513 and 514

   [b] Chemical materials and products - 599

2. Copra and coconut Kernel - 2212 and 2213
3. Dyeing, tanning and colouring materials - 532, 533 and 534
4. Fertilizers manufactured -.561
5. Gums, resins and lac - 2922
6. Hides and skins undressed - 211
7. Tobacco unmanufactured - 121
8. Vegetable oils and fats - 421 and 422
9. Animal oils and fats - 411
10. Leather and manufactures thereof - 611 and 612
11. Furskins, tanned or dressed - 613
12. Textile fibres, Yarn and thread :

   [a] Silk Yarn and thread - 6511

   [b] Cotton raw - 2631101 to 2631159 and 2631201 to 2631204

   [c] Cotton twist yarn and thread - 6513 and 6514

   [d] Jute raw - 2613

   [e] Synthetic fibre yarn and thread - 6516

   [f] Wool and wool tops - 2626 and 2628

   [g] Woollen yarn and Knitting Wool - 6512

13. Others* : 212, 221*, 241, 251, 261*, 262*, 263*, 265, 266, 267, 271, 275, 291, 292, 431, 515, 631, 632, 633, 651*, 664, 667 and 812

Note : (i) 221 excludes copra and coconut Kernel

(ii) 261 excludes raw silk

(iii) 262 excludes wool and wool tops

(iv) 263 excludes raw cotton

(v) 292 excludes Gums, resins and lac

(vi) 651 excludes. silken, Woollen, cotton twist and Synthetic fibre yarn and thread)

III. Raw-Materials and Intermediate Goods for Producing Consumer Goods :

1. Metal and Metal Manufactures :

[a] Iron and Steel - 691, 362, 693, 694, 695, 696, 697 and 698

[b] Non-ferrous metals

(i) Aluminium - 684

(ii) Copper - 682

(iii) Tin - 687

(iv) Zinc - 686

(v) Others - 681, 683, 685, 688 and 689

2. Petroleum and Petroleum Products :

[a] Petroleum crude and partly refined - 331

[b] Petroleum products - 332 and 521

3. Rubber, raw and manufactured :

[a] Natural, reclaimed and synthetic - 231

[b] Manufactured - 621 and 629

4. Others : 242, 243, 244, 273, 274, 276, 281, 282, 283, 284, 285, 286, 321, 341, 571, 661, 663, 671, 672, 673, 674, 675, 676, 677 ,678 and 679

IV. Capital Goods :

1. Machinery :

[a] Electrical - 722, 723,724, 725, 726 and 729

[b] Non Electrical - 711, 712, 714, 715, 717, 718 and 719

2. Transport Equipment :

[a] Railway locomotives and wagons - 731

[b] Road and Motor Vehicles - 732

[c] Bicycles - 7331101

[d] Aircraft - 734

[e] Others* : - 733 and 735

---

*(Note : 733 excludes bicycles)

See, Bepin* Behari : *Imports in a Developing Economy*, First Edition, 1965, pp. 176-181. Published by Vora & Co. Publishers Pvt. Ltd., 3 Round Building, Bombay.

APPENDIX TABLE - V.5

Percentage Share of Major Commodity Groups of Exports in India's Total Exports at Current Prices : 1965-66 to 1981-82

Year	*Consumer Goods*	*Intermediate Goods for producing consumer Goods*	*Intermediate Goods for producing Capital Goods*	*Total of Intermediate Goods*	*Capital Goods*
1	2	3	4	5	6
1965-66	65.47	19.54	13.60	33.14	1.39
1966-67	64.20	19.64	14.82	34.46	1.34
1967-68	62.56	18.50	17.33	35.83	1.61
1968-69	56.28	20.39	20.10	40.49	3.23
1969-70	53.30	21.50	21.26	42.46	3.94
1970-71	54.45	19.12	21.49	40.61	4.94
1971-72	58.84	20.88	15.63	36.51	4.65
1972-73	54.38	26.02	15.16	41.18	4.44
1973-74	56.82	24.64	13.89	38.53	4.65
1974-75	56.01	19.53	16.06	35.59	8.40
1975-76	54.55	19.04	19.91	38.95	6.50
1976-77	49.56	20.82	23.69	44.51	5.93
1977-78	51.66	22.25	18.65	40.91	7.44
1978-79	51.70	24.38	16.69	41.07	7.23
1979-80	54.96	24.14	12.00	36.14	8.90
1980-81	58.01	23.97	10.62	34.59	7.40
1981-82	54.13	24.08	13.73	37.81	8.06

Source : Calculated from Appendix Table V-1.

APPENDIX TABLE - V.6

Percentage Share of Major Commodity Groups of Exports in India's Total Exports at 1970-71 Prices : 1965-66 to 1981-82

Year	*Consumer Goods*	*Intermediate Goods for producing consumer Goods*	*Intermediate Goods for producing Capital Goods*	*Total of Intermediate Goods*	*Capital Goods*
1	2	3	4	5	6
1965-66	59.79	20.98	17.24	38.22	1.99
1966-67	59.04	23.60	15.68	39.28	1.68
1967-68	59.75	19.83	18.15	37.98	2.27
1968-69	52.68	20.23	19.67	39.90	7.42
1969-70	51.52	22.24	20.80	43.04	5.44
1970-71	56.00	16.82	22.10	38.92	5.08
1971-72	60.96	17.43	16.45	33.88	5.16
1972-73	57.86	20.75	15.83	36.58	5.56
1973-74	51.79	20.62	18.83	39.45	8.76
1974-75	48.83	20.22	23.68	43.90	7.27
1975-76	49.97	18.50	23.80	42.30	7.73
1976-77	49.21	19.46	24.77	44.23	6.56
1977-78	54.89	16.62	21.08	37.70	7.41
1978-79	56.02	15.52	20.00	35.52	8.46
1979-80	60.50	13.63	14.23	27.86	11.64
1980-81	66.04	15.75	10.36	26.11	7.85
1981-82	62.32	13.38	15.01	28.39	9.29

Source : Calculated from *Appendix Table V-2.*

APPENDIX TABLE - V.7

India's Per Capita N.N.P. at Current and Constant (1970-71) Prices : 1965-66 to 1981-82

Year	*Per Capita N.N.P. of India at Current Prices [in Rs.]*	*Per Capita N.N.P. of India at Constant (1970-71) Prices [in Rs.]*
1	2	3
1965-66	425.5	558.8
1966-67	481.8	551.5
1967-68	554.4	587.3
1968-69	552.3	589.1
1969-70	597.5	612.6
1970-71	632.8	632.8
1971-72	660.2	626.6
1972-73	711.5	604.1
1973-74	870.9	621.2
1974-75	1005.9	617.6
1975-76	1024.2	661.1
1976-77	1067.7	649.5
1977-78	1191.4	693.2
1978-79	1251.9	415.8
1979-80	1332.9	662.5
1980-81	1571.4	700.4
1981-82	1749.5	719.9

Source : National Account Statistics : (1970-71 to 1981-82), February 1983, Central Statistical Organisation, Department of Statistics, Ministry of Planning, Government of India, Appendix A-1, pp. 150-153.

APPENDIX TABLE V.8

List of the Countries Excluded

[A] Countries for which the financial statistics are not reported in International Financial Statistics :

Angola, Bulgeria, British, West Indies, Cambodia, Chad, Cuba, Czechoslovakia, Dahomey, Formasa, Guinea, Laos, Mozambique, Poland, Pureto Rico, Rhodesia and U.S.S.R.

[B] Countries for which data on 'National Income' at market prices are not reported in IFS : Afghanistan, Algeria, Argentina, Antigua & Barbuda, Baharin, Bahms, Bangladesh, Barbados, Belize, Burma, Burundi, Central African Republic, Congo, Dominica, Egypt, Ethiopia, Guatemala, Lebanon, Liberia, Medagascar, Lali, Malwi, Malaysia, Mexico, Mauritius, Nepal, Niger, Nigeria, Oman, Qatar, Rwanda, Syrian Arab Republic, St. Lucia, St. Vinicent, Suriname, Trinidad and Tobago, Uganda, Upper Volta, Uniter Arab Emirates, Yemen P.D. Republic, Yugoslavia and Zimbabwe.

[C] Countries for which the available statistics on exports and national income differ with respect to time of reporting and units of currency:

Bolvia, Bostwana, Cameroon, Ecuador, Haiti, India, Indonesia, Kuwait, Lesotho, New Zealand, Pakistan, Serra Leone, Sudan, Swaziland, etc.

Note : (i) Countries listed in [A], [B] and [C] are excluded for Table 5.5-A.
(ii) Countries listed in [A] and [B] are excluded for 5.5-B

APPENDIX TABLE-V.9

Countries Grouped by Level of Economic Development

[A] Highly Developed Countries :

Australia
Belgium
Canada
Czechoslovakia
Denmark
Finland
France
Germany
Israel
Japan
Kuwait
Netherlands
New Zealand
Norway
Sweden
Switzerland
U.S.S.R.
United Kingdom
United States

[B] Intermediate Countries :

Argentina
Austria
Bulgeria
Chile
Costa Rica
Cuba
Greece
Hungary
Ireland
Italy
Jamaica
Labanon
Libya
Mexico
Panama
Poland
Portugal
Purcto Rico
Republic of South Africa
Romania
Singapore
Spain
Uruguay
Veneuela
Yugoslavia

[C] Underdeveloped Countries :

Africa :

Algeria
Angola
Cameroon
Chad
Congo
Dahomey
Ethiopia
Malagasy Republic
Malawi
Mali
Morocco
Mozambique
Niger
Nigeria
Togo
Tunisia
Uganda
United Arab Republic
Upper Volta
Zambia
Americas

Ghana	Rhodesia	Bolivia
Guinea	Rwanda	Brazil
Ivory Coast	Senegal	British West Indies
Kenya	Sudan	Colombia
Liberia	Tanzania	Dominican Republic
Ecuador	Hondruas	
El Salvador	Nicaragua	
Guatemala	Paraguay	
Haiti	Pem	

Asia :

Afghanistan	Laos	Vietnam
Burma	Malaysia	Yemen
Combodia	Nepal	(Europe)
Ceylon	North Korea	Albania
China	Pakistan	
Formasa	Philippines	
India	Saudi Arabia	
Indonesia	South Korea	
Iran	Syria	
Iraq	Thailand	
Jordon	Turkey	

Source : *United Nations Statistical Office*, Centre for International Studies, 1971.

6

Structure of Indian Exports - II

Introduction

The preceding chapter being confined to an analysis of structure of India's exports at macro (i.e. aggregated) and micro (i.e. disaggregated) levels in terms of current prices as well as constant prices over a period of 1965-66 to 1981-82 and also with some well-established hypotheses examined therein, did not cover an analysis of trends and structure of India's foreign trade in general and India's export trade in particular at current prices with reference to the following :

[a] India's foreign trade over a period of 1966-67 to 1988-89

[b] India's export trade with special reference to India's principal exports by various commodity groups over a period of 1970-71 to 1986-87.

[c] An analysis of structural behaviour of India's export trade in terms of the following aspects over a period of 1965-66 to 1981-82 :

(i) Traditional and non-traditional exports.

(ii) Primary exports and manufactured exports.

(iii) Commodity composition of Indian exports according to market environment and SITC Commodity groups.

(iv) Direction of India's exports in terms of regional destination.

The Present Chapter

In order to systematize the study of Indian exports with reference to above, the present chapter is designed to examine and analyse the structural behaviour of India's exports over a period of time specified respectively with reference to the issues as detailed below :

As far as the foreign trade of India is concerned the following issues deserve to be examined.

(i) What has been the average percentage rates of growth per annum of exports and imports ?

(ii) What has been the percentage share of Indian exports in world exports ?

(iii) What has been the behaviour of percentage share of exports, imports and trade deficit in Gross National Product ?

As regards, India's export trade with special reference to India's principal exports by various commodity groups (i.e. Agricultural and Allied products, Ores and Minerals, manufactured goods, Mineral fuels and Lubricants and others) over a period of 1970-71 to 1986-87, we intend to examine what has happened to the percentage share of each commodity group in total exports ?

Further, with reference to the structural behaviour of Indian exports over a period of 1965-66 to 1981-82, the following aspects are intended to be examined :

(i) What has happened to the percentage share of various categories of commodity exports in total exports over time ?

(ii) What has been the average percentage rates of growth per annum of various categories of commodity exports ?

(iii) Has there been a diversification or concentration of Indian exports ?

(iv) What has happened to the stability of various categories of commodity exports ?

(v) Whether there is or not a relation between various categories of commodity exports with economic development ?

Trends in India's Foreign Trade : [1966-67 to 1988-89]

The trends in India's foreign trade can be discerned from Table 6.1. A glance at the table reveals the fact that as for as India's foreign trade is concerned, the year 1973-74 is the remarkable turning point as during period thereafter, the value figures of exports and imports seem to have magnified as compared to the earlier period. This state of affairs can be attributed to the oil price hike in the middle of the year 1973

TABLE 6.1

Imports, Exports and Trade Balance : 1966-67 to 1988-89

(Rs. Crores)

Years	*Imports*		*Exports*		*Trade Balance*	*Exports as % of World Exports*	*As % of GNP*		
	Amount	*% Increase*	*Amount*	*% Increase*			*Imports*	*Exports*	*Trade Deficit*
(1)	(2)	(3)	(4)	(5)	(6)	(7)	(8)	(9)	(10)
1966-67	2078	---	1157	---	-921	0.95	7.1	3.9	3.1
1967-68	2008	-3.4	1199	3.6	-809	0.74	5.8	3.5	2.3
1968-69	1909	-4.9	1358	13.3	-551	0.73	5.2	3.7	1.5
1969-70	1582	-17.1	1413	4.1	-169	0.67	3.9	3.5	0.4
1970-71	1634	3.3	1535	8.6	-99	0.63	3.8	3.6	0.2
1971-72	1825	11.7	1608	4.8	-217	0.58	4.0	3.5	0.5
1972-73	1867	2.3	1971	22.5	-104	0.58	3.7	3.9	+0.2
1973-74	2955	58.3	2533	28.1	-432	0.50	4.8	4.1	0.7
1974-75	4519	52.9	3329	31.9	-1190	0.46	6.2	4.6	1.6
1975-76	5265	16.5	4042	21.4	-1223	0.49	6.7	5.1	1.6
1976-77	5074	-3.6	5142	27.2	+68	0.55	6.0	6.1	+0.1
1977-78	6020	18.8	5408	5.2	-612	0.56	6.3	5.6	0.6
1978-79	6811	13.1	5726	5.9	-1059	0.51	6.5	5.5	1.0
1979-80	9143	34.2	6418	12.1	-2725	0.47	8.0	5.6	2.4
1980-81	12549	37.3	6711	4.6	-5838	0.43	9.2	4.9	4.3

Contd.

TABLE 6.1 (Contd.)

(1)	(2)	(3)	(4)	(5)	(6)	(7)	(8)	(9)	(10)
1981-82	13608	8.4	7806	16.3	-5802	0.42	8.5	4.9	3.6
1982-83	14293	5.0	8803	12.3	-5490	0.50	8.1	5.0	3.1
1983-84	15831	10.8	9771	11.0	-6060	0.50	7.7	4.7	2.9
1984-85	17134	8.2	11744	20.2	-5390	0.52	7.5	5.1	2.4
1985-86	19658	14.7	10895	-7.2	-8763	0.47	7.5	4.2	3.4
1986-87	20201	2.8	12452	14.3	-7749	0.44	6.9	4.3	2.7
1987-88	22399	10.9	15741	26.4	-6658	0.45	6.8	4.8	2.0
1988-89*	27693	23.6	20281	28.8	-7412	0.45	7.2	5.2	1.9

* Provisional

Source : Basic Statistics Relating to the Indian Economy, Vol. I, All India (August, 1989) Centre For Monitoring Indian Economy, Bombay

which led to an increase in the value figure of imports by 58.3% in the year 1973-74 as compared to 2.3% increase in the year 1972-73 and an increase in the value figures of exports by 22.5% in the year 1972-73 as compared to 4.8% increase in the year 1971-72.

Further, India being a developing country needs in creasing imports which gets reflected into increase in negative trade balance from Rs. 921 crores in 1966-67 to Rs. 7412 crores (i.e. 30.64% an average per annum) in 1988-89 . This increase in negative trade balance is also due to a world wide phenomenon of inflation consequent upon increase in oil prices.

As far as the average annual rates of growth is concerned, Indian imports registered a growth rate 13.81% during 1966-67 to 1988-89, 17.33% during 1970-71 to 1988-89 and 19.49% during 1973-74 to 1988-89. However, Indian exports registered a growth rate of 14.36% during 1966-67 to 1988-89, 15.52% during 1970-71 to 1988-89 and 16.19% during 1973-74 to 1988-89. We can see that after 1970-71 the growth rates of exports remained less than that of imports and after 1973-74 the growth rates of imports and exports remained higher due to the reasons cited earlier.

As far as Indian exports in relation to world exports are concerned, we perceive that the share of Indian exports in world exports in terms of percentage not only remained less than one percent during the period under consideration but it shows a declining trend of 0.95% in the year 1966-67 to 0.45% in the year 1988-89. This state of affairs is quite obvious, as India is one among many exporting countries of the world. However, it indicates that the Indian economy has many miles to go about to enhance the competitive strength of Indian exports in the world market.

As regards, the share of Indian imports in India's Gross national product, it is noticeable that it does not exhibit any systematic trend behaviour. This can be seen from the fact that the percentage share of Indian imports in GNP declined from 7.1% in the year 1966-67 to 6.5% in the year 1978-89 and thereafter it increased to 9.2% in the year 1980-81. However, it declined from 8.5% in the year 1987-88. The fluctuations in the share of Indian imports in GNP can be attributed to the effects of the interplay of macro-economic policy variables and fluctuations in the world business activity.

Further, as far as the share of Indian exports in the GNP is concerned, it shows a systematic increasing trend of 3.9% in the year 1966-67 to 5.2% in the year 1988-89. This reasonably good performance of Indian exports can be attributed to the export-oriented trade policy adopted by the Government of Indian. Further, there has been a fall in percentage share of trade deficit in GNP from 3.1% in the year 1966-67 to 1.9% in the year 1988-89.

India's Export Trade by Commodity Groups 1970-71 to 1986-87

As an analysis of India's foreign trade at global level does not focus on the structural behaviour of India's principal exports by various commodity groups (i.e. Agricultural and Allied Products, Ores and Mineral fuels and Lubricants and others) over time, we present an analysis of structural behaviour of commodity exports by groups.

In order to undertake an analysis of India's exports by various commodity groups, we have selected the period of 1970-71 to 1986-87 with an exclusion of the period of 1966-67 to 1969-79. However, the justification for the exclusion of the period lies in the fact that the period is too remote in the past from the point of view of relative economic significance of certain commodity group of exports viz. manufactured goods. It is only after the year 1970-71 that the increasing relative significance of certain commodity groups of exports is felt in relation to total exports and also in relation to other commodity groups of exports.

As far as the classification of India's principal exports in to various commodity groups referred above is concerned, India's commodity exports for the period 1970-71 to 1981-82 have been regrouped as per the classification for the period 1982-83 to 1986-87.[1]*

The structural behaviour of India's principal exports by various commodity groups in terms of their percentage shares in total exports over the period under consideration it can be visualized from Table 6.2 which reveals a very systematic trend behaviour of exports of Agricultural and Allied products, Ores and Minerals (excluding coal) and Manufactured Goods.

In case of agricultural and allied products exports, its percentage share in total exports systematically shows a decline from 39.22% in the year 1970-71 to 27.48% in the year 1986-87. Similarly, it is also visible that the percentage share of ores and minerals displays a decline from 9.57% in the year 1970-71 to 5.76% in the year 1986-87. The declining

*For Classification, see Appendix Table - VI.1

TABLE 6.2

India's Principal Exports by Commodity Groups : (1970-71 to 1986-87)

(Rs. Crores)

Years	I Agricultural and Allied products		II Ores and Minerals (excl. Coal)		III Manufactured Goods		IV Mineral fuels & Lubricants (Incl. Coal)		V Others		Total Exports
	Value Rs. Crores	% Share In Total	Value Rs. Crores	. % Share In Total	Value Rs. Crores	% Share In Total	Value Rs. Crores	% Share In Total	Value Rs. Crores	% Share In Total	Value Rs. Crores
(1)	(2)	(3)	(4)	(5)	(6)	(7)	(8)	(9)	(10)	(11)	(12)
1970-71	602.1	39.22	146.9	9.57	482.7	31.44	12.6	0.82	290.9	18.95	1535.2
1971-72	705.8	43.89	130.7	8.31	473.8	29.46	11.6	0.72	286.3	17.80	1608.2
1972-73	771.9	39.17	135.1	6.86	660.9	33.55	32.0	1.62	370.9	18.82	1970.8
1973-74	957.7	38.67	155.3	6.15	943.9	37.41	15.3	0.61	433.2	17.16	2523.4
1974-75	1371.0	41.18	196.2	5.89	1114.7	33.49	20.4	0.62	626.6	18.82	3328.9
1975-76	1541.4	39.10	245.9	6.24	1345.7	34.14	35.6	0.90	773.2	19.02	3941.8
1976-77	1485.9	28.89	275.0	5.35	2205.1	42.87	32.7	0.64	1144.5	22.25	5143.2
1977-78	1677.8	31.02	269.0	4.97	2453.9	45.39	27.8	0.51	979.4	18.11	5407.9
1978-79	1497.9	26.16	267.2	4.67	3016.5	52.68	19.8	0.34	924.9	16.15	5726.3
1979-80	1882.6	29.33	319.0	4.97	3021.7	47.08	21.2	0.33	1173.9	18.29	6418.4

(Contd.)

Table 6.2 (Contd.)

(1)	(2)	(3)	(4)	(5)	(6)	(7)	(8)	(9)	(10)	(11)	(12)
1980-81	1927.4	28.72	333.7	4.97	2995.7	44.64	27.9	0.42	1426.0	21.25	6710.7
1981-82	1777.4	22.80	380.3	4.88	3555.7	45.61	24.3	0.31	2058.5	26.40	7796.2
1982-83	2451.0	27.84	490.8	5.57	4551.1	51.70	1240.4	14.09	70.2	0.80	8803.5
1983-84	2621.7	26.83	506.2	5.18	4964.4	50.87	1590.0	16.27	83.4	0.85	9770.7
1984-85	2996.5	25.52	637.6	5.43	6210.1	52.88	1822.9	15.52	76.6	0.65	11743.7
1985-86	3018.3	27.70	784.7	7.20	6374.2	58.51	654.9	6.02	62.5	0.57	10894.6
1986-87	3422.0	27.48	717.2	5.76	7808.4	62.71	417.6	3.35	87.2	0.70	12452.4

Note : (i) The classification of India's principal exports into various commodity groups has been adopted as per the classification given in *Economic Survey* Government of India, New Delhi, 1988-89, pp. S-74-75.

(ii) The Value figures of exports of Commodity group IV : Mineral fuels and lubricants are exclusive of coal for the years 1970-71 to 1981-82, whereas for subsequent period the value figures are inclusive of coal.

Source : Estimated on the basis of information given in *Appendix Table : IV.2 and VI-3* for the years 1970-71 to 1981-82 and 1982-83 to 1986-87 respectively.

share of these two commodity groups of exports in total exports can be attributed to the fact that India being fundamentally an agricultural country (i.e. primary producing country), its exports are bound to be predominated by primary products for which world demand elasticities and domestic production elasticities are very low. And hence indicates greater degree of diversificatio.. of India's exports over time.

Further, it is pertinently important to note that the percentage share of exports of agricultural and allied products in total exports exceeded the percentage share of exports of manufactured goods in total exports during the years 1970-71 to 1975-76. However, the year 1976-77 marks a turning point as regards the relative position of both these groups of exports, as the percentage share of exports of manufactured goods in total exports exceeded the share of exports of agricultural and allied products in total exports during 1976-77 to 1986-87, thus reflected a trend reversal in terms of percentage share. Inspite of this phenomenon of trend reversal of these two commodity groups of exports, we can see that the percentage share of exports of manufactured goods in total exports shows a systematic increasing trend of 31.44% in the year 1970-71 to 62.71% in the year 1986-87. This state of affairs can be attributed to an increasing tendency towards diversification of India's exports over time because of progressive character of the Indian economy.

Moreover, the percentage share of exports of mineral fuels and lubricants (excluding coal) in total exports remained less that one percent during 1970-71 to 1981-82 shows a systematic declining trend. However during 1982-83 to 1986-87, the percentage share of this commodity group (including coal) in total exports though declining remained greater that one percent.

In case of other exports (inclusive of coal) during 1970-71 to 1981-82 shows a declining trend in terms of its percentage share in total exports. However during 1982-83 to 1986-87 this commodity group (excluding of coal) shows that its percentage share in total exports remained less than one percent.

Indian Exports During 1965-66 to 1981-82

In order to undertake an analysis of structural behaviour of Indian exports, we have excluded the period of 1982-83 to 1987-88 on account of non-availability of commodity wise data on Indian exports. However, it is intended here to examine the structural behaviour of Indian exports with reference to the following :

(i) Traditional and non-traditions exports.

(ii) Primary exports and manufactured exports.

(iii) Commodity composition of Indian exports according to market environment and SITC commodity groups.

(iv) Direction of India's export trade in terms of regional destination.

With reference to above, the following aspects of exports are intended to be examined.

[a] Percentage share of various commodity groups in total exports.

[b] Rates of growth of exports by commodity groups.

[c] Degree of diversification or concentration of exports.

[d] Statiblity of Indian exports by commodity group.

[e] Relation between commodity exports and economic development.

Percentage share of various commodity groups of exports in total exports :

An analysis of structural behaviour of exports in terms of change in the percentage share of various commodity groups of exports in total exports is indicative of change in relative significance of various commodity groups of exports over time. Therefore, we, present below an analysis of traditional and non-traditional exports of India.

Traditional and Non-Traditional Exports

The structural behaviour of traditional and non-traditional exports of India can be seen from Table 6.3, wherein traditional exports are defined as an aggregation of the exports of Tea, Cotton textiles, Jute textiles, Mica, Cashew Kernel, Metalliferrous ores, Spices, Tobacco and Leather products and non-traditional exports are defined as total exports less traditional exports. A glance at the table reveals the fact that the percentage share of traditional exports in total exports shows a systematic declining trend of 64.70% in the year 1965-66 to 28.62% in the year 1981-82, whereas the percentage share of non-traditional exports displays a systematic increasing trend of 35.30% in the year 1965-66 to 71.38% in the year 1981-82. However, it is important to note that the year 1973-74 marks a turning point in regard to relative importance of traditional and non-traditional exports in relation to total exports as there has been trend reversal in terms of relative share in total exports which can be seen from the fact that the percentage share of traditional exports exceeded the percentage share of non-traditional exports during 1965-66 to 1972-73 and during 1973-74 to 1981-82, the percentage share of non-traditional exports exceeded the share of traditional exports.

TABLE 6.3

Traditional and Non-Traditional Exports of India

Year	Traditional Exports**		Non-Traditional Exports		Total Exports
	Value in Crores of Rupees	Percentage of Total Exports	Value in Crores of Rupees	Percentage of Total Exports	Value in Crores of Rupees
(1)	(2)	(3)	(4)	(5)	(6)
1965-66*	825.0	64.70	450.1	35.30	1275.1
1966-67*	752.2	65.04	404.4	34.96	1156.6
1967-68	760.0	63.40	438.7	36.60	1198.7
1968-69	777.1	57.19	581.7	42.81	1358.8
1969-70	774.7	54.82	638.5	45.18	1413.2
1970-71	790.1	51.46	745.1	48.54	1535.2
1971-72	876.5	54.50	731.7	45.50	1608.2
1972-73	1001.5	51.07	959.4	48.93	1960.9
1973-74	1121.6	44.45	1401.8	55.55	2523.4
1974-75	1324.3	39.78	2004.5	60.22	3328.8
1975-76	1396.6	35.43	2545.0	64.57	3941.6
1976-77	1650.7	32.10	3491.6	67.90	5142.3
1977-78	2015.4	37.27	3392.5	62.73	5407.9
1978-79	1731.6	30.24	3994.5	69.76	5726.1
1979-80	2275.5	33.37	4542.8	66.63	6818.3
1980-81	2172.7	32.38	4538.0	67.62	6710.7
1981-82	2234.0	28.62	5571.9	71.38	7805.9

* The value figures are adjusted at post-devaluation rate by multiplying the figures with 1.575, the increased value of pre-devaluation Rupee.

** Traditional Exports include Tea, Cotton Textile, Jute Textiles, Mica, Cashew Kernel, Metalliferrous Ores, Spices, Tobacco and Leather products.

Source : Estimated on the basis of information available in the various issues of *Basic Statistics Relating to the Indian Economy*, published by Central Statistical Organisation, Department of Statistics, Ministry of Planning, Government of India, New Delhi.

The declining share of traditional exports and increasing share of non-traditional exports over time positively confirms to the well established hypothesis as regards developing country India under consideration. India, being basically a primary producing and developing country, the share of non-traditional exports is bound to rise and that of traditional exports to decline on account of diversification of exports over time.

However, a pertinent question arises as to what has been the nature of trend behaviour in terms of variation in percentage share of primary and manufactured goods exports over time ? Therefore, we present below an analysis of primary and manufactured goods exports with reference to above, table 6.4 reflects the structural behaviour of Indian exports consisting of primary and manufactured goods exports.

Primary and Manufactured Goods Exports

Primary Exports : The primary exports are defined as an aggregation of commodity exports under sections 0 to 4 of Standard International Trade classification commodity groups.

Manufactured Goods Exports : The manufactured goods exports are defined as an aggregation of exports under sections 5 to 8 of SITC commodity groups.

Further, it is important to note that the manufactured goods exports consists of traditional manufactured goods exports and non-traditional manufactured goods exports.

Traditional Manufacturing Goods Exports : This groups consists of exports of cotton textile, Jute textiles, Leather manufactured products and manufactured Tobacco.

Non-Traditional Manufacturing Goods : This group of exports consists of manufactured goods less traditional manufactured goods.

Having presented a conceptual and definitional explanation of commodity groups of exports, a quantitative analysis as evident from Table 6.4 follows hereafter.

It is evident from Table 6.4 that the percentage share of primary exports in total exports shows a systematically declining trend of 51.35% in 1965-66 to 40.72% in the year 1981-82, whereas the percentage share of exports of manufactured goods in total exports reveals a systematically rising trend of 48.19% in the year 1965-66 to 59.12% in the year 1981-82. However, it is important to note that during 1968-69 to 1981-

TABLE 6.4

Primary, Traditional and Non-Traditional Manufactured Exports of India

Years	Primary Exports		Manufactured Exports								Total Exports
			Total		Traditional			Non-Traditional			
	Value in Crores of Rupees	Percentage of Total Exports	Value in crores of Rupees	Percentage of Total Exports	Value in Crores of Rupees	Percentage of Total Manfactured Exports	Percentage of Total Exports	Value In Crores of Rupees	Percentage of Total Manufactured Exports	Percentage of Total Exports	Value in Crores of Rupees
(1)	(2)	(3)	(4)	(5)	(6)	(7)	(8)	(9)	(10)	(11)	(12)
1965-66	648.7	51.35	608.8	48.19	432.4	71.02	34.23	176.4	28.97	13.96	1263.3
1966-67	599.9	52.03	548.4	47.57	.386.8	70.53	33.51	161.6	29.47	14.02	1152.9
1967-68	605.5	50.76	581.4	48.74	360.5	62	30.22	220.9	38	18.52	1192.8
1968-69	634	46.74	716.8	52.83	374.6	52.26	27.62	342.2	47.74	25.23	1356.3
1969-70	625	44.37	778.7	55.28	387.4	49.75	27.5	391.3	50.25	27.78	1408.7
1970-71	716.7	47.02	803.2	52.69	361.8	45.04	23.73	441.4	54.96	28.95	1524.4
1971-72	740.5	46.19	857.3	53.47	444.1	51.8	27.7	413.2	48.2	25.77	1603.2
1972-73	897.4	45.91	1051.7	53.81	550	52.3	28.14	501.7	47.7	25.67	1954.5
1973-74	1159.5	46.04	1352	53.69	605.8	44.81	24.05	746.2	55.19	29.63	2518.3
1974-75	1588.6	47.08	1728	52	613.6	35.51	18.46	1114.4	64.49	33.52	3323.3
1975-76	1935.4	49.23	1988.6	50.58	612.8	30.82	15.59	1357.8	69.18	35	3931.3
1976-77	2091.2	40.77	3029	59.05	761.2	25.13	14.84	2267.8	74.87	44.21	5129.1

(Contd.)

Table 6.4 (Contd.)

(1)	(2)	(3)	(4)	(5)	(6)	(7)	(8)	(9)	(10)	(11)	(12)
1977-78	2186.8	40.77	3164.1	59	760.7	24.04	14.18	2403.4	75.96	44.81	5363.2
1978-79	2123.6	37.21	3570	62.56	757.7	21.22	13.27	2812.3	78.78	49.28	5706.6
1979-80	2559.2	39.97	3827	59.77	1134.6	29.65	17.72	2692.4	70.35	42.05	6402.4
1980-81	2707.1	40.61	3942.9	29.15	983.6	24.95	14.75	2959.3	75.05	42.05	6402.4
1981-82	3175.4	40.72	4610.2	59.12	969.4	21.03	12.43	3640.8	78.97	46.69	7798.3

Note : (i) Primary Exports : Exports under section 0 to 4

(ii) Manufactured exports : Exports under section 5 to 8

(iii) Traditional Manufactured exports : These include Cotton and Jute Textiles, Leather Manufactured Products and Manufactured Tobacco

(iv) Non-Traditional Manufactured Exports : These are (ii) minus (iii)

Source : *Appendix Table : IV-4*

82, the percentage age share of exports of manufactured goods in total exports exceeded the percentage share of primary exports which confirms to the commonly held belief that this would be the state of affairs with reference to a developing country like India under consideration. Further, it becomes clear that in value terms the exports of primary goods increased from Rs. 648.7 crores in 1965-66 to Rs. 3175.4 crores in 1981-82, whereas the exports of manufactured goods increased from Rs. 608.8 crores in 1965-66 to Rs. 4610.2 crores in 1981-82.

Thus, we can see that though in value terms, both these commodity groups of exports seem to be rising, but in relative terms, they clearly indicate a reverse trend behaviour over time.

Moreover, it is intelligible from the table that the traditional manufactured and non-traditional manufactured groups of exports though seem to be rising in value terms, indicate reverse trend behaviour in relative terms. This can be seen from the fact that in value terms, the exports of traditional manufactured goods increased from Rs. 432.4 crores in 1965-66 to Rs. 969.4 crores in 1981-82 and the exports of non-traditional manufactured goods increased from Rs. 176.4 crores in 1965-66 to Rs. 3640.8 Crores in 1981-82. However, in relative terms, both these commodity groups of exports indicate a reverse trend behaviour not only in relation to the exports of total manufactured goods, but also in relation to total exports.

The percentage of traditional manufactured goods exports in total manufactured goods exports declined from 71.02% in the year 1965-66 to 21.03 in the year 1981-82. Similarly, its share in the total exports also declined from 34.23% in the year 1965-66 to 12.3% in the year 1981-82. However, the percentage share of non-traditional manufactured goods exports in total manufactured goods exports increased from 28.97% in the year 1965-66 to 78.97% in the year 1981-82 and similarly, its percentage share in total export also increased from 13.96% in the year 1965-66 to 46.69% in the year 1981-82.

Thus, we can see that though the percentage share of total manufactured goods exports in total exports increased over a period of time indicate however a reverse trend behaviour in terms of percentage share, if the total manufactured goods exports are seggregated in two subgroups as mentioned earlier.

Since the structural behaviour of exports can also be viewed from the change in the commodity composition of exports, we present below an analysis of commodity composition of Indian exports according to market environment and SITC (Standard International Trade Classification) commodity groups.

Commodity Composition of Indian Exports According to Market Environment :

As far as Indian exports are concerned, the commodity exports can be classified into the monopolistic, oligopolistic, competitive and other exports. The classification is based on the nature of competition faced by commodity exports in the world market with reference to the same, we present below the details of classification.

Monopolistic Exports : Exports under this category include, Jute textiles, Mica, cashew Kernel and Lac.

Oligopolistic Exports : Exports under this category include Tea, Cotton textiles, Tobacco, Managanese ores, Black Pepper and Castor oil.

Competitive Exports : Exports under this category include Coffee, Raw Cotton, Raw Wool, Hides and Skins, Groundnut oil, Linseed oil, Coal and coke and Iron ore.

Other Exports : These exports are equal to total exports less an aggregation of rest of the exports under monopolistic, oligopolistic and competitive environment.

It becomes clear from Table 6.5 that all the commodity groups of exports according to market environment reflect an increase in value terms over a period under consideration. However, the percentage share of monopolistic exports in total exports shows a systematically declining trend of 27.04% in the year 1965-66 to 6.24% in the year 1981-82 and the oligopolistic exports also shows a declining trend of 27.46% in the year 1965-66 to 12.28% in the year 1981-82. The declining share of monopolistic and oligopolistic exports in total exports indicates that monopolistic and oligopolistic strength of Indian exports has declined over a period of time under consideration. This can be attributed to an entry of new exporters in the world market for exports and diversification of exports. However, the percentage share of competitive exports does not indicate a systematic trend behaviour which can be seen from the fact that the share of competitive exports increased from 13.82% in the

TABLE 6.5

Commodity Composition of Indian Exports According to Market Environment

Years	*Monopolistic Environment*		*Oligopolistic Environment*		*Competitive Environment*		*Other Exports*		*Total Exports*
	Value In Crores of Rupees	Percentage of Total Export	Value in Crores of Rupees	Percentage of Total Export	Value in Crores of Rupees	Percentage of Total Export	Value in Crores of Rupees	Percentage of Total Export	Value in Crores of Rupees
(1)	(2)	(3)	(4)	(5)	(6)	(7)	(8)	(9)	(10)
1965-66*	344.8	27.04	350.1	27.46	176.2	13.82	404	31.68	1275.1
1966-67	315.5	27.28	281.4	24.33	185.2	16.01	374.9	32.38	11556.6
1967-68	297.3	24.8	314.5	26.24	176	14.68	410.9	34.28	1198.7
1968-69	297.4	21.89	306.7	22.57	202.1	14.87	552.6	40.67	1358.8
1969-70	284.1	20.1	287.4	20.34	220	15.57	621.7	43.99	1413.2
1970-71	263.1	17.14	314	20.45	239.9	15.63	718.2	46.78	1535.2
1971-72	339.6	21.12	327.3	20.35	238.4	14.82	702.9	43.71	1608.2
1972-73	341.6	17.42	382.3	19.5	344.8	17.58	892.2	45.5	1960.9
1973-74	329.3	13.05	493.1	19.54	389.6	15.44	1311.4	51.97	2523.4
1974-75	457.5	13.74	553.4	16.62	391.4	11.76	1926.5	57.88	3328.8
1975-76	371.8	9.43	561.6	14.25	550.5	13.97	2457.7	62.35	3941.6
1976-77	334.3	6.5	769.8	14.97	679.8	13.22	3358.4	65.31	5142.3
1977-78	418.1	7.73	1024	18.93	697.5	12.9	3268.3	60.44	5407.9
1978-79	275.1	4.8	758.7	13.25	725.8	12.68	3966.5	69.27	5726.1

(Contd.)

TABLE 6.5 (Contd.)

1	2	3	4	5	6	7	8	9	10
1979-80	486.2	7.13	827.1	12.13	968.8	14.21	4536.2	66.53	6818.3
1980-81	501.3	7.47	903.1	13.46	963.8	14.36	4342.5	64.71	6710.7
1981-82	486.8	6.24	958.3	12.28	819.3	10.49	5541.5	70.99	7805.9

* The Value figures are adjusted at post-devaluation rate by multiplying the figures with 1.575, the increased value of pre-devaluation rupee.

Note : (i) Monopolistic exports : These are Jute Textiles, Mica, Cashew Kernel and Lac.

(ii) These are Tea, Cotton Textile, Tobacco, Mangenese Ores, Black Pepper & Castor Oil.

(iii) Competitive exports : These included Coffee, Raw Cotton, Raw Wool, Hides and Skins, Groundnut Oil, Linseed Oil, Coal and Cocke and Iron Ore.

(iv) Other exports are total exports minus total of (i), (ii) and (iii).

Source : Estimated on the basis of information available in the various issues of *Basic Statistics Relating to Indian Economy*, Published by Central Statistical Organisation, Department of Statistics, Ministry of Planning, Government of India, New Delhi.

year 1965-66 to 17.58% in the year 1972-73 and thereafter, in the year 1973-74 it declined to 15.44%. It is also visible that during 1973-74 to 1981-82, the percentage share of competitive exports show a systematically declining trend of 15.44% in the year 1973-74 to 10.49% in the year 1981-82. This declining trend after 1973-74 weakened the competitive strength of Indian exports in general and competitive exports in particular. Whereas, we find that other exports show a systematically increasing trend in percentage share in total exports from 31.68% in the year 1965-66 to 70.99% in the year 1981-82.

Thus we can perceive that over a period of time the competitive strength of Indian exports in general declined.

The Commodity Composition of Indian Exports

According to SITC Commodity Sections

As far as the commodity composition of Indian exports according to SITC commodity groups is concerned, Table 6.6 reveals important changes in the relative position of SITC commodity groups by sections.

With reference to above, it can be seen that the percentage share of Section-0, Food and Live Animals in total exports declined from 30.10% in the Year 1965-66 to 24.61% in the year 1981-82. Similarly, the percentage share of Section-2, crude Materials inedible except Fuel show a decline from 16.82% in the year 1965-66 to 9.94% in the year 1981-82 and the share of Section-6, Manufactured Goods classified chiefly by materials in total exports declined from 42.76% in the year 1965-66 to 33.07% in the year 1981-82, whereas the share of commodity Section-9, Commodities and Transactions not classified according to kind in total exports also shows a decline from 0.46% in the year 1965-66 to 0.16% in the year 1981-82 and its share however, remained less than one percent through out the period under consideration.

However, reverse trend behaviour in terms of percentage share can be discerned with regard to the commodity Section-5, 7 and 8 of SITC commodity groups. The share of chemicals increased from 1.43% in the year 1965-66 to 4.81% in the year 1981-82 and that of Machinery and Transport Equipment systematically increased from 1.31% in the year 1965-66 to 13.32% in the year 1981-82.

Moreover, the commodity Section-1, 3 and 4 do not show any systematic trend behaviour of their percentage share in the total exports.

TABLE 6.6

Commodity Composition of Indian Exports According to Standard International Trade Classification : (Percentage Distribution)

Years	0	1	2	3	4	5	6	7	8	9	
	Food and Live Animals	*Bever-ages And Tobacco*	*Crude Materials Inedible except Fuels*	*Mineral Fuels Lubricants & Related Materials*	*Animal & Vegetable Oils & Fats*	*Chemi-cals*	*Manufac-tured Goods Classified Chiefly by Materials*	*Machinery and Transport Equipment*	*Miscella-neous Manufac-tured Articles*	*Commodity and Transaction of not classified according to kind*	*Total Export = Total Sections 0 to 9*
(1)	(2)	(3)	(4)	(5)	(6)	(7)	(8)	(9)	(10)	(11)	(12)
1965-66	30.1	2.71	16.82	1.16	0.56	1.43	42.76	1.31	2.69	0.46	100.00
1966-67	30.61	1.96	18.1	1.09	0.27	1.29	42.56	1.34	2.38	0.4	100.00
1967-68	30.37	2.98	16.29	0.77	0.35	1.32	42.82	1.6	3.01	0.49	100.00
1968-69	26.85	2.49	15.63	0.89	0.88	1.75	44.46	3.21	3.43	0.41	100.00
1969-70	24.53	2.37	16.43	0.67	0.36	2.15	44.72	3.93	4.48	0.36	100.00
1970-71	27.07	2.14	16.51	0.83	0.47	2.39	40.39	4.93	4.98	0.29	100.00
1971-72	27.15	2.81	15.01	0.72	0.49	2.29	41.37	4.6	5.29	0.35	100.00
1972-73	26.69	3.28	13.01	1.63	1.3	2.07	41.65	4.31	5.78	0.28	100.00
1973-74	26.95	2.82	14.39	0.61	1.27	2.31	39.67	4.61	7.1	0.27	100.00

1974-75	30.67	2.48	13.01	0.61	1.04	3.13	35.11	6.42	7.33	0.2	100.00
1975-76	31.53	2.51	13.41	0.9	0.88	2.28	33.92	6.49	7.9	0.18	100.00
1976-77	25.35	2.01	11.74	0.64	1.02	2.32	41.28	5.81	9.65	0.17	100.00
1977-78	28.6	2.19	9	0.52	0.46	2.33	40.84	6.25	9.58	0.23	100.00
1978-79	25.53	2.05	8.98	0.34	0.31	2.7	40.79	6.92	12.51	0.23	100.00
1979-80	26.6	1.81	10.41	0.33	0.82	3.25	37.45	7	12.08	0.25	100.00
1980-81	25.58	2.12	12.2	0.42	0.29	3.52	34.72	7.88	13.03	0.24	100.00
1981-82	24.61	3.03	9.94	2.88	0.26	4.81	33.07	7.92	13.32	0.16	100.00

Source : Calculated from *Appendix Table* : IV-4

Thus, we can see that the commodity composition of Indian exports in terms of percentage share in total exports increased for commodity Sections-5, 7 and 8, whereas it declined for the commodity Section-0, 2, 6 and 9.

Commodity Concentration Index of Indian Exports According to Market Environment and SITC Commodity Sections

In order to ascertain, whether there has been a diversification or concentration of Indian exports over time, we have estimated the commodity concentration index[1] for Indian exports according to market environment and commodity sections of SITC commodity groups for the period of 1965-66 to 1981-82, using the formula given below :

$$\text{Commodity concentration Index, } C = \sqrt{\Sigma\,(Xi/X)^2}\ .\ 100.$$

Where Xi referes to exports of ith item and X refers to the total exports from India.

As far as the interpretation of commodity concentration index is concerned, lower the value of the index more evenly are the exports distributed and vice-versa and declining trend of index indicates greater diversification of exports and vice-versa. However, it is pertinent to note that the value of the index depends on the type of classification adopted.

Table 6.7 indicates the estimated values of commodity concentration index of Indian exports over time. Accordingly, we can see that the commodity concentration index shows a declining trend for both the SITC commodity sections and exports according to market environment. As far as the SITC commodity sections are concerned, the concentration index declined from 55.14 in 1965-66 to 45.59 (i.e. a decline by 9.43%) in the year 1981-82, and for Indian exports according to market environment the index declined from 49.94 in the year 1965-66 to 17.13 (i.e. a decline by 65.34%) in the year 1981-82 reflecting greater degree of diversification of Indian exports according to market environment as compared to Indian exports according to SITC commodity sections. This implies that greater the degree of aggregation involved in classification of Indian exports greater will be the decline in the index and greater will be the diversification of Indian exports. However, it is important to note that since, the concentration index has declined for both the commodity groups of exports. This also implies that the economic fortunes of India has not been dependent on a few commodities exports, but on a wide range of commodities.

1. Michaely Michael, *Op. cit.*, pp. 722-736

TABLE 6.7

Commodity Concentration Index of Indian Exports 1965-66 to 1981-82

Year	*Commodity Concentration Index of Indian Exports According to*	
	SITC Commodity Sections[1]	*Market Environment*[2]
(1)	(2)	(3)
1965-66	55.14	49.94
1966-67	55.59	39.91
1967-68	55.18	38.97
1968-69	54.54	34.78
1969-70	54.02	32.56
1970-71	51.93	30.92
1971-72	52.32	32.86
1972-73	51.84	31.51
1973-74	50.93	28.12
1974-75	49.55	24.56
1975-76	49.42	22.07
1976-77	51.21	21.00
1977-78	52.04	24.18
1978-79	51.02	18.96
1979-80	49.27	20.00
1980-81	47.52	21.05
1981-82	45.59	17.31

Source : 1. Calculated from *Appendix Table* : VI-4. 2. Calculated from *Table* : 6.5.

Direction of Indian Exports According to Regional Destination

Since change in the direction of Indian exports according to regional destination is also an indicator of structural change, we present below an analysis of structural change in Indian exports as per regional destination.

India is having trade relations with many regions of the world in which all countries of the world are classified in to Regions 0 to 9. As far as regional classification of April 1966. Since the period under consideration is 1965-66 to 1981-82 and the new regional classification of April 1977 was made applicable thereafter, we have reclassified the regions after April 1977 according to the regional classification of April 1966* in order to ensure comparability over time.

It can be seen from Table 6.8 on Direction of India's exports, that the percentage share of exports in total exports in terms of regional destination of Region 1 North American countries, Region-2, Latin American Countries, Region-3, other American countries and Region-8, European Free Trade Area countries shows a systematically declining in trend of 20.86% to 12.98%, 1.30% to 0.24, 0.20% to 0.05 and 19.38% to 8.16% respectively in the year 1965-66 and 1981-82.

However, it is noticeable that the percentage share of exports in total exports in terms of regional destination of Region-5, other Asian and Oceanian countries, Region-6, East European countries and Region-7, European Common Market Countries indicates a rising trend of 3.58% to 10.58%, 19.50% to 26.34% and 6.83% to 12.27% respectively in the year 1965-66 and 1981-82. As far as Region-0, African Countries and Region-9, other European Countries are concerned, the percentage share in total exports does not show any clear cut trend that can be concluded.

Thus we can see that the Regions-5, 6 and 7 are gaining increasing relative importance, whereas Regions-1, 2, 3 and 8 are loosing relative importance in India's export trade over the period under consideration. Moreover, the percentage share of exports in total exports accounted for by Region-4, Economic and Social Commission For Asia and the Pacific Countries increased from 19.73% in the year 1965-66 to 29.93% in the year 1975-76, however, thereafter it declined to 22.75% in 1981-82.

Growth Rates of Indian Exports during 1965-66 to 1981-82

Since, the structural behaviour of Indian exports can as well be assessed in terms of rates of growth of exports over time, we have estimated, the average percentage rates of growth of exports per annum at current prices of various commodity groups of exports viz. Traditional and Non-Traditional, Primary and Manufactured Goods comprising, Traditional Manufactured Goods and Non-Traditional Manufactured Goods, and Exports according to Market Environment comprising, Monopolistic, Oligopolistic, Competitive and other by using the formula given below :

---

*See. for Correspondence between the Two Classification. *AppendixTable* : VI.5.

TABLE 6.8

Direction of Indian Exports : (Percentage Distribution)

Years	Region-0	Region-1	Region-2	Region-3	Region-4	Region-5	Region-6	Region-7	Region-8	Region-9	
	African Countries	*North American Countries*	*Latin American Countries*	*Other American Countries*	*Economic & Social Commission for Asia & the Pacific Countries*	*Other Asian & Oceanian Countries*	*East European Countries*	*European Common Market Countries*	*European Free Trade Area Countries*	*Other European Countries*	*Total Export = Total of all regions*
(1)	(2)	(3)	(4)	(5)	(6)	(7)	(8)	(9)	(10)	(11)	(12)
1965-66	7.59	20.86	1.3	0.2	19.73	3.58	19.5	6.83	19.38	1.03	100.00
1966-67	6.19	21.68	0.86	0.2	20.95	3.36	19.58	7.69	18.65	0.84	100.00
1967-68	5.87	19.79	0.45	0.16	22.64	3.67	18.83	7.41	20.32	0.86	100.00
1968-69	5.36	19.4	0.27	0.15	25.33	4.94	19.63	8.17	15.95	0.8	100.00
1969-70	6.25	18.73	0.33	0.15	26.67	5.15	21.83	7.12	12.96	0.81	100.00
1970-71	9.07	15.4	0.54	0.13	26.8	4.71	23.72	6.44	12.38	0.81	100.00
1971-72	8.23	18.85	0.79	0.17	26.37	3.9	21.43	7.72	11.72	0.82	100.00
1972-73	5.18	15.53	0.21	0.11	28.42	3.71	24.02	11.34	10.51	0.97	100.00
1973-74	4.03	14.94	0.48	0.1	29.27	5.61	19.35	12.79	12.27	1.16	100.00
1974-75	7.15	12.59	0.6	0.11	27.38	8.73	20.58	11.08	10.82	0.98	100.00
1975-76	6.87	13.93	0.33	0.16	29.93	8.28	17.17	10	12.5	0.83	100.00
1976-77	6.07	12.01	0.29	0.15	24.76	11.06	15.41	16.29	12.96	1	100.00
1977-78	6.44	13.36	0.21	0.11	23.73	10.63	17.34	15.47	11.86	0.85	100.00

(Contd.)

Table 6.8 (Contd.)

(1)	(2)	(3)	(4)	(5)	(6)	(7)	(8)	(9)	(10)	(11)	(12)
1978-79	5.92	14.35	0.24	0.12	26.94	10.6	11.53	17.4	11.96	0.91	100.00
1979-80	5.18	13.56	0.28	0.09	27.08	9.64	13.92	18.24	10.86	1.15	100.00
1980-81	6.49	12.03	0.48	0.06	24.9	9.11	22.79	14.65	8.78	0.71	100.00
1981-82	5.81	12.98	0.24	0.05	22.75	10.58	26.34	12.27	8.16	0.82	100.00

Source : Calculated from *Appendix Table* : IV-6.

$$\text{Average Percentage Rate of Growth of Export Per Annum} = \frac{\sum \frac{y_t - y_{t-1}}{y_{t-1}}}{n-1} \cdot 100$$

Where Y_t, refers to the value of exports in year 't'

Y_{t-1} refers to the value of exports in year t-1

n refers to the total number of observations.

In order to undertake an analysis of growth rates of exports, we have estimated the rates of growth of exports of various commodity groups over a period of 1965-66 to 1981-82 and 1972-73 to 1981-82 as the later period experienced a transmission of world wide phenomenon of inflationary price rise consequent upon a sudden oil price hike in the middle of 1973 which affected the value of exports.

Growth Rates of Exports for Various Commodity Groups

It becomes evident from Table 6.9 that during 1965-66 to 1981-82, the total exports registered a growth rate of 12.58% per annum on an average. However, it should be noted that the non-traditional exports increased at the rate of 18.20% per annum greater than that of 7.05% per annum of traditional exports. Similarly, the exports of non-traditional goods increased at the rate of 22.49% per annum greater than that of exports of traditional manufactured goods of 6.25% per annum and the total manufactured exports increased at a rate of 14.23% per annum greater than that of primary exports of 11.14% per annum. Further, within the group of exports, according to market environment the other export increased at a rate greater than that of monopolistic, Oligopolistic and competitive exports of 4.87%, 7.80% and 11.19% per annum respectively. A similar picture emerges as regards, the inter-commodity comparision of growth rates of various commodity groups of exports during sub-periods 1965-66 to 1972-73 and 1972-73 to 1981-82.

However, an altogether a different picture as regards, the growth rates of exports of various commodity groups is perceived, if the pattern of growth rates is compared by sub-periods 1965-66 to 1972-73 and 1972-73 to 1981-82. As far as the latter period is concerned, the total exports increased at a rate of 17.15% per annum, greater than that of 6.72% per annum during the former period.

TABLE 6.9

Rates of Growth of Indian Exports by Various Commodity Groups

Name of the Various Commodity Groups of Indian Exports	*Average Percentage Rates of Growth of Exports per annum at Current Prices*		
	Period 1965-66 to 1981-82	*Period 1965-66 to 1972-73*	*Period 1972-73 to 1981-82*
[A] Traditional & Non-Traditional[1]			
(i) Traditional	7.50	3.05	10.16
(ii) Non-Traditional	18.20	12.39	22.73
[B] Primary & Manufactured[2]			
(i) Primary	11.14	5.27	15.71
(ii) **Total Manufactured**	14.23	8.50	18.69
(a) Traditional	6.25	4.28	7.78
(b) Non-Traditional	22.49	17.40	26.45
[C] According to Market Conditions[3]			
(i) Monopolistic	4.87	0.51	8.26
(ii) Oligopolistic	7.80	1.95	12.35
(iii) Competitive	11.01	10.98	11.36
(iv) Others	19.01	12.82	23.83
[D] Total Exports[4]	12.58	6.72	17.15

Source : 1. Calculated from *Table* : 6.3
2. Calculated from *Table* : 6.4
3 & 4. Calculated from *Table* : 6.5

Further, the similar picture emerges as regards, the growth rates of exports of various commodity groups in the sense that the growth rates of various commodity groups of exports are higher during 1972-73 to 1981-82 as compared to that of during 1965-66 to 1981-82.

Thus, we can see that the average percentage rates of growth of exports of various commodity groups are higher during 1972-73 to 1981-'82 as compared to that of during 1965-66 to 1972-73. These higher growth rates of exports after 1972-73 can be attributed to the resultant effects of world wide phenomenon of inflationary price rise consequent upon oil price hike in the middle of the year 1973.

Instability Index of Indian Exports by Various Commodity Groups

As far as the structural behaviour of Indian exports is concerned, it can be assessed in terms of instability index indicating, year-to-year percentage variation adjusted for trend. Therefore, in order to assess the relative instability of various commodity groups of exports at current prices the instability index of exports has been estimated by using the formula given by J.D. Coppock.[2] Accordingly, the instability index equals the anti-log of the square root of the logarithmic variance of series is given by

$$V \log = \frac{1}{N-1} \cdot \sum\left[\log X_{t-1} - \log X_t - \frac{1}{N-1} \cdot \sum(\log X_{t+1} - \log X_t)\right]^2$$

Where, N and X refer to number of years and value of exports respectively and subscripts indicate the date.

Thus, the resulting instability index is a closer approximation to the year-to-year percentage variation adjusted for trend.

It becomes evident from Table 6.10 that during the period of 1965-66 to 1981-82, the traditional exports are more stable with an instability index of 11.83 than that of non-traditional exports with an index of 15.81. Whereas within the group of primary and manufactured exports, the primary exports are more stable with an index of 11.57 than that of manufactured exports with an index 13.12. However, within the manufactured exports group, the traditional manufactured exports are more stable with an index of 20.38. Moreover, within the group of exports according to market conditions, the competitive exports are more stable with an index of 15.60 than those of monopolistic, oligopolistic and others with index values, 25.84, 17.81 and 16.15 respectively.

2. Coppock. J.D., Op.cit. p.24.

TABLE 6.10
Instability Index of Indian Exports by Various Commodity Groups

Name of the Various Commodity Groups of Indian Exports	*Instability Index of Indian Exports at Current Prices*
	Period : 1965-66 to 1981-82
[A] Traditional & Non-Traditional[1]	
(i) Traditional	11.83
(ii) Non-Traditional	15.81
[B] Primary & Manufactured[2]	
(i) Primary	11.57
(ii) **Total Manufactured**	13.12
(a) Traditional	15.51
(b) Non-Traditional	20.38
[C] According to Market Conditions[3]	
(i) Monopolistic	25.84
(ii) Oligopolistic	17.81
(iii) Competitive	15.60
(iv) Others	16.15
[D] Total Exports[4]	11.24

Source : 1. Calculated from *Table* : 6.3
2. Calculated from *Table* : 6.4
3 & 4. Calculated from *Table* : 6.5

Thus, it becomes clear from the analysis given above, that the primary exports, traditional exports, traditional manufactured exports and competitive exports are more stable as compared to exports of manufactured goods, non-traditional exports, non-traditional manufactured exports and monopolistic and oligopolistic exports respectively during the period of 1965-66 to 1981-82.

Relation Between Indian Exports and Economic Development

In order to ascertain as to which commodity groups of Indian exports are relatively of a greater significance in relation to economic development of India over a period of 1965-66 to 1981-82, we have run a simple linear regression of the proportion of a given commodity group of exports in total exports (Y) on per capita income (X) at current prices, as per capita income being an indicator of economic development. The regression model that is estimated is given below :

$$Y_t = a + bX_t$$

Where, Y refer to the proportion of a given commodity group of exports in total exports

X refers to the per capita income at current prices

Subscript, t refers to time.

It becomes clear from table 6.11 that out of ten regression equations estimated for ten commodity groups of exports, four of them viz. non-traditional exports, total manufactured exports, non-traditional manufactured exports and others exports are of relatively greater significance in relation to economic development of India as their proportion in total exports very directly with per capita income over a period of 1965-66 to 1981-82 which can be inferred from the fact that their slope coefficients have not only positive sign but their t values are statistically significant at 1 per cent level of confidence and their R^2 values are reasonably high implying that greater proportion of variation in the dependent variable (Y) can be explained by independent variable (X).

However, it can be seen that the other six commodity groups of exports viz. traditional exports, primary exports, traditional manufactured exports, monopolistic exports, Oligopolistic exports and competitive exports are of relatively lesser significance in relation to economic development of India as their proportions in total exports very inversely with per capita income over period under consideration which can be inferred from the fact that their slope co-efficients have not only negative sign but their t-values are significant at 1 per cent level of confidence and their values of R^2. (except in case of competitive exports) are reasonably high indicating that greater proportion of variation in the dependent variable (Y) can be explained by independent Variable (X).

TABLE 6.11

Relation Between Proportion of Each Commodity Group of Exports in Total Indian Exports (Y) and Per Capita Income (X) at Current Prices : 1965-66 to 1981-82

Sr. No.	*Name of the Category of Commodity Exports of India*	*Estimated Regression Equation*	R^2
1.	Traditional	Y = 0.7334147 – 0.0003003X (22.727)** (9.299)**	0.8524
2.	Non-Traditional	Y = 0.2665852 + 0.0003003X (8.197)** (9.228)**	0.8504
3.	Primary	Y = 0.5308617 – 0.0000869X (29.945)** (4.898)**	0.6158
4.	Total Manufactured	Y = 0.4640778 + 0.0000887X (25.554)** (4.881)**	0.6142
5.	Traditional Manufactured	Y = 0.3793949 – 0.0001703X (18.153)** (8.143)**	0.8156
6.	Non-Traditional Manufactured	Y = 0.0844906 + 0.0002591X (2.676)* (8.202)**	0.8176
7.	Monopolistic	Y = 0.3117909 – 0.0001768X (13.923)** (7.890)**	0.8062
8.	Oligopolistic	Y = 0.2855567 – 0.0001076X (19.919)** (7.500)**	0.7897
9.	Competitive	Y = 0.1680366 – 0.0000279X (19.635)** (3.258)**	0.4147
10.	Others	Y = 0.2344235 + 0.0003154X (7.088)** (9.440)**	0.8559

Note : * Significant at 5 percent level
** Significant at 1 percent level

Source: (i) For items with Sr. No. 1 and 2 estimated from *Table* : 6.3.
(ii) For items with Sr. No. 3, 4, 5 and 6 estimated from *Table* : 6.4.
(iii) For items with Sr. No. 7, 8, 9 and 10 estimated from *Table* : 6.5 and for all items, *Appendix Table V-7*.

Further, in order to examine, the relation between SITC Sections of Commodity exports of Indian and economic development, we estimated in a similar way as above, the regression of the proportion of each SITC section of commodity exports of India in total exports (Y) and per capita income (X) at current prices over a period of 1965-66 to 1981-82.

As far as SITC Sections-0, 1, 3 and 4 of commodity exports of India are concerned, their estimated regression equations being statistically insignificant are not presented here and therefore are excluded from the perview of the present study.

TABLE 6.12

Relation Between Proportion of Exports of SITC Commodity Groups in Total Indian Exports (Y) and Per Capita Income (X) at Current Prices : 1965-66 to 1981-82

Section No.	*Name of the SITC Section of Commodity Exports of India*	*Estimated Regression Equation*	*R^2*
2.	Crude Materials inedible except Fuel	Y = 0.1934537 – 0.0000625X (20.253)** (6.539)**	0.7413
5.	Chemical	Y = 0.0060353 + 0.0000198X (2.265)* (7.426)**	0.7879
6.	Manufactured Goods Classified Chiefly by materials	Y = 0.4651093 – 0.0000721X (31.066)** (4.812)**	0.6064
7.	Machinery & Transport Equipment	Y = 0.0039459 + 0.0000496X (0.670) (8.417)**	0.8254
8.	Miscellaneous Manufactured Articles	Y = 0.0121430 + 0.0000923X (2.206)* (16.762)**	0.9496
9.	Commodities and Transactions not classified According to Kind	Y = 0.0047684 – 0.00000201X (11.561)** (4.846)**	0.6308

Note : * Significant at 5 percent level
** Significant at 1 percent level

Source : *Estimated from Appendix Table VI-4 and Appendix Table V-7*

It becomes evident from Table 6.12 (see p. 189) that out of six regression equations estimated for six SITC Sections of commodity exports of India, three of them, viz. Section-5, Chemicals, Section-7, Machinery and Transport Equipment and Section-8, Miscellaneous Manufactured Articles are of a relatively greater importance in relation to economic development of India as their proportion in total exports vary directly with per capita income over time which can be inferred from the fact that their slope coefficients have not only positive signs but their t-values are statistically significant at 1 per cent level of confidence and their values of R2 are reasonably high indicating that greater proportion of variation in the dependent variable (Y) is explained by independent variable (X).

However, it can be seen that the other three SITC Sections of commodity exports, viz., Section-2, Crude Materials inedible except Fuels, Section-6, Manufactured Goods classified chiefly by materials and Section-9, Commodities and Transactions not classified, according to kind are of a lesser importance in relation to economic development of India as their proportion in total exports vary inversely with per capita income over time which can be inferred from the fact that their slope coefficients have not only negative sings but their 't' - values are statistically significant a 1 per cent level of confidence and their values of R^2 are reasonably high indicating that greater proportion of variation in the dependent variable (Y) is explained by independent variable (X).

Hence, we can conclude that the commodity exports of Chemicals, Machinery and Transport Equipment and Miscellaneous Manufactured Articles are of a greater importance to the economic development of India over time as compared to the commodity exports of Crude materials inedible except Fuels, Manufactured Goods classified chiefly by materials and Commodities and Transactions not classified according to kind.

(See Appendix Tables from P. 189 to 201)

Appendix Table VI.1

Classification Table of Indian Exports into Various Groups : 1970-71 to 1981-82

Sr. No.	*Name of Commodity Group*	*Name of the commodity*
(1)	(2)	(3)
I.	Agricultural and Allied Products	Jute Manufactures, Tea, Oil cakes, Tobacco, Cashew Kernel, Coffee, Sugar, Pepper, Raw Cotton. Fish and Fish preparations, Vegetable Oils (essential & non-essential) Hides & Skins & furskins.
II.	Ores and Minerals (excluding Coal)	Iron Ore, Mica and Managanese Ore
III.	Manufactured goods	Cotton fabrics, coir yarn and manufactures, Leather and Leather products (Excluding footwear), Engineering goods, Iron & Steel (excluding ferro-managanese Ores and ferro alloys), Chemicals and Chemical products, Art silk fabrics, Footwear, Cotton apparel, Handicrafts.
IV.	Mineral Fuels & Lubricants (including Coal)	Mineral fuels & Lubricants
V.	Others	Other exports including silver.

Note : Prepared on the basis of classification given in *Appendix Table VI.3*

APPENDIX TABLE VI.2

India's Principal Exports (1970-71 to 1981-82)

(Rs. Crores)

Sr. No.	Commodity	1970-71	1971-72	1972-73	1973-74	1974-75	1975-76
1	2	3	4	5	6	7	8
1.	Jute Manufactures	190.4	265.3	250	227.5	296.8	248.3
2.	Tea	148.3	156.3	147.3	146	228.1	236.8
3.	Cotton Fabrics :	75.3	76.6	100.9	195.1	158.9	158.7
	[a] Mill made	67.5	66.6	84.4	162.7	129.37	119.4
	[b] Handloom	7.8	10	16.5	32.4	29.2	39.3
4.	Coir Yarn and Manufactures	13	13.4	14.3	15.3	17.9	19
5.	Iron Ore	117.3	104.7	109.8	132.9	160.4	213.8
6.	Oil Cakes	55.4	40.2	74.8	178.2	96	86.1
7.	Leather & Leather Mfgs. (Exlg. footwear)	72.2	90.8	174.5	172.2	145	201.3
8.	Cashew Kernel	52.1	61.3	68.8	74.4	118.2	96.1
9.	Tobacco	32.6	45.1	63.9	70.9	82.2	98.4
10.	Engineering Goods	130.4	122.3	141	201.7	356.7	408.7
11.	Coffee	25.1	22.1	32.9	46	51.4	66.7
12.	Mica	15.6	15.4	16.6	13	18.2	14.6
13.	Sugar	27.6	30.2	13.3	42.2	339	472.3
14.	Peepar	15.3	14.8	14.3	29.5	34.5	33.9
15.	Manganese Ore	14	10.6	8.7	9.4	17.6	17.5

16.	Raw Cotton	14	16.3	21.6	32.4	15.2	38.8
17.	Mineral Fuel & Lubricants	12.6	11.6	32	15.3	20.4	35.6
18.	Iron & Steel (Exclg. ferro - manganese and ferro-alloys)	67.2	25.5	23.1	26.2	21.1	68.2
19.	Chemicals & Allied Products	29.4	30.4	35.3	50.3	92.9	84.5
20.	Fish & Fish Preparations	30.5	42	54.5	89.2	66.2	126.6
21.	Art Silk Fabrics	5.3	7.5	9.6	28.3	18.4	15.1
22.	Footwear	11.4	11.6	12.6	13.8	20.3	21.2
23.	Vegetable Oils (essential and non-essential)	10.8	11.5	29.6	37.9	43	37.2
24.	Cotton Apparel	8.6	14	29.9	67.4	96.9	144.9
25.	Handicrafts	69.9	81.7	119.7	173.6	186.6	224.1
26.	Hides & Skins & Furskins	0	0.7	0.9	1.5	0.4	0.2
27.	Silver	0	0	0	0	0	0
28.	Others	290.9	286.3	370.9	433.2	626.6	773.2
29.	Total Exports	1535.2	1608.2	1970.8	2523.4	328.9	3941.8

APPENDIX TABLE VI-2 (Contd.)

(Rs. Crores)

Sr. No.	*Commodity*	*1976-77*	*1977-78*	*1978-79*	*1979-80*	*1980-81*	*1981-82†*
1	2	3	4	5	6	7	8
1.	Jute Manufactures	200.8	244	166.9	336.1	330	250.1
2.	Tea	292.9	569.7	340.5	367.8	425.5	373.3
3.	Cotton Fabrics :	254	224.8	224.3	287.4	276.5	272.5
	[a] Mill made	200.8	143.4	163.2	216.3	188.4	0
	[b] Handloom	53.2	81.4	61.1	71.1	88.1	0
4.	Coir Yarn and Manufactures	24	23.9	26.4	36.6	26.2	25.8
5.	Iron Ore	238.5	240.8	232.9	285.2	303.3	343.4
6.	Oil Cakes	223.8	133.3	109.9	127.5	125.1	139.4
7.	Leather & Leather Mfgs. (Exlg. footwear)	263.5	248	327.7	485.6	337.1	374.1
8.	Cashew Kernel	106	149.5	80.2	118.1	140.1	168.8
9.	Tobacco	102.1	117.2	116.3	113.5	140.7	227.8
10.	Engineering Goods	554.4	617.4	700.7	739.1	727	817.3
11.	Coffee	114.1	194.4	144	163.3	214.2	132.5
12.	Mica	17.4	17.3	18.9	20.6	17.7	27.9
13.	Sugar	148.1	19.5	131	128.9	40.6	40.3
14.	Peppar	38.2	49.1	147.9	149.4*	111.4*	112.5*
15.	Manganese Ore	19.1	10.9	15.4	13.2	12.7	9
16.	Raw Cotton	27	0.7	16	75.1	164.9	35
17.	Mineral Fuel & Lubricants	32.7	27.8	19.8	21.2	24.9	24.3

18.	Iron & Steel (Exclg. ferro - manganese and ferro-alloys)	283	185.4	221.9	32.78	69.7	70.1
19.	Chemicals & Allied Products	109.1	116.7	148.1	197.8	225.6	347.3
20.	Fish & Fish Preparations	180.3	174.3	226.3	253.4	212.9	274.4
21.	Art Silk Fabrics	28.9	26.8	38.9	32.4	21.5	26.5
22.	Footwear	28.8	24	26.3	33.9	40.1	40.4
23.	Vegetable Oils (essential and non-essential)	52.6	26.1	18.9	49.5	22	23.3
24.	Cotton Apparel	257	235.1	345.5	343.7	378.2	547.9**
25.	Handicrafts	402.4	751.8	956.7	832.5	893.8	1033.8
26.	Hides & Skins & Furskins	0	0	0	0	0	0
27.	Silver 0	78.6	103.5	2.2	0	0	
28.	Others 1144.5	900.8	821.4	1171.7	1426	2058.5	
29.	Total Exports	5143.2	5407.9	5726.3	6418.4	6710.7	7796.2

Notes : * Spices
** inclusives readymade Garments
† Provisional

Source : *Economic Survey, Government of India, New Delhi, Various Issues*

APPENDIX TABLE VI.3

India's Principal Exports (1982-83 to 1987-88)

(Rs. Crores)

Sr. No.	*Commodity*	*1982-83*	*1983-84*	*1984-85*	*1985-86*	*1986-87*	*1987-88*
I.	Agricultural & Allied Products : of which	2451.0	2621.7	2996.5	3018.3	3422.0	N.A.
1.	Coffee	187.1	181.7	210.2	264.9	296.7	263.2
2.	Tea & Mate	369.8	515.2	766.6	626.3	576.8	592.4
3.	Oil cakes	148.6	151.6	136.9	134.0	189.8	173.3
4.	Tobacco	247.4	178.1	178.3	169.6	185.3	134.6
5.	Cashew Kernels	135.4	150.8	179.7	225.1	327.6	306.7
6.	Spices	94.6	116.7	206.7	277.8	279.0	309.3
7.	Sugar & Molasses	66.9	174.3	35.2	15.8	1.4	0.8
8.	Raw Cotton	107.8	157.0	59.7	68.2	204.7	95.5
9.	Rice	217.9	113.6	169.2	196.3	197.3	324.6
10.	Fish & Fish Preparations	364.2	364.0	381.4	409.0	539.0	525.1
11.	Meat & Meat Preparations	80.5	71.7	82.5	73.8	75.5	85.5
12.	Fruits, Vegetables & Pulses (Excl. Cashew Kernel & Processed fruits & Juices)	153.8	104.6	136.6	124.0	155.8	150.8
13.	Miscellaneous processed foods (incl. processed fruits & Juices)	80.2	63.2	76.8	82.4	75.5	65.9
II.	Ores & Mineral (Excl. Coal) : of which	490.8	506.2	637.6	784.7	717.2	703.3
14.	Mice	20.1	17.9	19.6	20.9	19.6	23.2
15.	Iron Ore	380.5	401.6	459.4	578.8	546.6	542.8

III.	Manufactured Goods : of which	4551.1	4969.4	6210.1	6374.2	7808.4	N.A.
16.	Textile fabric & Manufactures (excl. Carpet hand made) of which	1556.1	1481.3	1717.5	1795.1	2178.8	3088.8
	(i) Cotton Yarn, Fabrics made ups etc.	419.6	428.8	620.4	573.7	637.2	1063.8
	(ii) Readymade garments of all textile Materials	590.8	725.6	935.3	1067.0	1330.5	1792.1
17.	Coir Yarn & Manufactures	26.3	24.9	27.9	33.7	33.5	29.4
18.	Jute Manufactures (incl. twist & yarn)	206.3	170.9	341.3	261.8	244.0	242.8
19.	Leather & Leather Manufactured (incl. leather footwear, leather - travel goods & Leather garments)	414.6	492.5	724.1	769.9	922.4	1148.5
20.	Handicrafts (incl. Carpet hand-made)	1440.4	1599.3	1750.8	1881.4	2547.6	3253.3
	of which Gems and Jewellery	1014.8	1294.1	1237.1	1502.7	2074.3	2613.5
21.	Chemical and allied products	348.3	327.6	482.9	497.5	583.2	823.4
22.	Machinery, Transport equipment & Metal Manufactures (incl. Iron & Steel)	867.7	807.2	956.1	954.1	1132.7	1433.0
IV.	Mineral fuels & Lubricants (incl. coal)	1240.4	1590.0	1822.9	654.9	417.6	656.5
V.	Others :	70.2	83.4	76.6	62.5	87.2	N.A.
VI.	Total :	8803.5	9770.7	11743.7	10894.6	12452.4	15741.2

Source : *Economic Survey*, Government of India, New Delhi, 1988-89, S. 74, 75.

APPENDIX TABLE VI.4

Commodity Composition of India Exports According to Standard International Trade Classification

(Rs. Crores)

	0	1	2	3	4	5	6	7	8	9	
Years	Food and Live Animals	Beverages and Tobacco	Crude Materials Inedible except Fuels	Mineral Fuels Lubricants & Related Materials	Animal & Vegetable Oils & Fats	Chemical	Manufacture Good Classified Chiefly by Materials	Machinery and Transport Equipment	Miscella-neous Manufac-tured Articles	Commodity and Transport of not classified according to kind	Total Export* = Total Sections 0 to 9
(1)	(2)	(3)	(4)	(5)	(6)	(7)	(8)	(9)	(10)	(11)	(12)
1965-66**	380.2	34.2	212.5	14.7	7.1	18.1	541.2	16.5	34	5.8	1263.3
1966-67**	352.9	22.6	208.7	12.6	3.1	14.9	490.6	15.4	27.5	4.6	1152.9
1967-68	362.2	35.6	194.3	9.2	4.2	15.7	510.7	19.1	35.9	5.9	1192.8
1968-69	364.1	33.8	212	12.1	12	23.7	603	43.6	46.5	5.5	1356.3
1969-70	345.6	33.4	231.4	9.5	5.1	30.3	630	55.4	63	5	1408.7
1970-71	412.7	32.6	251.7	12.6	7.1	36.4	615.7	75.1	76	4.5	1524.4
1971-72	435.3	45.1	240.6	11.6	7.9	35.4	663.3	73.8	84.8	5.4	1603.2
1972-73	521.6	64.1	254.3	31.9	25.5	40.4	814.1	84.3	112.9	5.4	1954.5
1973-74	678.8	71	362.3	15.3	32.1	58.2	999	116	178.8	6.8	2518.3

1974-75	1016.2	82.3	432.3	20.4	34.4	104.1	1166.9	213.5	243.5	6.7	3323.3
1975-76	1239.4	98.5	527.1	35.6	34.8	89.5	1333.4	255.2	310.5	7.3	3931.3
1976-77	1300.5	103	602.2	33	52.5	119.1	2117.5	297.8	494.6	8.9	5129.1
1977-78	1533.8	117.7	482.6	27.8	24.9	125	2190.3	335.3	513.5	12.3	5363.2
1978-79	1456.9	117	512.4	19.4	17.9	153.8	2327.5	395.1	693.6	13	5706.6
1979-80	1703.3	115.4	666.6	21.2	52.4	208.4	2397.6	447.3	773.7	16.2	6402.4
1980-81	1705.1	141.3	813.6	27.8	19.3	234.6	2314.3	525.5	868.5	15.8	6665.8
1981-82	1919.2	236.4	775	224.9	19.9	375.4	2578.9	617.4	1038.5	12.7	7798.3

* Total exports are exclusive of re-exports

** The value figures are adjusted at post-devaluation rate by multiplying the figures with 1.575. the increased value of pre-devaluation rupee.

Source : *Monthly Statistics of the Foreign Trade of India. vol. I. Exports and Re-Exports*, Published by Directorate General of Commercial Intelligence and Statistics. Government of India. for the Years 1965-66 to 1981-82

Appendix Table VI.5

Correspondence Table of Regional Classification

Regional Classification of countries, of April 1966		*Corresponding Regions and Countries of Regional Classification of April 1977*
Region No.	*Name of the Region*	
(1)	(2)	(3)
0	Africa	Region Nos. 1, 2, 3 and 4
1.	North America	Canada and U.S.A.
2.	Latin America	Region No. 6 and **Countries :** Costa Rica, Cuba, Dominican Republic, El Salvador, Gutemala, Haiti, Hondruas British, Nicaragua, Panama Canal Zone and Panama Republic.
3.	Other American Countries	**Countries :** American Samoa, Antigua, Bahamass, Barabados, Bermuda, British Virgin Islands, Dominica, Fulkland - Islands, French Guiana, French West Indies Gayman Islands, Grenada, Guyana, Hondruas (not British), Jamaica, Martinique, Monteserrat, Netherland Autillies, Pureto Rico, St. Pierre Miquelon, St. Lucia, St. Ritts-Nevis-Anguilla, St. Vinicent, Surinam, Trinidad and Tobago, Turks, and Caicos Islands and Virgin Islands of U.S.
4.	Economic and Social Commission for Asia and the Pacific	**Countries :** Afghanistan, Australia, Bangladesh, Republic (formerly Formasa), Hong Kong, Indonesia, Iran, Japan, Kampuchia Democratic Republic.
	ESCAP Countries	Korea Republic, Korea Democratic Republic, Laos, Malaysia, Nepal, New Zeland, Pakistan, Philippines, Singapore, Sri lanka, Thailand, Vietnam Democratic Republic.

(Contd.)

Appendix Table : VI.5 (Contd.)

Regional Classification of countries, of April 1966		*Corresponding Regions and Countries of Regional Classification of April 1977*
Region No.	*Name of the Region*	
(1)	(2)	(3)
5.	Other Asian and Oceanian Countries	**Countries :** Behrein Island, Brunei, Christmas Islands, Cocos Islands, Cook Island, Cyprus, Fiji Island, French Polynesia, Gilbert and Ellice Islands, Gaum, Iraqe, Israel, Jordon, Kuwait, Lebanon, Macao, Maldive Islands, Mongolia, Nauru Republic of Neutral Zone, New Caledonia, New Herbrides, Nice Islands, Norfolk Islands, Oman, Pacific Island, Papu and New Guin, Pictarin Islands, Portugese Timor, Qutar, Sabah, Sarwak, Saudi Arabia, Solomon Islands, Syrian Arab Republic, Tonga, Tuvalu, Tokelan Islands, United Arab Emirates, Wallis and Futuna Islands, Western Samoa, Yemen People's Democratic Republic, Yemen Arab Republic.
6.	East European Countries	Region No. 15 and Yugoslavia
7.	European Common Market Countries	**Countries :** Belgi im, France, Federal Republic of Germany, Italy, Luxmberg and Netherlands
8.	European Free Trade Area Countries	**Countries :** Austria, Denmark, Norway, Portugal, Sweden, Switzerland and United Kingdom.
9.	Other European Countries	**Countries :** Albania, Andorra, Channel Islands, Gibraltar, Greece, Liechtenstein, Malta, Spain, Turkey, Ferore Islands, Finland, Greenland, Iceland and Ireland.

Note : Prepared on the basis of Regional Classification of April 1966 and April 1977 Given in *'Monthly Statistics of the Foreign Trade of India. Vol. I. Exports & Re-Exports' Published by Directorate General of Commercial Intelligence and Statistics,* Government of India, March 1967 and March 1978.

APPENDIX TABLE VI.6

Direction of Indian Exports

(Rupees in crores)

Years	Region-0 African Countries	Region-1 North American Countries	Region-2 Latin American Countries	Region-3 Other American Countries	Region-4 Economic & Social Commission for Asia & the Pacific Countries	Region-5 Other Asian & Oceanian Countries	Region-6 East European Countries	Region-7 European Common Market Countries	Region-8 European Free Trade Area Countries	Region-9 Other European Countries	Total* Export = Total of all regions
(1)	(2)	(3)	(4)	(5)	(6)	(7)	(8)	(9)	(10)	(11)	(12)
1965-66**	95.9	263.5	16.4	2.5	249.3	45.2	246.3	86.3	244.8	13.1	1263.3
1966-67**	71.4	250	9.9	2.3	241.5	38.7	225.7	88.7	215	9.7	1152.9
1967-68	70	236	5.4	1.9	270.1	43.8	224.6	88.4	242.4	10.2	1192.8
1968-69	42.7	263.1	3.7	2	343.6	67	266.2	110.8	216.3	10.9	1356.3
1969-70	88.1	263.9	4.6	2.1	375.7	72.6	307.5	100.3	182.5	11.4	1408.7
1970-71	138.2	234.7	8.3	2	408.6	71.8	361.6	98.2	188.7	12.3	1524.4
1971-72	131.9	302.2	12.6	2.8	422.8	62.6	343.6	123.8	188	13.2	1603.5
1972-73@	101	303.5	4.2	2.2	555.4	72.6	469.5	221.7	205.3	19	1654.4
1973-74@	101.6	376.3	12.1	2.6	737.1	141.3	487.4	321.9	308.7	29.3	2518.3
1974-75@	237.5	418.3	19.9	3.6	909.9	290.1	684	368.1	359.3	32.6	3323.3
1975-76	270	547.8	13	6.4	1176.5	325.4	674.9	393.5	491.5	32.3	3931.3
1976-77	311.4	616.1	15	7.9	1269.8	567.5	790.2	835.5	664.8	50.9	5129.1

1977-78	345.2	716.5	11	6.1	1272.8	569.9	929.9	829.8	636.3	45.6	5363.1
1978-79	337.9	819.3	13.8	7.1	1539.7	604.7	657.9	993	682.4	52.2	5708
1979-80	331.7	868.2	17.8	6	1733.6	617.2	891.3	1167.6	695.5	73.5	6402.4
1980-81	432.3	801.6	32.2	4.2	1659.7	607.2	1519.3	976.5	585.5	47.3	6665.8
1981-82†	441.9	987	18	4	1729.2	804	2002.4	932.5	620.4	62.7	7602.1

* Total value figures of total exports are exclusive of re-export

** The value figures are adjusted at post-devaluation rate by multiplying the figures with 1.575, the increased value of pre-devaluation rupee.

@ Region No. 7 excludes Denmark, Ireland and U.K. and Region No. 9 includes Ireland.

† The value figures of total exports are exclusive of the exports of crude oil of Rs. 196.2 crores as country details do not include.

Note : On account of change in regional classification of the various countries of the world in April 1977, the correspondence between the *Regional Classification of April 1966 and of April 1977* has been made according to the *Regional Classification of April 1966.* (For Correspondence between the two, see *Appendix Table VI-5.*

Source : *Monthly Statistics of the Foreign Trade of India, Vol. I, Exports and Re-Exports,* Published by Directorate General of Commercial Intelligence and Statistics, Government of India, for the Years 1965-66 to 1981-82..

7

Main Findings and Conclusions

The central theme of the present study has been to examine and analyse India's export trade with special reference to price and quantity trends and structure over time.

With reference to above, an empirical investigation has been carried out in a stepwise fashion whose main findings and conclusions are presented hereafter.

After having examined a brief survey on empirical research done so far, a detail explanation of methodology adopted to estimation of value, price and quantum indices for Indian exports by various commodity groups is presented and trends of quantity and price is analysed by various commodity groups. The structure of India's exports in money terms as well as in real terms, both at aggregated and disaggregated levels is examined. Further, a separate analysis of Indian exports has been carried out for the periods : 1965-66 to 1981-82 and 1970-71 to 1986-87.

As far as the construction of price and quantum indices of exports and imports indicating price and quantity trends over time is concerned, it has been a matter of common practice among various countries of the world to construct the price and quantum indices of exports and imports at highest degree of aggregation in terms of section of SITC Commodity groups. With reference to this, it is however, important to note that greater the degree of aggregation involved, greater will be the possibility of ignoring the relative importance of a commodity belonging to a respective section and hence the price and quantum indices of exports and imports may not be able to present a clear picture of price and quantity trends overtime.

Further, it is important to note that the estimated price and quantum indices of exports at a greater degree of disaggregation will be more meaningful in terms of its implications as compared to that of at greater degree of aggregation.

The present work therefore, has been designed to construct Paaschee price index and Laspeyre's quantum index of Indian exports at a higher degree of disaggregation of Three-Digit Level of RITC Commodity groups for the period of 1965-66 to 1981-82 with 1970-71 as the base year.

With reference to above, it is important to note that the construction of price and quantum indices of Indian exports has been done by making necessary adjustments in view of incomplete coverage of commodity of exports and non-export of a commodity either in the base year or in the current year. However, adjustments were also made in case of non-availability of data on quantity of exports.

Further, the price and quantity trends in Indian exports are examined by various commodity groups Viz. (a) Consumer goods, (b) Intermediate goods for producing consumer goods, (c) Intermediate goods for producing capital goods and (d) Capital goods. With reference to the same, the value, price and quantum indices have been estimated by using Paaschee price index method and Laspeyre's quantum 'index method'. This enabled us to examine the effects of changes in prices and quantity on value of exports more meaningfully.

So far as the effects of changes in the price and quantity on value of total exports, during 1965-66 to 1970-71 are concerned, our findings reveal the fact that the price effect has been more prominent than the quantum effect. The fall in the value of exports by 27.75% has been due to a greater percentage fall in price by 40.07% than the increase in the quantity by 9.65%.

However, during the period of 1970-71 to 1981-82 the opposite came to be true as the increase in the value of total exports by 336.89% has been due to a greater increase in the quantity by 122.18% than the increase in price by 110.14%.

With reference to the relative prices of primary products and manufactured products, it has been found that over a period of time under consideration the variations in prices have been more favourable to manufactured products as compared to that of primary products. This can be discerned from the fact that the export price index of manufactured products has increased by 268.33% as against the increase in the price index of primary products by 181.03% during the period of 1965-66 to 1981-82.

As regards, a relation between export prices and domestic prices, it is found that the movements in export prices have been lower than the domestic prices. The export price index has registered an increase of 197.35% as compared to an increase in the domestic price index of 287.14%. This indicates that Indian exports have been more profitable to be sold in the domestic market than in the world market.

As far as the behaviour of price indices of major commodity groups of exports is concerned, we find that during 1965-66 to 1981-82, the price index number of consumer goods increased by 154.14% or at an average annual rate of 9.07%, while the price indices of intermediate goods for producing consumer goods, and intermediate goods for producing capital goods increased by 304.64% or at an average annual rate of 17.92% and by 271.52% or at an average annual rate of 15.97% respectively. However, the price index of capital goods increased by 295.95% or at an average annual rate of 17.41%.

With reference to quantum index, our results reveal that the quantum index of total exports during 1965-66 to 1981-82 increased by 102.63%, whereas the volume indices of exports of consumer goods, intermediate goods for producing consumer goods, intermediate goods for producing capital goods and capital goods increased by 111.20%, 29.23%, 76.38% and 846.14% respectively. The maximum increase in the volume index number of capital goods can be attributable mainly to increase in the volume index of the exports of machinery and transport equipment.

In order to examine the structural behaviour of Indian exports, a macro level analysis has been carried out in terms of share of exports to NNP, share of Indian exports in world exports, growth rates of exports and instability coefficients of exports, whose relevent conclusions are furnished below :

(i) The proportion of exports to NNP over a period under consideration reveal an increasing trend behaviour indicating an increasing tendency towards outward orientation of the Indian economy and increasing tendency for comparative advantage.

(ii) An Inter-country analysis of national income and exports in terms of proportion of exports to national income comprising of 55 countries of the world grouped into (a) highly developed (b) intermediate and (c) underdeveloped in accordance with their level of economic development reveals that the proportion of exports to national income shows a rising trend over time.

(iii) As regard, the relation between exports and economic development, considering per capita income as a rough indicator of economic development, we have regressed the proportion of exports to NNP on per-capita income. Our regression results shows that with an economic development of a country, India being under consideration, the proportion of exports to NNP has increased over time indicating an increasing tendency for outward orientation of the economy.

(iv) In view of the assessment of the export performance of India in relation to world exports, our findings reveal that there has been a precipitous decline in the share of India's exports in world exports from 0.95% in 1966-67 to 0.45% in 1988-89 indicating a relative stagnation of Indian exports.

(v) As far as the growth rates of Indian exports are concerned, our empirical findings reveal that the total exports grew at the rate of 6.76% over the period of 1965-66 to 1981-82.

From among the major commodity groups of exports, the exports of capital goods registered a highest rate of growth of 15.75%. However, the exports of consumer goods, intermediate goods for producing consumer goods and intermediate goods for producing capital goods grew at the rates of 6.96%, 4.15% and 5.82% respectively.

Moreover, from among the principal commodities of exports, the exports of Sugar and Honey, Gums, Resins and Lac, Vegetable Oils & Fats, Textile Fibre Yarn and Thread and Petroleum and Petroleum products registered a decline in their growth rate of -3.61%, -2.81%, - 1.53%, -2.57% and -3.81% respectively.

However, it is important to note that the maximum growth rate of exports is revealed by export of Machinery and minimum growth rate is revealed by exports of Fruits, nuts and Vegetables.

(vi) As far as instability coefficient of exports is concerned, it has been estimated for major commodity groups of exports at current prices and constant prices for the period of 1965-66 to 1981-82.

From among the major commodity groups of exports, our findings show that except intermediate goods for producing capital goods with an instability index of 24.58, the rest of the commodity groups of exports, viz, consumer goods intermediate goods for producing consumer goods, capital goods and total exports are more stable at current prices with an index of 11.39, 12.73, 34.28 and 10.18, than at constant prices with an index of 17.66, 26.18, 55.13 and 16.63 respectively.

Further, in the context of Indian exports, the hypothesis that as compared to the exports of primary products, the exports of manufactured products are more unstable which has come to be true as is evident from our findings that the exports of manufactured products show an instability index of 21.96 at current prices and 24.20 at constant prices. While the exports of primary products show an index of 11.22 at current prices and 18.30 at constant prices during the period of 1965-66 to 1981-82. Thus we can perceive that the exports of manufactured products are more unstable at current as well as constant prices in relation to the exports of primary products.

Further, the structural change in Indian exports has been examined at current as well as at constant prices at micro (i.e. disaggregated) level. With reference to degree of commodity concentration in the composition of Indian exports and in terms of shift in the share of major commodity groups of exports viz. consumer goods, intermediate goods for producing consumer goods, intermediate goods for producing capital goods in the total exports.

In order to examine the degree of commodity concentration in Indian exports at Three-Digit Level of commodity groups, the commodity concentration index at current and constant prices was calculated. With reference to the same, our findings show that there has been a declining tendency of degree of commodity concentration in the composition of Indian exports in money terms as well as in real terms. However, it becomes clear that exports are more diversified in money terms than in real terms over the period 1965-66 to 1981-82 as the same index in money terms declined by 35.87%, while it declined in real terms by

32.46%.

This declining tendency of commodity concentration index over a period under consideration, is indicative of the fact that with the passage of time, the Indian exports have tended to be increasingly diversified.

In view of the empirical investigation of the relation between exports and economic development of India, our findings in terms of estimated regression equations reveal that the share of capital goods in total exports being positively related to per capita income, the economic development tends to raise the share of exports of capital goods in total exports which is in consonance with our expectation. This is so because with economic development, the capital base of the country tends to improve remarkably which gets reflected into the increased production and exports of capital goods.

Further, an analysis of India's foreign trade in general and India's export trade in particular, the following conclusions need to be explicitly spelt out.

(i) As far as the average annual rates of growth is concerned, our findings reveal that, Indian imports registered a growth rate of 13.81% per annum during 1966-67 to 1988-89, 17.33% during 1970-71 to 1988-89 and 19.49% during 1973-74 to 1988-89. However, Indian exports registered a growth rate of 14.36% during 1966-67 to 1988-89, 15.52% during 1970-71 to 1988-89 and 16.19% during 1973-74 to 1988-89. Thus, we can see that after 1970-71 the growth rates of exports remained less than that of imports and after 1973-74 the growth rates of imports and exports remained higher than that of prior to 1973-74. This state of affairs can be attributed to the oil price hike in the middle of 1973 which led to an increase in the value figures of exports.

(ii) As regards, the share of Indian exports in GNP, our findings reveal a systematically increasing trend of 3.9% in the year 1966-67 to 5.2% in the year 1988-89 indicating an increasing tendency towards outward orientation of the Indian economy overtime consequent upon an adoption of exports oriented trade policy by the Government of India.

Further, in order to examine the structural behaviour of Indian exports, a separate study has been made for the period of 1970-71 to 1986-87 and 1981-82. However, our main findings regarding the structural behaviour of Indian exports by various commodity groups Viz., agricultural and allied products, ores and minerals, (excluding coal), manufactured goods, and mineral fuels and lubricants (including coal) are furnished hereafter.

As regards, India's exports during the period of 1970-71 to 1986-87, our findings show that the percentage share of exports of agricultural and allied products in total exports declined from 39.22% in 1970-71 to 27.48% in 1986-87, whereas the share of exports of manufactured goods increased from 31.44% in 1970-71 to 62.71% in 1986-87. This trend reversal of share of exports in total exports indicates that the Indian exports over a period of time under consideration have diversified. However, the percentage share of exports of ores and minerals is shown to have declined from 9.57% in 1970-71 to 5.76% in 1986-87.

Having briefly, summarised, the main findings of structural behaviour of Indian exports during 1970-71 to 1986-87, the main findings as regards, the structural behaviour of Indian exports during 1965-66 to 1981-82 are in order.

(i) The percentage shares of exports of traditional goods, primary products and traditional manufactured products in total exports have declined during the period under consideration. Whereas, the shares of exports of non-traditional goods, non-traditional manufactured goods, and total manufactured goods increased over time. Thus, our findings are indicative of increasing degree of diversification of Indian exports.

(ii) The commodity composition of Indian exports according to market conditions is indicative of the fact that the monopolistic and oligopolistic strength of Indian export has declined which can be seen from their declining shares in total exports overtime.

(iii) As far as the commodity composition of Indian exports by SITC commodity groups is concerned, our findings show that the shares of exports of chemicals, machinery and transport equipment and miscellaneous manufactured goods in total exports increased over time, whereas that of food and live animals and manufactured goods classified chiefly by materials declined.

(iv) As regards, the commodity concentration index indicating the degree of diversification or concentration of commodity exports of India, our results show that the value of index has precipitously declined for exports according to market conditions indicating greater degree of diversification of Indian exports over time.

(v) As regards, the direction of India's exports in terms of regional destination, our findings show that there has been an increase in the relative importance of Economic Regions, 5, 6 and 7 i.e. other Oceanian countries, Eastern European Countries and European Common Market Countries respectively, as their percentage share in our total exports increased overtime.

(vi) As far as the relation of each commodity group of exports and economic development is concerned, our results show that the exports of non-traditional goods, total manufactured goods and non-traditional manufactured goods are of greater importance in India's economic development as their percentage shares in total exports vary positively with India's per capita income which is evidenced by our estimated regression equations.

Moreover, similar results hold in case of exports of chemicals, machinery and transport equipment and miscellaneous manufactured goods.

BIBLIOGRAPHY

Books

Adams F.G. : *An Econometric analysis of International Trade : an Interrelated Explanations of Exports and improts of DECD Countries*, 1969.

Agarwal B.M. : Indo-Japanese Trade Relations - A Diagnosis. Allaekh Publishers, Delhi, 1974.

Alan Brown and Egon Neuberger : *International Trade and Finance.* University of California, 1968.

Allen R.G.D.: *International Trade Economics.* New York, John Wiley & Sons, Inc. 1953.

: *International Trade Statistics* London. John Wiley & Sons, Inc. 1953.

American Economic Association : *Readings in the Theory of International Trade*. Toronto, The Blakison Co., 1949.

: *Readings in the Theory of International Trade*. London, George, Allen & Unwin Limited, 1955.

: *Readings in International Economics.* London, George Allen & Unwin Limited, 1969.

Arora R.S. : *A Practical Guide to Foreign Trade in India.* New Delhi, National Publising House, 1967.

Baldwin R.E. (ed.) : *Trade, Growth and Balance of Payments.* Amsterdam : North Holland Publishing Co., 1964.

Baldwin R.E. : *Economic Development and exports Growth : A Study of Northern Rodesia.* New York Cambridge University Press, 1966.

Baldwin R.E. : *Determinants of the Commodity Structure of United States Trade SSRI Series.* University of Wisconsin, October, 1969.

Behari Bipin : *Imports in a Developing Economy.* Bombay, Vora & Co., 1965.

Behari Bipin : *Current Economic Problems.* Bombay, Vikas Publications, 1969.

Bela Balassa : *Trade Prospects for Developing Countries.* Illinois, Richard, D. Irwin, 1964.

Bellugro Conference : *New Direction for World Trade : A Chatham House Report*, Proceeding of a conference held at Bellagro, September 1963, London, Oxford University Press, 1964.

Banerji Ranadev : *The Development Impact of Barter in Developing Countries : The Case of India.* Development Centre of the Organisation for Economic Co-operation and Development, 1977.

Bhagwati J.N., Jones R.W., Mundell R.A. & Vanrk J. : *Trade, Balance of Payments and Growth : Papers in International Economics in Honour of C.P. Kindleberger.* London North Holland Publishing Co. 1971.

Bhagwati J.N. and Eckans R.S. (eds.) : *Foreign Aid.* Harnondsworth : Penguin Book Ltd. 1970.

Bhagwati J.N. (ed.) : *International Trade.* Harmondsworth : Penguin Books Ltd. 1969.

Bhagwati J.N. and Padma Desai : *India : Planning for Industrialisation and Trade Policies since 1951.* Oxford, Published on behalf of DECD Centre, 1970.

:*Trade, Tar`ff and Growth : Cambridge*, The MIT Press, 1969.

Bhardwaj R. : *Structural Basis of India's Foreign Trade.* University of Bombay, 1961.

Bright Singh D.: *Economics of Development with special Reference to India.* Bombay : Asia Publishing House, 1971.

Caves R.E. : *Trade and Economic structure.* Cambridge, Massachusetts, 1960.

Chatterjee P.K.: *Foreign Capital and Economic Development, with Special Reference to India.* Calcutta, Progressive Publishers, 1971.

Cohen B.I. : *The Stagation of Indian Exports. 1951-61*, Unpublished Ph.D. Thesis, Harvard University, June 1963.

Coppock J.D. : *International Economic Instability.* New York, McGraw-Hill Book co., 1962.

Datta B and Others : *Economic Development and Exports : A Study of the Impact of Indian Economic Development on Exports*. Calcutta; The World Press Private Ltd., 1962.

Datta Asha L. : *India's Economic Relations with tne USSR and East Europe.* Cambridge, 1972.

Department of Commercial Intelligence & Statistics : *A Guide to Current Official Statistics of Trade Shipping and Custom Revenue of India.* Government of India. Third Edition, 1978.

Dharam Kumar : *India and the EEC.* Bombay, Asia Publishing House, 1966.

De Vries B.A. : *The Export Experience of Developing Countries.* Baltimore : Johns Hopkins Press, 1967.

Economic and Scientific Research Foundation : *Prospectives for India's Trade with Developing Countries*, New Delhi, 1966.

Eltis W.A., Scott M.F. and Wolfe J.N. (ed.) :*Induction : Growth and Trade : Essays in Honour of Sir Roy Harrod*, Oxford Calrendon Press, 1970.

Golden Jubilee Symposium of Indian Economic Conference 1967 : *Development Trade and Aid.* Bombay, Popular Prakashan, 1969.

Johnson H.G. : *Economic Policies Trades Less Developed Countries.* London, George Allen and Unwin Ltd., 1967.

Johnson H.G. : *International Trade and Economic Growth.* London : George Allen and Unwin Ltd., 1967.

Gupte D.B. : *Exports in Developing Economy - A Case Study of Indian.* Baroda, The M.S. University Unpublished Ph.D. Thesis, 1973.

Halder Animesh : *India's Export Pattern, An Analysis on Potential Diversification.* Calcutta, Minerva Associates, Pvt. Ltd. 1976.

Haberler G. : *International Trade and Economic Development.* Egypt, Cairo, National Bank of Egypt, 1959.

Harrod R. and Hague D.C. : *International Trade Theory in a Developing World.* London, Macmillan, 1969.

Indian Institute of Foreign Trade : *Trade with East European Countries.* New Delhi, IIFT, 1973.

Kemp M.C. : *A Contribution to the General Equilibrium Theory of Preferential Trading : Contribution to Economic Analysis.* North Holland Publishing Co., 1969.

Khan M.S. : *India's Economic Development and International Economic Relations.* Bombay, Asia Publishing House, 1961.

Kindeberget C.P. : *The Terms of Trade, A European Case Study.* London, Chapman and Hall Ltd., 1956.

: *Foreign Trade and the National Economy.* New Heaven and London, Yale University Press, 1962.

Lakdawala D.T. : *International Aspects of India's Economic Development.* Oxford University Press, 1954.

Lipsey R.E. : *Price and Quantity Trends in the Foreign Trade of United States.* Princeton University Press, 1954.

Macbean A.I. : *Export Instability and Economic Development,* London, George Allen and Unwin Ltd., 1966.

Maizels Alfred : *Exports and Economic Growth of Developing Countries.* Cambridge, Cambridge University Press, 1968.

Meier G.M. : *The International Economics of Development.* New York, Harper & Row Publishers, 1963.

: *International Trade and Development.* Harper & Row, New York, Inc., 1963.

Meyor F.V. : *The Terms of Trade.* Compenhagen, Munksgad, 1962.

Nambiar R.G. : *Resource Structure of India's Foreign Trade.* Baroda, The M.S. University unpublished Ph.D. Thesis, 1971.

Panchmukhi V.R. : *Trade Policies of India : A Quantitative Analysis.* Delhi, Concept Publishing House, 1978.

Raj K.N. : *Indian Economic Growth, Performance and Prospects.* Delhi, Allied Publishers, 1965.

Rowe J.W.F. : *Primary Commodities in International Trade,* Combridge University Press, 1965.

Sachs Ignancy : *Foreign Trade and Economic Development of Underdeveloped Countries.* Bombay, Asia Publishing House, 1955.

Salvi P.G. : *New Directions in India's Trade Policy*, Bombay, Vora & Co., 1964.

Sen Sunanda : *India's Bilateral Trade and Payment Agreements*, Calcutta, Bookland Pvt. Ltd., 1965.

Sharma R.K. : *The Economic of Indo-Soviet Trade*. Bombay, Allied Publisher Pvt. Ltd., 1979.

Simha S.L. and Hemalatha D. : *Oil, International Payments and Reforms*. Madras Institute for Financial Management and Research, 1975.

Singh Manmohan : *India's Export Trends*. Oxford Clarendon Press, 1964.

Singh Manmohan : *"Survey of Research on International Trade Payment"* Unpublished Report, National Council of Social Science Research, New Delhi, 1971.

Tandon J.K. : *Indo-German Economic Relations*. National Publishing House, 1978.

Theberge James D. : *Economics of Trade and Development*. New York John Wiley & Sons, Inc. 1968.

The Gazetter of India, Vol. III : *Economic Structure and Activities*.

Government of India, Ministry of Education and Social Welfare.

United Nations : *International Compensation for Fluctuations in Commodity Trade*. New York, 1961.

United Nations Secretariat : *Instability in Export Markets of Underdeveloped Countries*, United Nations, Department Economic Affairs, 1952.

Vassil Vassilev : *Policy in the Soviet Block on aid to Developing Countries*, Paris, OECD Development Centre, 1969.

Venek Joroslav : *General Equilibrium of International Discrimination*. Cambridge, The Harward University Press, 1965.

Verghese S.K. : *India's Foreign Trade*. Bombay, Allied Publishers Pvt. Ltd., 1964.

Wells S.J. : *British Export Performance : A Comparative Study*. London, Cambridge University Press, 1964.

Yates P.L. : *Forty Years of Foreign Trade.* New York, The Macmillon Co., 1959.

Youngil Lim : *"Export Industries and Pattern of Economic Growth in Ceylon".* Unpublished Ph.D. Thesis, The University of California, Los Angeles, 1985.

Articles & Papers

Ahuja : "India's Trade with Eastern Europe - A Comment", *Indian Economic Journal* Vol. IX, January 1962.

Alt Richard : "Comment on Dr. Rao's 'Export and Development" *Indian Economic Journal*, Jan-Mar 1968.

Ambegronker Nalini : "India's Trade with Eastern European Countries : Trend and Problems", *Reserve Bank of India Bulletin*, March 1974.

Artus J.R. : "The Behaviour of Export Prices for Manufacturers", *IMF Staff Papers*, November 1970.

Ayal E.B. : "The Impact of Export Taxes on the Domestic Economy of Underdeveloped Countries" *Journal of Development Studies*, July 1965.

Balassa B. : "Some Observations on Mr. Backerman's 'Export - propelled' Growth Model", *The Economic Journal*, December 1963.

: "Trade Policies in Developing Countries", *American Economic Review*, May 1971.

Baldwin R.E. : "Export Technology and Development from a Subsistence Level", *Economic Journal* Vol. 73, March 1969.

Ball R.J. and Drake P.S. : "Export Growth and the Balance of Payments" *Manchester School of Economics and Social Studies*, May 1962.

Bansal G.L. : "A Note on Multi-Country Trade", *American Economic Review*, XL II, September 1952.

Berrill, K. : "International Trade and Economic Growth" *Economic History Review*, April 1960.

Bhagwati J.N. : "Contributions to Indian Economic Analysis - A survey"

American Economic Review, 1969.

Bhatia Romesh : "The Oil Crisis. : An Economic Analysis and Policy Imperatives", *Economic and Political Weekly*, 27th July, 1974.

Caves R.E. : "Trade and Development : A Traditional View", *Economic Development and Cultural Change*, October 1964.

Cairncross A.K. : "International Trade and Economic Development", *Kyklos*, 1960, Fasc. 4.

Chandra N.K. : "USSR and Third World : Unequal Distribution of Gains", *Economic and Political Weekly*, Annual Number 1977.

Chisti Sumitra and Artam Parkash : "Import Possibilities for India Under Rupee Payment Agreements". *Foreign Trade Review*, July-September 1969.

Chisti Sumitra : "India's Trade with Developing Countries under Bilateral Trade and payment Agreements : An Analysis of India's Trade with Afghanistan, Egypt and Sudan", *Foreign Trade Review*, April-July 1973.

Cohen B. : "A Comment on S.J. Patel's Analysis of Indian Exports", *Indian Economic Journal,* September, 1963.

: "Stagnation of Indian Exports, 1951-61" *Quartely Journal of Economics*, Novermber 1964.

: "The Less - Developed Countries' Exports Primary Products", *Economic Journal*, June 1988.

Commerce Research : "Foreign Trade of India" *Commerce* Bureau *Annual*, 1971.

: "One Honoured Exporters : A Feature", *Commerce*, April, 1, 1972.

Cooper Richard N. : "Growth and Trade, Some Hypothesis about Long Term Trends", *Journal of Economic History*, 1964.

Corden W.M. : "Industrialization and Trade", *Australian Economic Papers*, (Jan-Dec. 1964)

: "Growth, Terms of Trade and Comparative Advantage", *Economica Interzionale*, August, 1959.

Dave S.A. : "India's Trade Relations with East European Countries : 1952-1953 to 1956-60. A Study in Bilateralism", *Indian Economic Journal*, IX, July 1961.

: "India's Trade with East European Countries" *Indian Economic Journal*, IX, April 1962.

De Costa G.C. : "Devaluation and Balance of Payments" *Economic and Political Weekly*, October 1966.

: "Devaluation and Exports - An Interim Report", *Economic and Political Weekly*, September 1967.

De Varies B.A. and Kessing F.A.G. : "The Use of Bilateral Trade Agreementswith Third Countries", *IMF Staff Papers*, August 1956.

Dholakia Ravindra H. & Joshi Pravin R. : "On Chenery's Measures of Import Substitution", *Journal of The Maharaja Sayajirao University of Baroda*, (Social Science), Vol. XXXI-XXXII, No. 2, 1982-83.

Diwan Romesh K. : "Import Structure and Policy" *Foreign Trade Review*, April-June 1968.

Dubey V. : "A Survey of Recent Trands in India's Foreign Trade", *Indian Economic Journal*, April, 1963.

Dutt M.M. : "A Prototype Model of India's Foreign Sector", *International Economic Review*, January 1964.

: "Re-examination of the Import Structure of India : A Reply", *Review of Economics and Statistics*, August 1976.

Ellisworth P.T. : "The Terms of Trade Between Primary Producing and Industrial Countries, *International Economic Affairs*, 1956.

Ely Devors : "Statistics of United Kingdom : Terms Trade, *The Manchester School of Economics and Social Studies*, September 1954.

Goldstein M. and Khan M.S. : "Large Versus Small Price Changes and the Demand for Imports", *IMF Staff Papers*, March 1976.

Gulati I.S. : "Oil Price and Developing Countries" *Economic and Political Weekly*, 26th April 1975.

Harberger A.C. : "Some Evidence on the International Price-Mechanism", *Journal of Political Economy*, December 1957.

Haberler G. : "Introduction to Problems of International Economics", *Review of Economics and Statistics*, February 1958.

Halder A. and Richards J.H. : "Structural Characteristics of India's Foreign Trade and its Effects on the Instability of Export Receipts", *Indian Economic Journal*, October - December 1963.

Hang Sheng Cheng : "Statistical Estimates of Elasticities and Propensitites in International Trade", *IMF Staff Papers*, April 1959.

Helgerdf F. : "The Case for Multilateral Trade" *American Economic Review*, March 1943.

Houthakker H.S. : "The Calculation of Bilateral Trade Patterns in a Ricardian Model with intermediate products and barriers to Trade", *Journal of International Economics*, Vol. 6, No. 3, August 1976.

Houthakker H.S. and Stephen P. Magee : "Income and Price Elasticities in World Trade", *Review of Economics and Statistics*, Vol. 51, May 1969.

Johnson H.G. : "Increasing Productivity, Income-Price Trends and Trade Balance", *The Economic Journal*, September 1954.

Joshi P.R. : "Recent Developments in The Theory of Balance of payments - A Survey", *Essays on Recent Developments in Economics. The Maharaja Sayajirao University Economics Series No. 9. Department of Economics. Faculty of Arts. The M.S. University of Baroda*, Baroda, 1982.

Joshi P.R. : "Heckscher-Ohlin Model and Factor Price Equalisation Theorem Under Alternative Conditions - A Geometrical Exposition", *Special Number in International Economics, Indian Economic Journal*, Vol. 34, Jan-March, 1987, No. 3.

Katrak H. : "Commodity Concentration and Export Fluctuations - A Probability Analysis" *Journal of Development Studies*, July 1973.

Kemp M.C. : "The Relation Between Changes in International Demand and the Terms of Trade", *Econometrica*, 1956.

: "Errors of Measurement and Bias in Estimation of Import Demand

Parameters", *Economic Record, XXXVIII*, Septermber 1962.

Khalaf, Nadim G. : "Country Size and Trade Concentration", *Journal of Development Studies*, October 1974.

Khan M.S. : "Import and Export Demand in Developing Countries", *IMF Staff Papers*, November 1974.

: "Structure and Behaviour of Imports of Venezuela", *Review of Economics and Statistics*, 1975.

Kilani K.R.F.: "Changing Pattern of India's Foreign Trade", *Industrial Times*, August 1961.

Kreinin M.E.: "Price Elasticities in International Trade", *Review of Economics and Statistics*, November 1967.

Kubursi A.A. : "The Import structure of Labenon - A Qantitative Analysis", *Journal of Developing Areas*, October 1974.

Leamer D. Edward : "The commodity Composition of International Trade - An Empirical Analysis", *Oxford Economic Papers*, November 1974.

Lewis W.A. : "World Production, Prices and Trade 1870-1960", *Manchester School of Economic and Social Studies*, May 1952.

Manual Perez Guerro : "International Trade and the Challenge of Growth of Developing Countries" *Foreign Trade Review*, January - March 1972.

Massell Benton F. : "Export Concentration and Fluctuations in Export Earnings : A Cross-section Analysis", *American Economic Review*, March 1964.

Mc Doungall G.D. : "India's Balance of Payments", *Bulletin of Oxford Institute of Statistics*, May 1964.

Mc Gilvray J. and Simposon D. : "The commodity Structure of Anglo-Irish Trade", *Review of Economics and Statistics*, 1973., 55 (4).

Michaely Michael : "Concentration of Exports and Imports - An International Comparision" *The Economic Journal*, December 1958.

Morgan Theodore : "The Long Run Terms of Trade Between Agriculture and Manufacturing", *Economic Development and Cultural Change*,

October 1959.

Murti V.N. and Sastri V.K. : "Foreign Demand for Certain Indian Exports", *Reserve Bank of India Bulletin*, Bombay, RBI, May 1950.

Murti V.N. : "Elasticity of Demand for Certain India's Imports and Exports", *Sankhya*, XI, December 1951.

Naya S. : "Fluctuations in Export Earnings and Economic Pattern of Asian Countries", *Economic Development and Cultural Change*, Part. I, July 1973.

Nayyar Deepak : "India's Export Performance in the 1970's" *Economic and Political Weekly*, May 15, 1976.

Obrien : "On Commodity Concentration and Exports in Developing Countries", *Economia Interzionale*, November 1972.

Ohleson L. : "On Unit Prices and their Use in the Analysis of International Specialisation pattern with Heterogeneous Industries", *Journal of International Economics*, August 1974.

Ocrrutt Guy H. : "Measurement of Price Elasticities in International Trade", *Review of Economics and Statistics*, May 1950.

Patnaik S. Chandra : "Indo-Soviet Economic Relations and its impact on Indian Economy" *Indian Economic Journal, Vol. 24, No. 5, Conference Number 1976.*

Rajan M.S. and Mehta : "India's Foreign Policy and Trade Promotion", *Foreign Trade Review*, October-December 1972.

Rao M. Jagadeswara and Reddy K. Chenchi : "India's Trade with Scocialist Countries: 1951-1952 to 1973-74" *Indian Economic Journal*, Vol. 24, No. 5, *Conference Number*, 1976.

Rao Y.A. : "The Pattern of India's Foreign Trade in Relation to Economic Development" *Indian Economic Journal*, January 1956.

Richter H. : "Average Value and Volume Indices of Imports by Areas and Origin and by Commodity Categories of Metropolition OEEC Member Countries", *International Statistical Review*, 1956.

Satri V.K. : "India's External Trade : Some Problems", *Indian Economic Journal*, July 1955.

Sebastain M. : "Does India by dear from and Sell Cheap to the Soviet Union" ? *Economic and Political Weekly*, Vol. III, Dec, 1, 1973.

Sharma M.L. : "India's Foreign Trade, A Review" *Foreign Trade Review*, July - September 1976.

Sharma O.P. : "Demand Conditions of India's Exports to the Socialist Countries, Some Issues and Contraversies", *Indian Economic Journal*, Vol. 24, No. 5, Conference Number, 1976.

Sharma O.P. : "Trends and Determinants of India's Export Performance, 1961-1974", *Foreign Trade Review*, October - December 1976.

Shetty S. Vasudeva : "India's Trade with Socialist Countries of East Europe Under Bilateral Trade and Payment Agreements", *Indian Economic Journal*, Vol. 24, No. 5, Conference Number 1976.

Singer H.W. : "The Distribution of Gains Between Investing and Borrowing Countries" *American Economic Review*, May 1950.

Stern Joseph J. : "A Note on the Structure of Pakistan's Trade", *Pakistan Development Review*, Vol. IX, Summer 1964.

Studenmund A.H. : "A Cross-Sectional Analysis of the Law of Declining International Trade", *Western Economic Journal*, December 1973.

Thirnvenkatachani K. : "Indo-Soviet Trade - A Perspective" *Indian Economic Journal*, Vol. 24, No. 5, *Conference Number*, 1976.

Wu S.Y. & Wassink D. : "Three Phase of Growth in a Developing Economic Relative to International Trade", *Indian Economic Journal*, 1970.

[illegible] The [illegible]

[illegible]

[illegible]

[illegible]

[illegible]

[illegible]

[illegible]

[illegible]

[illegible]

[illegible]